BHASWAR MUKHERJEE calls himself an accidental writer. He has a degree in mechanical engineering and an MBA from IIM Bangalore. After close to eighteen years in multinational banks (Bank of America and HSBC), he quit in 2005 to set up his own company, Bridgepoint Solutions Pvt Ltd, which provides consultancy and learning solutions in the banking domain.

His short story, 'Unrequited', was selected by author Neelam Chandra Saxena in a contest launched by Readomania and was one of the two winning entries. 'Acceptance' was selected by author Sudha Murty and published by Penguin India in their anthology, *Something Happened on the Way to Heaven*. Another story, 'Garib Rath', was picked up by author Ravinder Singh for his anthology, *Tell Me a Story*, and published by Penguin India. His contribution, 'Leap of Faith', featured in *Crossed and Knotted* (Readomania), India's first composite novel, a Limca Book of Records entry. In 2016, his short story, 'It Was Not Their War', was selected by author Ashwin Sanghi as one of the winners and published in the anthology by the *Times of India* in the Write India Contest Season 1. In 2019-20, his short stories for TOI-Season 3 were shortlisted for the top ten by authors Nayantara Sahgal, Amitav Ghosh, Upamanyu Chatterjee and Vivek Shanbhag for their respective prompts.

Bhaswar has contributed to eleven anthologies and his solo anthology, *It Happens: Stories of Human Relationships*, was published in May 2020, for which the Navi Mumbai Chamber of Business and Industries in association with Great Human University recognized him as the 'Best Storyteller 2021' at the Indian Authors Conference and Awards, November 2021.

THE COUNTERFEITER

ABDUL KARIM TELGI & THE STAMP SCAM

BHASWAR MUKHERJEE

Om Books International

First published in 2022 by

Om Books International

Corporate & Editorial Office
A-12, Sector 64, Noida 201 301
Uttar Pradesh, India
Phone: +91 120 477 4100
Email: editorial@ombooks.com
Website: www.ombooksinternational.com

Sales Office
107, Ansari Road, Darya Ganj,
New Delhi 110 002, India
Phone: +91 11 4000 9000
Fax: +91 11 2327 8091
Email: sales@ombooks.com
Website: www.ombooks.com

ISBN: 978-93-92834-16-5

Printed in India

10 9 8 7 6 5 4 3 2 1

This book is dedicated to all who hope and strive for a corruption-free India

Contents

Acknowledgements

I can almost see you raise your eyebrows in surprise. Why a book on the Telgi scam, two decades after its heady run, and four years after the death of its architect Abdul Karim Ladsaab Telgi in prison? Why this treatise of a dated white-collar crime when newer and bigger scams assail our systems even before we have recovered from the earlier one?

Two reasons. First, because Telgi's is a rare rags-to-riches story of an ordinary individual, made possible equally by a complicit system of lawmakers, law keepers and government officials as much as the machinations of the antagonist. And for the intriguing unanswered questions, including the size of the crime that remain and continue to challenge our collective reason.

Second, while there have been innumerable articles, newspaper reports and even a book, there hasn't yet been a detailed chronicle of his audacious journey into the world of grime and crime, from womb to grave and beyond. For both the devil and possible learnings are in the detail.

I have been merely a *sutradhar* (chronicler) of the Telgi saga and this book wouldn't have been possible without the invaluable contribution of the following to whom I am deeply grateful.

To Suhail Mathur of The Book Bakers, my agent and guide, who first mooted the idea of this book. We had been shooting the breeze and blue-sky gazing on a non-fiction project for a while and when he suggested Telgi, I had similar reactions as many of you might have. Yet when he provided me reasons cogent and persuasive, I latched on, like a homing pigeon.

To Om Books International, my publishers, who approved the project expeditiously and provided the wind beneath my wings. To their team, for their invaluable suggestions, meticulous editing, cover design and the look and feel of the book.

To Dipankar Bose, a friend and an advocate (Partner, S. Jalan & Co., Kolkata), who helped me navigate the choppy waters of case filings and judgments, criminal applications, appeals, writ petitions, et al. Without his help, this painstaking effort to reconstruct Telgi's crimes through copious court papers may have never seen the light of day.

To my millennial daughter Anuta, whose enthusiasm in reading all my efforts matches her zest at providing her brutally honest feedback on each. Coming from a generation removed from mine, it provides me the much-needed perspective. To my wife who stoically bore the cross of enhanced household chores for the time that I was chained to my desk, yet never failed to encourage me and goad me on.

Finally, dear readers, my gratitude to you, as you hold this book in your hand. I sincerely hope that you will enjoy this telling of the Telgi saga as much as I have enjoyed putting it together. Do feel free to provide your feedback liberally, laudatory or otherwise, for that is the only way I can ever hope to become better at my craft.

Introduction: A Contextual Framework

India's ranking in the Corruption Perceptions Index (CPI) for 2020, an annual compilation exercise by Transparency International, slipped to 86 from 80 in 2019. The index, which ranks 180 countries and territories by their perceived levels of public sector corruption, according to experts and business people, uses a score scale of 0 to 100, where 0 is highly corruptible and 100 very clean. A country with a higher score has a better rank. India's score in 2020 was 40, just one point below its 2019 score of 41. Yet, the country's rank fell by six places. Whether the score is 40 or 41, India's score was below the average score of 43, which is clearly disappointing.

We may be tempted to stoically accept this poor performance, given our direct and indirect experiences with bribery and corruption at all levels, notwithstanding every government promising us clean governance. However, let's not forget that this is a ranking for public sector corruption levels alone and, thus not a metric for corruption in other sectors which touch us. Some pessimists may even argue that on the CPI measure alone, India should languish somewhere at the bottom. Experts opine that the CPI doesn't reflect the real corruption level in any country, which is better measured by the integrity score.

That second statistic is the Index of Public Integrity (IPI) compiled and published by a team of researchers at the European

Research Centre for Anti-Corruption and State-Building at the Hertie School of Governance in Berlin. This focuses on the fact that while several indices show that corruption remains a key issue both in developing countries and in many modern societies, not many focus on how to control it. The common corruption indices tell us mainly about how citizens and experts perceive the state of corruption in their society. They do not tell us anything about the causes of corruption or about how the situation can be improved. The IPI's measure is a composite index consisting of six components: Judicial Independence, Administrative Burden, Trade Openness, Budget Transparency, E-Citizenship and Freedom of the Press. It aims to give an objective and comprehensive picture of the state of control of corruption in 117 countries, a study done biennially, the last conducted in 2019, in which India ranked a lowly 71.

In an interesting development, the Central Vigilance Commission (CVC) India, together with the Indian Institute of Management India, Ahmedabad (IIM-A) as consultants, has worked to create the Integrity Index (II). It is yet an evolutionary model which focuses on two aspects of integrity – the Integrity of Management and the Management of Integrity – arguing that the former is a prerequisite for the latter. The II for public organisations will be computed, based on evaluation of operational processes and perception of the same by internal and external stakeholders. Data for evaluation will be submitted online by the respective organisations on a participation basis. Therefore, the framework for computing integrity index relies only on primary data, unlike other tools developed elsewhere such as the CPI and the IPI. The II is expected to help the government departments in India assess where they stand on anti-corruption measures.

That said, the Indian experience with corruption over the years has been nothing short of frustrating. The Transparency International, which has the utopian vision statement of "We have one vision, a world free of corruption", defines corruption as "the abuse of entrusted power for private gain", a description which fits those complicit, whether they be politicians, or those charged with positions of authority or responsibility or power or those authorised to handle public wealth and livelihoods with care and concern.

India has seen a rash of such financial corruption couched in the more common moniker of 'scam' (defined as 'an illegal plan for making money, especially by tricking people'). The scams most entrenched in public memory, either for their size, audaciousness, political entanglement or systemic failures include Infrastructure Leasing and Financial Services (IL&FS, estimated Rs 100,000 crore, under probe currently), Nirav Modi (Rs 11,400 crores), Vijay Mallya (Rs 9,000 crores), coal block allocation or the Coalgate (Rs 1.86 lakh crore), 2G Spectrum (Rs 1.76 lakh crore), Commonwealth Games (Rs 70,000 crore), Satyam (Rs 14,000 crore), Saradha Group (Rs 30,000 crore), Mining Odisha (Rs 4 lakh crore), Fake Stamp or Telgi (Rs 25,000 crore) among others.

So, what appears to be the reasons for the pervasive decline of public morality in India that makes recurring scams a way of life? A country that is classified as a developing nation, the world's second most populous at 1.37 billion and the fifth largest contributor to world nominal GDP of USD 94.94 Tr (at USD 2.95 Tr-IMF October 21 World Economic Outlook) also has the dubious reputation of having an guesstimated stash of black money currently in Swiss and other offshore banks at about Rs 112 lakh crore or USD 1.5 trillion, roughly half the GDP of the nation! To put that in perspective, if we could get all the money back, it would facilitate a direct tax holiday for individuals and corporates for the next thirteen years!

It appears that there are four fundamental factors contributing to our poor standards of integrity and the value placed on morality:

- **Legal**: The non-existence of stringent laws and prohibition to inculcate public morality. Laws in India are often lenient in corruption cases, the judicial process long drawn out which encourage people to indulge in immorality and disintegrity. As the story develops here, we will see how an allegedly corrupt police inspector or a sub-inspector rose to the rank of assistant commissioner by the time that they could be arrested and punished!

Borders too are porous with poor examples of extradition laws being implemented, allowing flight not just of tainted capital, but perpetrators, too. Recent examples would be those of Mehul Choksi, Nirav Modi and Vijay Mallya.

- **Political**: Corruption and malpractices are not considered big crimes when political positions are decided. People guilty of immoral practices or having a history of graft are not ostracized, but instead occupy key positions. Our Constitution does not prevent those accused of corruption from holding political office. According to an *India Today* article of 25 May 2019, "Out of 539 winners analysed in Lok Sabha 2019, 233 MPs (Members of Parliament) have declared criminal cases against themselves. This is an increase of 44 percent in the number of MPs with declared criminal cases since 2009."

- **Social**: Indian society has been very accommodative when it comes to accepting corrupt or immoral individuals. People occupying high offices and venerated positions by using immoral methods are taken as role models of success. They thus encourage others with the example of their own lives and social acceptance.

- **Cultural**: The Indian culture of advocating inculcation of moral integrity remains much in theory. It doesn't prescribe strict or practical measures for implementation and practice. Immorality is not considered a taboo and those indulging in it are not discouraged.

In this context, what makes the stamp scam special, curious and audacious is the sheer innovation of an underdog – Abdul Karim Ladsaab Telgi. It has the overtones of a Bollywood potboiler, replete with chases, corrupt government officials and policemen, political blessings, bar dancers and yes, a murder too!

The untimely death of the antagonist, his posthumous exoneration, and the painful truth that little of his estimated Rs 17,000 crore aggrandisement was ever recovered, will serve as encouragement for the nefarious rather than a lesson for posterity. That the size of the scam can at best be a guesstimate between Rs 20,000 to Rs 30,000 crore, perpetrated by an individual and his motley group, and larger than the combined scammed amounts of Nirav Modi and Vijay Mallya, far more established and connected individuals, makes for a riveting read.

The Central Bureau of Investigation (CBI), which was handed over the investigation of 48 of the 200 cases by the Supreme Court in March 2004 following a hearing of a Public Interest Litigation (PIL), pegged the figure of the scam at a fraction of the amount, at nearly Rs 172 crore after two years of investigation, though initially, in several the cases filed/reopened by them, case histories show the amount swindled at around Rs 25,000 crore. The period considered by the CBI team was from 1993 and 2002 during which it found that the financial magnitude of the case rose sharply only after 1998, when Telgi began his own manufacturing unit using genuine machines which had been discarded by the India Security Press. The figure, however, in addition to having several riders appears grossly understated. Telgi apparently used to measure the amount of cash he had by *'boris'* (large gunny bags in which the ill-found wealth was stashed). His personal aggrandisement, the bribes paid to the police and politicians and the amount of money that he would spend on entertainment, too, don't quite add up. When Telgi expired, "... unpaid dues towards income tax alone was Rs 190 crore, with the first claim against him being raised in 2005 for an amount of Rs 120 crore" (*The Indian Express*, 27 October 2017).

Evidence of Telgi's having splurged Rs 93 lakh on a bar dancer on a single New Year eve night in 2000 is a well-established and oft-quoted lore, though again the amount varies, based on different reports. The CBI, by its own admission in its report, has recorded that the scamster had thirty-six properties across the country, 123 bank accounts in eighteen cities including Delhi, Mumbai, Bangalore, Chennai and Indore, had paid off Rs 12.38 crore to government officials, invested Rs 2.98 crore in dance bars and Rs 2 crore in film-making and also made a donation of Rs 14 crore for social causes, including purchase of ambulances, building small hospitals and contribution to celebration of festivals of all religions.

Curiously, in many of the legal cases and pronouncements, the value of the scam was pegged between Rs 25,000 and Rs 30,000 crore. For example, in Criminal Appeal No 660/2009 (which decided the appeal of the accused Telgi and his elder brother Abdul Rahim), in the Original Crime Report filed (CR No 109 of 1997), judges Ravi Malimath and John Michael Cuna JJ mentioned the scam value of Rs 25,000 crore many years *after* the CBI report. There have been allegations that political play in burying the scam had pegged the value so low in the CBI report.

The anatomy of the scam has been reconstructed from the many case filings and judgments, news articles and papers, references for which have been provided.

Those unaware of the rules for stamps and stamping in India may wish to first refer to the ready reckoner provided in the appendix at the end of this book. Though the Telgi scam predominantly played out well before the advent of e-stamping in India in 2013, the same has been provided for complete understanding of the domain and the developments in the digitisation of stamping.

However, the process of transition to e-stamping has been fraught with concern for the livelihood of thousands of stamp vendors (Telgi, too, was one). Details of their challenges have been added in the appendix. Clearly, unless they find alternative revenue streams, they will be marginalised or perish. Perhaps many already have. Telgi's stamp scam has certainly hastened the adoption of e-stamping and hence the demise of the standalone stamp vendor. Like the many scams before and after Telgi's, the biggest price has been paid by those vulnerable, rather than the ones responsible.

PART I

THE INITIATION

1

Humble Beginnings

Abdul Karim Ladsaab Telgi was born on 29 July 1961. He was the second of the three sons of Ladsaab Telgi. His elder brother was Abdul Rahim Telgi and his younger, Abdul Azeem Telgi.

The middle-class family struggled to make ends meet. Ladsaab Telgi was a Class IV employee in the Indian Railways. Though the job enabled Ladsaab to keep his family together, penury continued to be their faithful companion. Reportedly, the family couldn't afford two square meals a day. The family settled in the panchayat town of Khanapur, in Belgavi, in the Belgaum district of Karnataka, and Ladsaab managed to eke out a modest living in the small railway station of Khanapur.

When Abdul Karim was seven or eight years old, his father died. Reasons for Ladsaab's demise are unclear. He was, however, reportedly suffering from diabetes and remained distraught over his state of finances. Though Ladsaab's widow, Shariefa Bi, then in her twenties, secured his family pension of rupees sixty a month, it was clearly inadequate for the family. Her three sons assisted her in sourcing fruits such as chikoos, pears, cherries and mulberry from the nearby forests and selling them at the Khanapur railway station on a pushcart. The family would also pack their wares in boxes and containers and sell them to passengers on the mere twelve trains that stopped in Khanapur in the 1970s. Often, a brother or two would travel distances on the trains to expand sales, while another would manage their stationary cart at the station. Abdul Karim Telgi also worked at the Khanapur railway station canteen, to supplement the family's income.

Undeterred by the hardships, Abdul Karim completed his Class X from the Sarvodaya Vidyalaya English Medium High School in Khanapur (his brothers studied here, too) and joined the Gogte College of Commerce, Belgaum, from where he completed his BCom in 1984. His elder brother Abdul Rahim, too, was a BSc graduate, though younger brother Abdul Azeem dropped out of academics at the pre-university level.

Both Abdul Rahim and Abdul Azeem were accomplices in their mastermind brother's crimes in their later lives and their names find mention in the criminal records at the Bangalore City Market Police Station and the Pune Bund Garden Police Station, respectively. When the CBI took over the cases in 2004, Abdul Rahim Telgi died before charges could be filed in the Bangalore City Market case. Abdul Azeem, despite discontinuing education post-secondary level, worked as a labourer in the Gulf. He was apparently helped by Abdul Karim in his endeavours as a travel agent, and later returned to help his brother in his businesses, whether sending labourers to the Gulf or in the bogus stamp paper business. Allegedly, he was Abdul Karim's chief recruiter for the fake stamp paper distribution network. He was politically active, too, and a member of the national minority cell of the Congress party. When Abdul Azeez was arrested on 2 July 2003, he was the vice-president of the Khanapur Municipal Council in Karnataka. However, his relations with Abdul Karim's family appeared to have soured over time as evident during developments at Abdul Karim's funeral.

After completing his graduation, Abdul Karim Telgi, whose ambitions couldn't be contained in the cloistered confines of Khanapur, moved to the city of dreams, Mumbai, in search of a job.

He reportedly stayed with his friends for six to seven months and gained employment as a sales executive with M/s Filix India Ltd at a salary of Rs 3,800 a month. Filix India Ltd. supplied office furniture.

For someone so inured by childhood trials and tribulations and successful at having navigated the choppy waters of a chequered education, it was expected that Abdul Karim Telgi would scorch a path in his vocation as much as he had in his academics. Regrettably, that was not to be. Abdul Karim was lazy and failed to meet his sales target month on month. He was soon dismissed for non-performance, and was then able to secure a job as a manager under Mr Yusuf Usmail Turk at a budget stay lodge, Kishan Guest House, on Walton Road in Colaba. He worked there for about two-and-a-half years. During this period, he met Shahida Begum, the sister-in-law of Yusuf Usmail, and fell in love with her. Shahida resided in Shivajinagar, Bengaluru, at the time. Abdul Karim and Shahida married on 19 April 1987 with the blessings of both the families.

Abdul Karim's dreams soon began to outgrow Mumbai. He decided to try his luck in the Gulf. He landed a job and left for Saudi Arabia. However, his sloth was again his failing, and he soon lost that job. Reportedly, he tried his hand at odd jobs but, eventually disillusioned, returned to Mumbai within a couple of years. His goalpost in life at that point appeared to have clearly shifted: how to make money without hard work.

As one of the many in the 1980s who flocked to the Gulf with dreams of garnering wealth, Telgi had seen the lucrative business of travel agents, who helped such youths with their passage, up close. Initially, he borrowed money to rent a shop in Crawford Market in Mumbai and set up a business in manpower consulting and then started sending people to Gulf countries for employment. Business prospered and he opened his own company, Arabian Metro Travels. However, the painstaking and often slow success that comes with fair dealing was not Telgi's cup of tea. He soon realised that with the sharp competition among various travel agents, whose tribe was threatening to outgrow applicants for Gulf jobs, the only way that he could enhance revenues was to expand his clientele. And the easiest way to do so was to make those ineligible for immigration and travel (for various faults with their passports or other documents) eligible.

This involved creating false documents and forgery. He and his team began to make a plethora of fake documents that would facilitate smooth passage of the aspirants at the airport even if their passport had an ECR (emigration check required) stamp or other issues that could raise red flags for immigration officials. He also managed to use his contacts in the Middle East to illegally send these people abroad. As his fame as a 'fixer' spread, candidates began to flock to his doors. The business boomed for about three years. However, it was not all smooth sailing, and, in several cases, immigration clearances and passports were either refused or delayed. Telgi, in turn, denied returning the handsome advances that applicants paid him. Many resorted to filing police complaints and cases were registered against him under the Indian Penal Code (IPC) for cheating. Immigration officials, too, had become aware of the racket that Telgi was running and tipped off the police.

Police investigation revealed that Telgi was guilty of forgery and fraud under the Immigration Act as well as many sections under the India Penal Code (IPC). The Mumbai Police chased him to Khanapur village and arrested him in December 1993 under various sections of the IPC along with sections under the Immigration Act for cheating people by promising to send them abroad for employment. It must be mentioned here that Abdul Karim Telgi was famous and was loved in his village as Karim Lala. Though he splurged crores in personal enrichment in later life, he reportedly also spent Rs 14 crore in philanthropy with donations for ambulances, hospitals and other charitable purposes. A beneficiary of much of the largesse was Khanapur village and Belgaum district.

The Mumbai Police put Telgi behind bars for fraud and forgery at the M.R.A. Marg Police Station in south Mumbai. This was Telgi's first run-in with the law. However, the incarceration, instead of reforming him, became his springboard into the murky world of crime and corruption on an unprecedented scale.

While in custody, Telgi met Ram Ratan Soni, a stockbroker who had been jailed for forging share papers, specifically recycling used share transfer stamps. The idiom 'Thick as Thieves' found its ideal expression in their unholy nexus, though later the two fell out. In his book *Dangerous Minds*, author and former investigative journalist S. Hussain Zaidi mentions that Soni encouraged Telgi to think big and commit crime for crores and not 'loose change'. Soni indoctrinated Telgi into the world of stamps and stamp papers, and advised that the stamp-paper office was one of the most 'porous' and neglected government departments with poor checks and balances. If that could be exploited, the sky was the limit. Soni also told Telgi that he had a wide network of government officials, politicians and in the underworld, all the necessary ingredients for a mega scam. The seeds of the scam had been sown in hushed conversations in their dank and sordid cells, germinating to a heady resolve soon enough. Together, the two plotted to collaborate once they were released and began to plan their lives outside the prison.

2

A Little Help from Friends

Once Telgi and Ram Ratan Soni were released from prison (Telgi was released on bail), they realised that to sell counterfeit stamps, they had to be licensed vendors under the Bombay Stamp Act, 1958. Vendor licences were in great demand and a licence was awarded by the superintendent of stamps. Applications were in queue for close to three years. It was clear that they would need to grease the system to be able to 'expedite' their application.

Anil Gote, a politician, was elected to the legislative assembly in 1999 as a Samajwadi Janata Party candidate. Later, he joined the Bharatiya Janata Party (BJP) and became a member of the state assembly from Dhule, Maharashtra, in 2009, and was re-elected in October 2014 with a reduced majority. He resigned from the BJP in 2018 and joined the Nationalist Congress Party (NCP), a breakaway faction of the Indian National Congress (INC), in 2019. Telgi approached Anil Gote in late 1993. Gote was a journalist in those days, but aspired to be a politician, which made him well-connected. Telgi allegedly sought his help to gain access and to meet Vilasrao Deshmukh, revenue minister in the ruling Congress government. Whilst it is unknown how Telgi befriended Anil Gote and/or if he ever met Vilasrao Deshmukh, it is likely that Ram Ratan Soni's connections helped. It appears that upon Gote's recommendation, Deshmukh endorsed Telgi's application for a stamp vendor licence. Telgi applied for a stamp vendor's licence on 20 January 1994. The timelines here appear a little cramped as Telgi, as per case filings, was arrested in Crime No 91 of 93 in December 1993 (charges of cheating and under the Immigration Act discussed in the previous chapter) and released on bail.

Radheshyam Laxmanrao Mopalwar, the superintendent of stamps, cleared Telgi's application expeditiously and Telgi was able to secure a stamp-vending licence (number 12500) on 18 March 1994. Years later, in his confession from prison to a Pune magistrate on 4 February 2006 in case CR 355 of 1995, Telgi specifically named Mopalwar as partner in the crime. In his 153-page confession, Telgi alleged that "Mopalwar had not only cleared his application within a couple of months, while most had been waiting for years, but also gave him a licence that allowed him to sell all kinds of stamps, normally issued to very few vendors." He went on to state that after issuing the licence, Mopalwar befriended Telgi. The confession said: "Now, slowly Mopalwar started discussing stamps and stamp vending business. He told me that this is a very big business and that he will support me in every way. And he also promised me that he will give me the client list of general stamp office." (*The Indian Express*, 1 November 2006.)

Allegedly, Telgi paid a bribe of Rs 5 lakh for this list of large and important clients, who bought stamps and stamp papers in bulk. During the period that Telgi was an authorised stamp vendor, Mopalwar allegedly accepted gifts worth more than Rs 60 lakh from him. According to Telgi, after a misunderstanding between the two, possibly arising out of the case CR 355 in 1995, Mopalwar turned against him and reported his misdeeds. Not only was Mopalwar the whistle blower in this case, but he also cancelled Telgi's stamp vendor licence on 21 June 1995. Mopalwar was also the complainant and prosecution witness in two or three other cases registered against Telgi.

However, on 17 July 2009, a special CBI court named Mopalwar as an accused after Telgi moved an application in court in October 2008. Special judge Chitra Bhedi issued the necessary summons to Mopalwar to appear in court on 27 July 2009. Mopalwar was then the joint CEO of Maharashtra Industrial Development Corporation (MIDC). He was charged with "cheating, fraud and forgery and also some sections of the Bombay Stamp Act and the Prevention of Corruption Act (POCA)" (Zee News, 17 July 2009). The charges did not stick.

Anil Gote was arrested, much later in July 2003 for charges against him in the fake stamp scam and was imprisoned for four years.

Sanjay Singh's book, *Telgi Scam: Reporter ki Diary*, refers to the charge sheet against Gote's alleged proximity to Telgi on account of the following (as translated from Hindi):

- *Local address given by Telgi to become member of The Kisan Trust (KT) in Dhule was that of Anil Gote's house.*
- *Anil Gote and Telgi were present on the same platform of KT for a public function in Dhule two-and-a-half years after the date Telgi was declared a fugitive on 16 January 1996.*
- *Telgi donated Rs 26 lakh to KT headed by Gote in which he also made receipts of Rs 5 lakh each favouring Ram Jethmalani and Lalit Suri without their consent.* (Note: Both Ram Jethmalani and Lalit Suri denied receipt of any such funds.)
- *In 1994, Anil Gote used political influence to provide Telgi a stamp vending licence.*
- *Gote allegedly also requested the electricity board to give concessions in the recovery of Telgi's electricity dues.*
- *During 1997-2003, Anil Gote's stay at Hotel Ritz in Mumbai was paid for by Telgi, who also bore the expenses for Anil Gote's two trips to Delhi.*
- *At Telgi's behest, Gote wrote a recommendation for Ganga Prasad, general manager of India Security Press, and the then law minister Jethmalani forwarded the letter to Finance Minister Yashwant Sinha.*

A *Times of India* report of 13 November 2003 mentions that Gote had allegedly written to the Brihanmumbai Electric and Suburban Transport (BEST) general manager on 8 February 2001, "urging them to grant ten instalments to Telgi for the payment of electricity bills of Rs 3.64 lakh due from the Alankar Lodge near Crawford Market in south Mumbai" (linked to the fifth point above).

The charge sheet had apparently established that Telgi and Gote travelled together to Delhi by air on 26 November 1998, stayed at the Ashoka Hotel, and the bill for the stay was paid by Telgi. The duo stayed at Hotel Diplomat in Delhi once again for two days, from 28 October 1999.

Alankar Lodge near Crawford Market has a 'rich' history in the annals of the Telgi chronicles as a den of infamy. An article in the *Times of India* on 8 April 2011, reporting the sale of this lodge, mentions that it was used for nefarious purposes by Telgi in meeting with corrupt cops and for storing stocks of his fake stamps/papers. Though the Dawoodbhoy Fazalbhoy Education Trust owned the property, they had to fight a protracted three-and-a-half-year-long legal battle to wrest it back from the law-enforcement agencies, who had attached the same (in addition to other properties) to pay off the court fines and legal fees levied upon Telgi. It transpired that the property had been seized on the order of the MCOCA (Maharashtra Control of Organised Crime Act) court in the belief that the same belonged to Telgi.

The truth was that Telgi had 'bought' the property from the trust under the archaic 'pagdi' system in 1997, a form of tenancy that flourished in the yesteryears. Prior to 1999, there was no need to get into a contract with the landlord for a lease. Rent receipts took care of the whole process. Year after year, the rents would remain the same, as though it was never impacted by inflation. The pagdi would be a large upfront amount paid to the owner and substantially low rentals, with certain ownership rights, vested with the tenant. Hence Telgi was no more than a tenant and MCOCA had no locus-standii to have ordered the seizure of the property.

The Dawoodbhoy Fazalbhoy official said the trust was not aware that they were dealing with a scamster.

Besides the 2,000 square feet of premises at the Alankar Lodge, other properties belonging to Telgi, which were seized by the court, included a plush flat in Cuffe Parade, a printing office at Mint Road in Fort, two flats in Shirin Apartments in Colaba, and Sunny House at Mathuradas Estate in Colaba. It was in the 1,600-sq.-ft flat in Cuffe Parade that Telgi was found in January 2003, enjoying all creature comforts, though he was supposed to be in police custody (see chapter 'Murky Mumbai' which appears later in this chronicle).

The *Times of India* report of 13 November 2003 also mentions that the police had raided Telgi's Boatwala Chambers office in the Fort area on 10 June 2002 and seized several incriminating documents. These included counterfeit stamps and stamp papers valued over Rs 130 crore. Importantly, a photocopy of a letter, dated 2 June 1998, written by leading lawyer Ram Jethmalani, in his capacity as Union urban affairs minister was also discovered. This letter, addressed to then Union finance minister Yashwant Sinha had recommended a promotion for the India Security Press (ISP) Deputy General Manager Ganga Prakash, a prominent player in the Telgi saga. When Jethmalani was questioned on this letter, he confirmed having issued the same at the behest of Gote and Telgi, who had approached him with the request. Ganga Prakash was a key player who helped Telgi take the game to a different level, but more on that in the chapter, 'ISP: The Golden Goose'.

Armed with the expedited issuance of his stamp vendor licence in March 1994, Telgi took up offices in Handloom House, Garden Mansion Police Court Fort and at Hussain Manor, Bomanji Petit Street, Kemps Corner in Mumbai, both within the limits of M.R.A. Marg Police Station, where one of the earliest cases against Telgi and (inter-alia) Soni were registered.

3

First Steps

The operation was meticulously conducted. Telgi ran his business under the name 'Telgi AKL Government Licensed Stamp Vendor'. The contraction of the first three parts of his name, AKL, became popular in all subsequent cases and references. In the book, *Dangerous Minds*, S. Hussain Zaidi and Brajesh Singh write: "In an interesting aside, Abdul Karim Ladsaab Telgi is mentioned as AKL Telgi throughout the CBI charge-sheet. Subsequently, the acronym AKL became infamous in the annals of legal history, especially in the CBI dossiers. The only other acronym that gained as much notoriety is the similar-sounding UBL, terrorist Bin Laden's moniker in all Federal Bureau of Investigation (FBI) and Central Intelligence Agency (CIA) communiques, though his name was spelt as Osama."

The licence covered the sale of various judicial and non-judicial stamps, but not special adhesive stamps. Special adhesive stamps were required to be effaced/cancelled after affixation by the signature of an authorised signatory, so that they could not be reused or misused for other purposes (by removing them from the original document on which they had been affixed). A special adhesive stamp did not become a stamp unless it was so effaced and cancelled. Hence, special adhesive stamps were available only from the General Stamp Office (GSO) or its authorised outlets and stamp offices, and not from licensed stamp vendors.

A customer who wanted to get a document stamped with special adhesive stamps was expected to produce the document at the stamp office and pay for the value of the stamps. Thereupon, the officer concerned would stamp the instrument with the requisite number and value of stamps and efface stamps with a stamping machine and put his signature and date on the stamps. Often, when the stamping machine for effacement was non-functional or when the volumes of requests at a particular stamp office was high, rubber stamps would be used to cancel the special adhesive stamps and authorised by an officer in the stamp office, signing the same.

On 29 May 1995, an employee of Telgi's firm, Rakesh Sharma, who introduced himself as a sales executive, approached Manish Shantilal Parekh, a partner of M/s Purnanand & Company, a firm of advocates and solicitors. M/s Purnanand urgently required affixing special adhesive stamps on a couple of lease deeds that the firm had drawn up for two of its clients, M/s Lalbhai Realty Ltd. and M/s Arvind Fashion Limited. Rakesh promised to procure the necessary stamps expeditiously from the stamp office. Accordingly, the lawyers' firm handed over the deeds with the value of special adhesive stamps needed to be affixed marked in pencil, on each document. Manish Parekh offered to pay for them by payorders drawn in favour of 'Superintendent of Stamps'. Rakesh, however, declined to accept the payorders, advising that Telgi's firm had necessary credit from the state government stamp office against which they would secure the necessary purchases and that after stamps were affixed, a bill would be duly raised.

The documents were delivered by Telgi's representative the next day, duly bearing special adhesive stamps worth Rs 9,12,920 and Rs 7,46,030 respectively in the two lease deeds with copies bearing stamps of Rs 20 each. This representative was not Rakesh Sharma, who did not return – as part of Telgi's modus operandi, once a successful sale was made, the sales representative disappeared (for another sale) while another staff from Telgi's firm completed the operational aspects/transaction. The stamps were stamped with rubber seals of the 'Extended Sale Counter' at Bandra and appeared to have been duly cancelled in ink. Telgi's firm also raised a bill for the full amount and demanded payment of the same. Since Manish Parekh did not find a receipt issued by the stamp office for payment of stamp duty, he insisted on one. The receipt was, however, not forthcoming. Manish Parekh, therefore, asked his clerk, Rasiklal Shah, to inquire into the issuance of special adhesive stamps.

Rasiklal reported that the special adhesive stamps affixed had not been issued by the stamp office and that inquiries were being made at the extended sale counter in Bandra as well to ascertain whether the stamps had been issued there. Ultimately, it was revealed that even the extended sale counter at Bandra had not issued the stamps. Manish Parekh met the superintendent of stamps, Radheshyam Mopalwar, after seeking an appointment over telephone. According to Manish Parekh's deposition in court, he was surprised to find Telgi sitting with Mopalwar when Parekh visited Mopalwar's office. There, Telgi admitted that it was a mistake on the part of his employee and that the documents should be treated as 'cancelled'. Mopalwar advised Parekh that Telgi would be writing a letter to the lawyer's firm and the documents could be returned to Telgi against the letter. Telgi would then pass the documents on to the stamp authorities for verification.

The letter was duly issued by Telgi, who averred that an employee of his firm had sought the assistance of one Sanjay Gaikwad to stamp the documents and that Telgi had issued a cheque for Rs 16,58,500 to Sanjay Gaikwad as consideration. In the letter, Telgi also admitted that his licence as stamp vendor did not authorise him to sell special adhesive stamps and that the bill was issued to the lawyer's office by mistake. The letter requested the lawyer's office to return the stamped documents with his bill. He stated that the lawyer's office could then get a fresh set of documents stamped from the stamp office directly.

Any purchase of stamps from the treasury and all such transactions were duly recorded in the official registers. There was, however, absolutely nothing whatsoever to show that the stamps were in fact purchased by Sanjay Gaikwad or Telgi from the treasury. There were no records found in Telgi's office or none produced by him to prove that the said stamps were purchased by him. Any stamp office, including the extended sale counter at Bandra, could only accept cash payment up to Rs 50,000 from one person. Any amount more than that would require a written permission from General Stamp Office (GSO), Mumbai. Mopalwar confirmed that Abdul Telgi had returned to his office with the letter, along with a copy of the cheque for Rs 16,58,500 drawn in favour of appellant Sanjay Gaikwad. Incidentally, the original cheque never surfaced and the statement of Mahesh Rammasubramanian Nath, an employee of the bank on which the cheque was drawn, confirmed that the cheque was not presented for payment. Mopalwar examined the stamped documents and the rubber stamps affixed therein and found that they indeed resembled the ones used for effacement at the extended sale counter in Bandra.

Bhimaji Narayan Gosavi, the deputy superintendent of stamps at the extended sale counter in Bandra, confirmed that the special adhesive stamps worth Rs 16,58,500, shown to have been sold on 29 May 1995, were not sold from the extended sale counter.

Ismail Mohammad Patel, the sales supervisor authorised to act as proper officer at the extended sale counter at Bandra on 29 May 1995 and 30 May 1995, confirmed that the said signatures on the cancellation mark on the lease documents were not executed by him. He also confirmed that the stated rubber stamps appearing on the special adhesive stamp for effacement were not those of his office. The signature too did not belong to any authorised signatory of his office and had been forged. He denied seeking replacement for an impaired rubber stamp from a private agency and said that the special adhesive stamps on the documents were not issued by the stamp office in Bombay.

Krishnaji Thakya Raut, a peon at the extended sale counter in Bandra, clarified that as per the practice followed in the office, he pasted special adhesive stamps on the documents. He too denied receiving the said lease agreements.

Subhash Kashinath Patil, working as a clerk at the extended sale counter in Bandra, said no entries for sale of the said special adhesive stamps were entered in the official sales register on 29 May 1995. No entries were found in the register upon examining it.

Since the extended sale counter had reported that there was no such sale of special adhesive stamps on the relevant date, Mopalwar, the superintendent of stamps, Mumbai, lodged a complaint on 2 June 1995 with M.R.A. Marg Police Station. This led to a registration of Crime Report, C.R. No. 355 of 1995. The complaint was recorded by Assistant Police Inspector (API) Baburao Tulshiram Mukhedkar, who thereafter interrogated Abdul Telgi. The stamp vendor put the blame squarely on Sanjay Gaikwad with the story of the Rs 16.58 lakh cheque and tried to distance himself from the transaction. According to the statement of Baburao, the investigation of Sanjay Gaikwad led to Ram Ratan Soni. He, however, did not elaborate how the connection with Soni was found.

The interrogation of Ram Ratan Soni led to the discovery and seizure of rubber stamps from his residence at Sonawala Building, Dadi Seth Aguiry Lane, Kalbadevi. These included three round rubber stamps with the seal bearing the words 'Extended Sales Counter, Bandra, GSO, Bombay', a rectangular stamp with the words 'Proper officer, Extended Sales Counter, Bandra, General Stamp Office, Bombay' and the third, a date stamp. All these stamps were imitations and fake.

The stamped documents were sent to the deputy controller of stamps at Nashik for scientific investigation. Interestingly, both Sanjay Gaikwad and Abdul Telgi were able to secure bail in the case.

Police constable Vinod Mugatrao Khandale, who investigated the complaint filed by Mopalwar, failed to locate the alleged sales executive Rakesh Sharma, who had visited the lawyer's office. When the case came up for hearing later, the following emerged while questioning the staff in Telgi's offices:

a. Anil Jayram Bhambhani, a marketing executive in Abdul Telgi's firm (between October 1995 and November 1995), said that he used to secure orders for all types of stamps, including special adhesive stamps. He stated that in all orders for special adhesive stamps, he would collect the documents from the customers and deliver them to the office for getting them stamped. The stamped documents would then be delivered by a boy to the customers, who would collect the payments and deposit instruments at the office. Anil confirmed knowing Sanjay Gaikwad and seeing him in Telgi's office. He also confirmed that he knew Ram Ratan Soni, whom he had seen accompanying Sanjay Gaikwad on their visits to the office of Abdul Telgi. In fact, he had seen Soni deliver an envelope to Abdul Telgi, which contained stamps. When Telgi saw that Anil was in the room, he had immediately asked Anil to leave.
b. Fatima Ibrahim Malam was working as telephone operator in Telgi's office and identified both Soni and Gaikwad as frequent visitors to Telgi's office. Incidentally, Fatima was also wanted as a co-accused in C.R. No. 135 of 2002 registered with the Bund Garden Police Station at Pune but was subsequently not prosecuted. Neither Anil nor Fatima was aware of the sales executive, Rakesh Sharma.

The Forensic Science Laboratory where the stamped documents were sent along with specimen rubber stamp impressions reported that the rubber stamp impressions on stamps did not tally with the specimen impressions collected from the stamp office. Neither did the impressions match the fake rubber stamps seized from Soni's residence. Therefore, though Soni's complicity in this case could not be established, he was found guilty because he was in possession of rubber stamps for the purpose of counterfeiting. And was thus a participant along with the other accused persons in the conspiracy.

Sanjay Gaikwad, too, may have eventually escaped the allegations, despite the statements recorded from Telgi's office staff, had it not been for the intrepid Dilip Hanmantrao Mane, police superintendent, who was able to link a similar case in Kolkata and produce proof that Abdul Telgi and Sanjay Gaikwad had stayed together at the hotel Heera International in Kolkata at about the same time that the fraud was perpetrated there. Dilip Mane was also responsible for sending the documents to the Forensic Science Laboratory.

The report from the deputy works manager of India Security Press at Nashik, where the documents too were sent, certified that the stamps sent for examination were all genuine and matched the sequence numbers of the stamps produced at their press! The report further clarified that "Remnants of indented stamped impression were deciphered underneath the present stamped impression by ESOA technique and also paper fibre disturbances on the SPECIAL ADHESIVE stamps marked..."

This indicated that some of the special adhesive stamps had been obtained from older documents where they had been used previously and then the earlier cancellation/effacement markings erased and the stamps novated and reused. For the stamps which had not been so changed, it was concluded that they must have been obtained from documents where they had been earlier pasted upon (but not effaced/cancelled). Thus, it appeared that genuine special adhesive stamps were fraudulently obtained and then impressed with forged rubber stamps of the extended sales counter. The signature of the authorised officer too had been forged. Since there was no complaint of theft or misappropriation, obtaining special adhesive stamps fraudulently couldn't be established or charged, since inability to satisfactorily explain the source was itself not an offence. However, putting rubber stamp thereon amounted to forgery by making a false document.

The incident highlighted Telgi's modus operandi at this juncture; genuine stamps were mixed with previously used stamp and stamp papers and resold to new clients. For non-judicial stamp paper, the 'washing' process required was more extensive as all printing and writing on the stamps had to be erased in a manner that the original security paper, which had been overwritten, was not damaged and remained invisible to the naked eye.

Years later, when the case was transferred to the CBI and charges pressed, Telgi's lawyers tried to absolve him by arguing that there could be no charge of counterfeiting when special adhesive stamps on the documents in question were certified as genuine. The judge rejected the plea holding that special adhesive stamps became genuine stamps only upon rubber stamping it with the seal of office and effacing it duly with the signature of the proper officer. Since all rubber stamping, inking, cancellations and the signatures were fake, charges of counterfeiting, forgery and cheating (as the lawyer's firm which was duped had reported the case) were framed.

After Mopalwar cancelled Telgi's licence in June 1995, an arrest warrant was issued in his name. When Telgi found that the noose was tightening around him and felt that an arrest was imminent, he moved for anticipatory bail in the Bombay High Court on 15 November 1995. He was instructed to be present in the court. There was major police bandobast on 1 December 1995, the day his bail application was to be heard, for the police were confident that his application would be rejected, and they would be able to arrest him in the court itself. Yet, before the pronouncement of his bail rejection could be made, Telgi managed to slip past the police.

The police were at a total loss to explain how the slow and portly Telgi had managed to hoodwink so many policemen and escape. This event was cited as major failing of the Mumbai Police. Even years later, the courts sought an explanation for this lapse and decried the inaction of the state machinery of Maharashtra between this event and November 2001, when Telgi was eventually arrested by the Karnataka Police. (CA 91 of 2004 in Cri WP 865 of 2003 decided on 9 March 2004.)

Sometime towards the end of 1995, Soni and Telgi parted ways. Whether the fallout was because of Telgi's ambition to take the scam to the next level which Soni was not comfortable with, or due to their individual greed and aspirations, is not clear. Despite his second brush with the law, Telgi appeared to have become even more emboldened. He decided that he needed to deflect the heat piled by the police in Mumbai, and look at opportunities in other states, where he could operate safely. However, he decided to keep the production of counterfeit stamps in Mumbai under his control, and find licensed stamp vendors in other states and cities, on whom he could piggyback his business.

Details from the Criminal Appeals filed by some of the accused (Criminal Appeal 381/2010, 130/2011, 321/2010, 296/2010 decided on 14 July 2017 in the original Crime No. 545 of 2000 before the Upparpet Police Station, Bengaluru City) reveal that Telgi obtained men and material, equipment, machineries, premises, accessories, technical know-how etc., to design, develop, print, pack, transport and sell fake stamps/stamp papers etc., with the association of others. A printing press was set up in the name and style of M/s Mudran Offset Printers, at Mumbai. This press printed wedding and greeting cards by the day and fake stamp papers by night. Various firms and bank accounts were opened in Mumbai. With the help of his associates, who joined the crime syndicate, from time to time, he expanded his illegal business of sale and circulation of fake stamps/stamp papers to other parts of the country, including Bengaluru, Karnataka. He had even issued instructions on the way the fake stamp business should function in sync with his crime syndicate, titled 'Special Points', which were seized from the residence of one of the accused, Mohd. Sayeed, in Kolkata. The said document contained the details of the action to be followed in respect of running the outlets for sale and circulation of fake stamps, etc., a Standard Operating Procedure (SOP), if you will!

4

The City Market Case

From 1996, Telgi and his associates – namely, Badruddin, Vittal Maruti Sungar, Anwar Hussain, Raffi Ahmed, Ayub Buvaji, Anees Khan, A.D. Chetan, Sameer Fayaz Dastagir, Noor Ahmed, Amjad Khan, Nawaz Khan, Illiyas Ahmed, Byroji Rao, Mohd. Shoaib, Liyakath Hussain, Pradeep Kumar, Salik Wazir, Muzammil Ahmed Salik, Salauddin Ashraff Mohamed, Fayaz Ahmed, T. Thippaiah, Rehan Baig, Sirajuddin Nasipudi – were parties to the criminal and illegal acts of counterfeiting government stamps at Bengaluru and other parts of Karnataka, in a systematic and organized manner. The market in his home state was most promising and presented an opportunity Telgi was not going to let go.

Between 1996 and 2000, Telgi and his cabal arranged fake franking seals, embossing materials, composing letter blocks, rubber stamps, stationeries, other accessories, and instruments, etc., for the purpose of the manufacture of counterfeit stamps. There was a tectonic shift in the way fake stamps were produced post-1998, which will be discussed later. Fake stamps and stamp papers were regularly brought to Bengaluru by through courier services, or by his trusted acolytes, and stored. With the help of his associates, they were sold to different buyers as genuine. The accounts of such fake stamps/ stamp papers were maintained by Badruddin, on behalf of Telgi.

Firms were opened in the name of M/s Citizen Enterprises, M/s Prime Services, M/s Unique Services, M/s Unique Enterprises, M/s Cauvery Enterprises, M/s Sri Sai Enterprises, etc., in different cities across Karnataka. Telgi's crew induced genuine buyers like banks, insurance companies, private establishments, individuals through these firms, and supplied fake stamps/stamp papers and fabricated embossing/franking, as genuine, causing the state to suffer a huge revenue loss.

M/s Citizen Enterprises was set up as a proprietary firm in Bengaluru. Telgi's front man for this business was one Syed Mohiyuddin. Telgi had helped Syed obtain a stamp vending licence on 6 March 1996. The licence was initially granted for a year, which was thereafter renewed up to 31 March 1998. Syed realised sometime in December 1996 that the stamps being peddled were counterfeit, and that their operations were a fraud. But he dared not question the might of the Telgi brothers, who had garnered the reputation of being ruthless and well connected.

A few sales executives, who found out that they had been recruited to sell fake stamps and wanted to quit, had spoken to Syed in private at his residence. Syed said he was afraid of the Telgi brothers and feared for his life but would support the executives if they filed a police complaint against the Telgi brothers, who were running the business in his name.

The licence authorised Syed to sell non-judicial stamps up to Rs 25,000, judicial stamps up to Rs 1,000, court fee stamps, copying sheets and hundi papers. It did not permit him to sell any other type of stamps and stamp papers. Offices in rented premises in the name of M/s Citizen Enterprises were set up in 4th Block, Jayanagar, Bengaluru, and thereafter at Church Street, Brigade Gardens, Bengaluru. The entire setting up, the lease agreements, obtaining the vendor licence and collection of payments were all conducted in Syed's name, who acted as the front, but was orchestrated by Telgi.

Since Telgi was in Mumbai, his elder brother Abdul Rahim Telgi and his trusted men Badruddin, Vittal Maruti Sungar, Salik Wazir ran the business in Bengaluru. Since the stamps and stamp papers were all manufactured in Mumbai before they were couriered or personally delivered in Bengaluru, Syed was instructed to approach a local printer and get the Kannada word 'Karnataka' printed on the stamps i.e., on bill stamps of Rs 100 denomination, share transfer stamps of Rs 100, Rs 50, Rs 20, Rs 5 and Re 1 denominations, foreign bill stamps of Rs 20 denomination, insurance stamps of Rs 2 and Re 1 denominations. The glib explanation provided to the local printer for this strange request was they only wished to avoid payment of the interstate levy of 2 per cent between Karnataka and Maharashtra.

The local printer was thus made to believe that the stamps were genuine and duly purchased by their 'head office' in Maharashtra from the state treasury there. Syed would visit the local printer with plastic pouches containing small stamps of ten or fifteen sheets for the purpose of printing. He used to pay Rs 100 per pouch as printing charges. Syed would also bring typed letters of the word 'Karnataka' in Kannada.

Syed was assisted in his business by Shanal Jamedar Badruddin, Anand Thorat, Illiyas Ahmed, Sohail Khan and Sadiq Ibrahim Hudli. All the five, along with Abdul Rahim Telgi, stayed in Hotel Shalimar, N.R. Road, at City Market, Bengaluru, during the year 1996-97. A.K.L. Telgi would visit Bengaluru once a week from Mumbai, and wielded complete control over production, sale, distribution and collection. At that time Telgi was running his firm M/s Metro Exports, dealing in the sale of stamps and stamp papers, in Mumbai. 'Metro' was used as a chain name to for Telgi's other business interests like Metro Corporation and Metro Enterprises. His new office was on Mint Road, in the Fort area, an indication that his business was flourishing, and that he was moving up in life.

The business was run professionally as a sales organization to avoid surveillance. M/s Citizen Enterprises advertised for 'sales executives' and 'sales managers' in the local papers. Selected and qualified candidates (all graduates) would be called for interviews via a telegram or telephonically. After the interview, which would be directly conducted by either of the Telgi brothers or Salik Wazir, the candidates would be appointed to their posts. The candidates would be trained by one Mr Sudarshan for about a week about the different kinds of stamps, their applications and then taken to various banks, share brokers, companies, etc. They would be expected to collect orders for sale of stamps and even authorized to offer handsome discounts to secure business.

After obtaining the orders, the stamp papers were delivered by an office staff, who would also collect payment by way of cheques or payorders in the name of the firm.

Syed never interacted with the sales staff and (it would appear that) he was not allowed to. All discussions were limited to Wazir, the Telgi brothers and Sudarshan. All sales executives were given a photocopy of Syed's stamp vending licence for the purpose of his file or record and to show to customers who wanted to see the licence.

Apparently, several men who comprised Telgi's trusted inner circle and managed his businesses in different cities and towns were from his hometown in Khanapur. Many of them began to demand a greater and greater slice of Telgi's wealth, such as seeking cash to build their own houses in Khanapur. When they were refused, many turned witnesses against Telgi in the later years.

Among other corporates, Citizen Enterprises had sold stamps worth Rs 1,30,625 to Indian Bank, Raheja Towers, M.G. Road, Bengaluru, of which only stamps worth Rs 3,145 were genuine. The bank also placed an order for the supply of special adhesive stamps which Citizen Enterprises supplied.

It is strange that many customers, including banks, appeared to be unaware that special adhesive stamps could be procured only from stamp offices and not from licenced vendors. Like many customers, Indian Bank had made payments for these purchases vide cheques in favour of M/s Citizen Enterprises. In another case, fake stamps worth Rs 29,886 were sold to M/s Fanuc India Private Limited, on 9 September 1996. Shashikanth Barde, the works manager of the India Security Press, Nashik, who evaluated these stamps when CBI took over the case, confirmed that most stamps sold by M/s Citizen Enterprises were fake.

The complaints in the police stations against fake stamps being circulated began to grow and the eyes of the law were now on M/s Citizen Enterprises. On 10 April 1997, Police Inspector (PI) T.G. Sangram Singh, of the City Market Police Station, Bengaluru City, received a lead that men dealing in fake stamps were camping in Hotel Shalimar. It was not revealed where the tip-off came from. Inspector Sangram Singh called his juniors to his chamber at about 3:30 p.m. and planned to raid the hotel immediately. The police set up foolproof mechanism for the raid. The fruit vendor outside the police station was also summoned to accompany them. It appears that very often, the fruit and the vegetable vendors outside the police station were called in to sign as witnesses on documents. They knew that they had to comply; else they would find their carts removed the next morning.

Along with the constable and his junior police officer (PO) Vali Basha, Singh arrived at Hotel Shalimar in a police jeep. On the way, another police junior, who was helping in traffic management, was picked up. Another police officer, Venkatesh, joined them at the hotel. So, the posse for the raid was made of five policemen and two civilians (the fruit vendor and one Kalegowda).

Records say that Aslam was then the manager of Hotel Shalimar. He was in Room No. 310 when the police swooped down on the premises. His housekeeping staff called him on the intercom to inform that the police were making inquiries and they wanted to speak to him. Aslam was initially unwilling to provide information when the police interrogated him. Singh threatened to use force and only then did the manager reveal that the persons, whom the police were looking for, were in Room 101 and 104. He also said that Abdul Rahim Telgi had checked into the hotel on 1 April 1997. The police scrutinised the guest register of the hotel which confirmed that four rooms had been allotted to eight persons, but currently, only two were occupied.

They went to the first floor to conduct the raid, first in room 104 and then in room 101. They had to knock repeatedly and bang the doors before the occupants opened them. Inspector Singh and his junior went inside the two rooms, while the rest waited outside. They had to wait for over an hour. Six persons were apprehended from the two rooms: Shanal Jamedar Badruddin, Anand Thorat, Illiyas Ahmed, Sohail Khan, Sadiq Ibrahim Hudli (all employees of Citizen Enterprises) and Abdul Rahim Telgi. The material seized included two folded newspapers containing stamps of different denominations, three green covers containing counterfeit stamps of different denominations, nine covers of Shalimar Paints containing stamps of different denominations, two bundles of postal stamps, various other material and three to four suitcases. In the suitcases, along with personal effects, stamps, rubber stamps and stamp papers were found. The total value of the stamps and stamp papers seized was about Rs 300,000. They also found cash of Rs 26,000 in one of the suitcases.

After the seizure and the arrest of the six persons, Singh directed officer Basha and another constable to accompany him along with those arrested back to the police station. The rest were directed to return on foot. Hotel Shalimar is a half-hour walk from the police station. Upon reaching the police station, Singh called one of the officers, Venkataswamy, an assistant sub-inspector (ASI), to write the seizure *mahazar* and dictated the same to him. The mahazar is a panchnama (an evidentiary statement detailing the items found and times for the same) and contains the details and the boundaries of the spot where an offence or an accident has occurred. After Venkataswamy had completed writing the mahazar, Singh read the document which detailed the seizure of twenty-four items and cash worth Rs 26,000. Thereafter, the mahazar was signed by the police. The two civilians also witnessed the same and the procedure was completed by about 8:30 p.m. Significantly, while the five men were sent to the lock-up, Abdul Rahim Telgi was made to sit on a stool outside the lock-up, as he insisted that he was unwell.

During the questioning, one of the five men in the lock-up fainted, and Basha and another police constable took him to the hospital. He was released after minor first aid measures and brought back to the police station.

The next morning, when officer Basha and the constable returned, they found that out of six persons, only five were in the lock-up. Abdul Rahim Telgi was missing. They later learnt that late in the night, Telgi, along with a doctor friend, Salik Wazir, and Syed had approached Singh and his junior, and conspired to release Abdul Rahim Telgi. It appeared that Inspector Singh had received illegal gratification to let Telgi out. Not only was Abdul Rahim Telgi gone, but the records pertaining to the raid and seizure showed only five names in the mahazar. Abdul Rahim's name was missing. Accordingly, the initial FIR was filed against only five persons, and not six.

Nearly eight to ten days after the raid, Singh gave ASI Venkataswamy six packets of stamps. He directed Venkataswamy to travel to India Security Press in Nashik, along with constable Venkatappa.

At the India Security Press, the officials counted 144,790 stamps. They asked the police to deposit one rupee per stamp before they could examine the stamps for genuineness. As the police officers did not have the requisite money, Venkataswamy contacted Singh from Nashik. Singh advised them to speak to the officials of the India Security Press once more. The officers suggested that the police provide one sample stamp from each sheet, picked out at random. This would reduce the number of stamps to be examined significantly, and hence the charges. However, upon Inspector Singh's directions, no stamps were given to the officials of the press and the police returned to Bengaluru with the said packets of stamps, which were returned to Singh.

About five to six days later, Singh again gave Venkataswamy one packet containing some sample stamps to be carried to Nashik. Venkataswamy and Venkatappa went to Nashik again. A letter with the packet containing stamps was given to the officials of the

India Security Press, following which the policemen returned to Bengaluru. The report received from the India Security Press in due course confirmed that all the stamps were genuine!

Years later, this case (Crime Report-CR No. 109 of 1997), along with developments in trial and session courts, the judgments, the subsequent appeals by the accused, was one of the forty-eight cases transferred to the Central Bureau of Investigation (CBI) in March 2004 by a Supreme Court directive. The CBI sent all the 144,790 stamps, along with the requisite payment, to the India Security Press. The officials there confirmed that most of the stamps seized from Hotel Shalimar were fake.

5

A Lax Law

The notorious Bengaluru City Market case underscored the possible police complicity in helping Telgi and his cohort escape. The spotlight was on Inspector Sangram Singh who was found responsible and sentenced by the trial courts. As reported on 13 August 2004 in the *Frontline*, a magazine published by the the Hindu Group, the CBI arrested Sangram Singh and two of his former colleagues, inspectors Vali Basha and V.A. Khan (on 7 July 2004) for allegedly conniving with Telgi in the sale of fake stamp paper and subverting investigations.

The charges pertained to 1997-98 when all the three officers were attached to the City Market Police Station. According to the CBI, Sangram Singh received Rs 10 lakh for the release of Telgi's brother Abdul Rahim Telgi. Khan is alleged to have received Rs 2 lakh from Telgi in 1998 for foisting a case against a group that was trying to run a parallel stamp paper racket. While his appeal against the sentencing was pending, the same charges were levied by the CBI in October 2004 vide their fresh charge sheet, by which time Sangram Singh had already retired from the force as assistant commissioner of police (ACP). Though Sangram Singh was eventually absolved, this was an instance where judicial delays had allowed a potentially tainted police inspector rise to the ranks of an ACP!

The charges against Sangram Singh were as follows:

a. The hotel in which the raid was conducted was not within the jurisdiction of the City Market Police Station. Sangram Singh had no authority to conduct the raid or the investigation, since the same fell under the jurisdiction of the Kalasipalya Police Station. Notwithstanding, he proceeded to conduct the investigation and file a charge sheet.
b. That he allowed the two Telgi brothers, along with Wazir and Syed, to escape from the clutches of the law.
c. That he deliberately failed to conduct the investigation properly. Not only did he assist in the escape of Abdul Rahim Telgi, but also did not charge those arrested in the raid under the relevant sections and provisions, but for a lesser offence, under various sections of the Indian Penal Code (IPC).
d. That when India Security Press asked for samples of the stamps seized, he included only genuine stamps to get a clean report from ISP.

Sangram Singh's appeal against the CBI charge sheet (Criminal Appeal No 457 of 2009) was heard by the Supreme Court along with the appeals of the others charge sheeted (and sentenced by the earlier trial courts). The court also heard the fresh charge sheets by the CBI in which it implicated Sangram Singh in the above allegations and included A.K.L. Telgi, Wazir Ahmed Salik Vazeer, Syed Mohiddin, as accused along with the initial five (arrested from Hotel Shalimar). However, even before CBI could file the charge sheets, Abdul Rahim Telgi died, and the case subsisted with the remaining accused.

To prove the charges, the prosecution (CBI) examined 34 witnesses, and marked 213 exhibits, along with 113 material objects. The Supreme Court sentenced A.K.L. Telgi, Wazir Ahmed, Syed Mohiddin and the five arrested from Hotel Shalimar. However,

Sangram Singh was absolved of the charges on 4 September 2017, *in seriatim*, based on the following:

a. Assistant Commissioner of Police stated in the cross-examination that there was no clarification as to which jurisdiction Hotel Shalimar came under. Since the area map of the Chickpet subdivision was not collected by Sangram Singh, he would be unaware of the jurisdiction under which the hotel fell. It would thus be reasonable to presume that Sangram Singh had proceeded with the investigation in good faith. After completing the investigation, he had duly submitted his report to the Assistant Director of Prosecutions, who was expected to find out whether the charge sheet was in order, including the question of jurisdiction. However, there was no error of jurisdiction noticed by the Assistant Director of Prosecutions, and he had accepted the investigation report. Therefore, the allegation of lack of territorial jurisdiction was not acceptable.
b. The court ascribed circumstantial evidence at best on the alleged help by Sangram Singh in Abdul Rahim Telgi's escape. If that were true, the court opined, charges should have been made under Prevention of Corruption Act (POCA) and not the Indian Penal Code. However, the CBI had not filed any charges against Sangram Singh under POCA, for which he was exonerated on this count.
c. The allegation of the CBI that he deliberately failed to conduct the investigation properly was deemed ill-founded. Though it is true that the initial FIR was lodged against only five of the accused, and Abdul Rahim Telgi kept out of it, thereafter Inspector Singh had taken up further investigation of the case. During the investigation, various materials were unearthed, which involved Abdul Rahim Telgi. Therefore, when he filed the second charge sheet, Singh had arraigned Abdul Rahim Telgi as an accused. Singh could very well have

avoided charge sheeting Abdul Rahim Telgi, since his name was not shown in the initial FIR. Hence, the conspiracy theory of the CBI ran contrary to the material on record.

d. There was no evidence placed on record by the CBI to show that Sangram Singh had replaced fake stamps with genuine ones and sent them to the India Security Press. It is only an allegation that had subsisted without any evidence. Only because Sangram Singh hadn't mentioned the details of the stamps seized, charges of any criminal conspiracy or intention could not be made. The court also ruled that if subterfuge were indeed the objective of Sangram Singh, he would not have sent all the stamps seized in the first instance (which were returned as the police were unable to pay the charges for their examination).

In an interesting development (as per the same report of *Frontline*, 13 August 2004), retired ACP T.G. Sangram Singh, under arrest in connection with the multi-crore Telgi fake stamp paper scam, "opened a can of worms when he made a suo motu statement in a Bangalore city court (on 8 July 2004) that he had been made the fall guy in the case and blamed it on former Karnataka Chief Minister S.M. Krishna's attempt to protect Cabinet colleague R. Roshan Baig" (his role and that of his brother Rehan, a business associate of Telgi's, has been discussed later). According to Sangram Singh, he had been victimised to protect Roshan Baig and was the sufferer of the deep-seated conspiracy hatched by ex-CM Krishna, Union Minister for Urban Development and Parliamentary Affairs Ghulam Nabi Azad, Karnataka Minister for Water Resources M. Mallikarjuna Kharge, former Karnataka minister D.K. Shivakumar and Krishna's son-in-law V.G. Siddarath. These allegations were made notwithstanding the fact that all relevant Telgi cases had been shifted to the CBI in March 2004 and Sangram Singh had been arrested in July 2004 by the central agency and not the state machinery.

"Before entering the court, an emotional Sangram Singh told presspersons that he had gone to Chennai carrying Rs 20 crores meant for forest brigand Veerappan at the behest of ex-CM Krishna, Shivakumar, the then Additional Director-General of Police (Intelligence) P.S. Ramanujam, and the then Deputy Inspector-General of Police (Intelligence) T. Jayaprakash." Sangram Singh further said that during the period (between July to November 2000) that Kannada film actor Rajkumar who had been kidnapped by Veerappan remained a prisoner, Singh had visited Chennai twice and delivered Rs 20 crores to film actor Rajinikanth's manager (the ransom demanded by Veerappan for Rajkumar's release). This ransom had allegedly been financed from Telgi's tainted funds.

Sangram Singh's accusations were made in the First Additional City Metropolitan Magistrate Court and provided enough political ammunition to the BJP-led opposition to "stall the proceedings in the state legislature and demand Kharge's resignation". Though the Congress-led coalition in power was wounded by this development, Chief Minister Dharam Singh refused to succumb to the statements made by Sangram Singh, an accused in the scam. He futher confirmed that no ransom had been paid to anyone.

Notwithstanding the denials made by the government, as *Frontline* reported, the common perception was that the Krishna government, desperate to secure the release of Rajkumar, had indeed paid Veerappan. Sangram Singh found a supporter in his former boss, H.T. Sangliana, who oversaw the Veerappan operation for a short while. According to Sangliana, Sangram Singh's allegations about the involvement of Congress politicians in the stamp paper scam and the Veerappan ransom payoff 'were 100 per cent correct'. Talking to *Frontline*, Sangliana said that he saw no reason why Sangram Singh should lie. "He was an officer who always liked to give the impression that he could be relied upon to undertake any clandestine mission. They [the political establishment] have used him and discarded him. After I visited the terrain in which Veerappan operates, I gave the Krishna government a six-page letter and one of the points I made was that Veerappan should be given terms to surrender. The government didn't agree. They were probably afraid that all these issues (ransom, and who paid it) would come out if Veerappan surrendered, so they wanted him killed. Veerappan is also alleged to have paid the election campaign bills of several politicians. All this would come out if Veerappan surrendered." Former Karnataka Director-General of Police C. Dinakar, who was at the helm during the Rajkumar kidnapping, has also stated in his book *Veerappan's Prize Catch: Rajkumar*, that a huge ransom was paid to secure the actor's release. Yet questions remain about the amount, the source of the money and the channels through which it reached Veerappan.

The City Market case also brings to light the reason for corruption and crime perpetrated not just by criminals, but also by those entrusted as guardians of the law in public life. The fear of retribution for those who indulge is minimal, given the protracted judicial process and the often-inconclusive results of long-drawn-out litigations.

Telgi's operations had spread to other lucrative centres, too. In 1996, he teamed up with Vijay D. Patil and Abdul Hafiz, owners of M/s Capital Services, located in South Extension, New Delhi. Following a complaint (First Information Report-FIR No. 803/99) registered at the Defence Colony Police Station, a raid was conducted and accused Vijay D. Patil was found in possession of fake stamps. M.A. Hafiz had rented several premises and opened offices for Capital Services. The main office though was at Military Road, Anand Parbat, New Delhi. A current bank account number 4264 was also opened at Punjab National Bank, Dev Nagar, New Delhi. It was found that fake stamps were supplied to various persons/firms. Payments were received in cash and by way of cheques. Suhail Khan, Laxman Maruti Tirveer, Sachin Kalge and Navneet Kumar were also found involved in the racket. After the completion of investigation, charge sheets were filed against seven persons.

Charges were framed and the accused pleaded guilty. They were convicted vide order of 2 May 2009 and sentenced vide order dated 11 June 2009. However, many had already been languishing in jail for many years. For example, Vijay Patil had been in custody since 28 October 1999 and had already served seven years in prison (Criminal Application No. 44/2010, etc. refers). Those sentenced were unable to furnish the fines determined at over Rs 4 lakh each. The irony of justice was that the mastermind A.K.L. Telgi continued to elude the arm of the law or was able to bribe his way through.

Telgi had by now realised that the spoils were limited to the amount of money he could invest in purchasing genuine stamp papers and involved the tedium of 'washing' used stamp papers and reusing them. There have been reports that he would buy genuine stamps worth Rs 2.5 crore in a year using the various stamp vendors willing to act as a front for him and leverage the same with fakes three to four time the amount to achieve a turnover of Rs 10 crore or so in a year. With more and more cases of counterfeits being reported, he began to realise that the effort was simply not commensurate with the risks and the return.

The production of the counterfeits would have to be better and closer to perfect if his process of mixing them with originals were to succeed. It would be even better if they were so perfect that he wouldn't need to invest in originals at all. Perfection in fakes was also necessary if he had to steer clear of the skirmishes with the police. Run-ins with the police added to his operational expenses, with the speed money spent on buying his freedom. Without a licence himself, Telgi realised that he would have to depend on the vast army of stamp vendors across the country and exploit the most vulnerable of them. Syed Mohiyuddin was just one example of the many used by Telgi to act as a front for him, apply for stamp vendor licences and run his scam as proxy.

If the law couldn't jail him, A.K.L. Telgi refused to be imprisoned by the methods of his current business. The stage was ready – and porous enough – to take his game to the next level.

PART II

THE SCAM JUGGERNAUT

6

ISP: The Golden Goose

Telgi's methodology of producing and distributing counterfeit stamps had changed to lend his business greater economies of scale; he was bleeding government machinery to fatten his coffers. From the simple process of 'washing' and recycling used stamps and stamp papers, he was now printing counterfeits. Though this didn't have the risks of damage and wastage, it was imperfect and fraught with risk of detection. Though his racket had expanded in many states of the country, the fear of the fakes being found out and the law snapping at his heels continued to haunt Telgi. Moreover, the centralised modes of production in Mumbai did not allow the stamp king a pan-India footprint. He needed to collaborate with the like-minded in key locations to produce counterfeit stamps and stamp papers, which mirrored the real ones.

He remembered what his erstwhile partner in crime Ram Ratan Soni had told him some years before in prison about government departments being unmonitored and neglected. If they could start counterfeits of stamps, it would be like creating a parallel economy, and printing almost a proxy currency. Telgi wondered what the utopian model of the scam could be. What if he were able to produce exact replicas of genuine stamps and stamp papers? Those that were so good that they made detection nearly impossible?

Along with the lack of monitoring and neglect, could he exploit the paltry wages of the government officials, who controlled the printing of India's currency and stamps? What was the best way to game the system? The target institution would have to be close to Mumbai, where he had already established a network. And the India Security Press in Nashik, less than two hundred kilometres from Mumbai, seemed to be the perfect target. An idea had already begun to take shape in his devious mind.

The Security Printing and Minting Corporation of India Ltd. (SPMCIL) is a wholly owned Schedule 'A' Miniratna Category-1 company of the Government of India (GOI) incorporated on 13 January 2006. SPMCIL, technically a new entity, had centuries-old experience in security printing and minting. The management, control, maintenance and operations of erstwhile nine production units under the Currency and Coinage Division, Department of Economic Affairs, Ministry of Finance, GOI, were transferred to SPMCIL with effect from 10 February 2006. The Ministry of Finance exercises its administrative control over SPMCIL through the board of directors.

Ganga Prakash, deputy general manager at the India Security Press, Nashik Road, since March 1998, had joined the services of SPMCIL (in its earlier avatar) as a Class I officer on 9 April 1974. Initially inducted as an assistant master, he was a diligent worker. His clean employment record and hard work earned him promotions from time to time. In May 1992, he was deputed as the deputy general manager in GOI Mint, Noida. Subsequently, he was transferred to the Currency Notes Press, Nashik Road. He was thereafter promoted as deputy general manager and posted at the India Security Press, Nashik.

Other than currency notes, which were the remit of the Currency Notes Press, Nashik, and the Bank Note Press, Dewas, both the India Security Press (ISP) at Nashik and the Security Printing Press (SPP), Hyderabad, were engaged in printing, stocking and supplying a variety of security-related products such as non-judicial stamp papers, judicial stamp papers, revenue stamps, court-fee stamps, passport books, postal stamps, visas, university certificates, adhesive excise duty stamps. ISP-Nashik and SSP-Hyderabad would distribute to various organisations in accordance with the indents received and would also supply to various state governments, Union Territories and Central government departments, including Department of Posts, Ministry of Finance, Ministry of External Affairs, Ministry of Defence, Reserve Bank of India and to state municipal corporations, state election corporations, etc.

Under the aegis of SPMCIL, in addition to the four mints producing India's coinage and a security printing paper mill, the two security presses and the two currency presses were extremely important institutions as they were responsible for the printing, storage and distribution of all currency notes, stamps and stamp papers for the whole of India. These institutions needed security systems and protocols stronger than Fort Knox, but surprisingly functioned like most GOI departments and institutions at that time – lax and porous.

A.K.L. Telgi was able to infiltrate the India Security Press, working his way up from the security guards at the gate to one of the top offices, that of Deputy General Manager (DGM) Ganga Prakash. Allegedly, Ganga Prakash became Telgi's key inside man for the biggest con-job that India had ever witnessed. By Ganga Prakash's own representation dated 30 April 1998 addressed to the Joint Secretary, Government of India, Ministry of Finance, he admitted that he had come in contact with A.K.L. Telgi in the middle of 1998, soon after he had taken charge as DGM, ISP-Nashik.

The role of Ganga Prakash came to light much later by when much of the 'fake-genuine' stamps had flooded the market. Owing to the efforts of the central and state investigating agencies, in 2001-02, the fake stamp racket, running into crores of rupees, was detected in Karnataka and then in the Pune-Mumbai-Thane belt. The tentacles of his crime had apparently spread to several other states and were being slowly unravelled. Seizure of the stamps and stamp papers put forth a strange conundrum. They appeared genuine, even matching the coded production numbers of ISP-Nashik, but the revenue against these stamps and stamp papers appeared to have eluded the coffers of the India government. Also, whether by design or inefficiency, whenever ISP failed to stick to its obligation of supplying the indented quantity of stamp paper, Telgi and others would use the opportunity to sell fake papers and fill the gap, or even oversupply to meet the demands of a burgeoning market.

On 2 January 2004, *Frontline* carried an article highlighting that, "...the Karnataka Revenue Department despite falling revenues, was just a silent spectator. For example, the total number of non-judicial stamps indented by Karnataka from ISP in 1997-98 was around Rs 563 crore and the corresponding value of stamp duty registered was Rs 538 crore. In 1998-99, the indented sum fell to Rs 537 crore, and the value of stamp duty registered plummeted to Rs 477 crore. In 1999-2000, the value of stamp duty registered was Rs 583 crore, against stamps to the tune of Rs 433 crore indented from ISP. In 2000-01, though the number of stamps requisitioned was only Rs 386 crore, the value of stamp duty registered was Rs 741.46 crore. In other words, though the Karnataka government had registered stamp sales of Rs 741.46 crore on paper, the beneficiaries were the sellers of fake stamps" – to the extent of Rs 355.46 crore, almost equal to the sum indented from ISP!

The business was clearly very profitable. The perpetrator was enjoying much more than the growing difference between the amount indented and the registered stamp sales, which was riding north. There were many stamped deeds prepared for various transactions that were not registered. After the scam was exposed the following year, which put a rein on the sales of fake stamp paper, against an indent of Rs 766 crore worth of stamp papers, the stamp duty registered was a more equitable and satisfying Rs 799 crore.

The allegations ran deeper. Where the demand for stamps and stamp papers was growing in a linear manner, or sometimes stagnant or declining in line with the vicissitudes of the Indian economy, the supply had suddenly become unlimited as both ISP and Telgi were able to 'supply' the stamps. It was alleged that in such situations, the production of genuine stamps from ISP would be directed to fake addresses and lie there unused, while the same production codes and batch numbers would be passed on to Telgi, when he created the duplicates of the stamp papers. His replaced lot, replicas of the originals, would then cater to the needs of the open market, institutions as well as government departments.

A conspiracy as deep-rooted as this wouldn't have played out without the blessings of a senior person in-charge of the operations of ISP, an onus which rested squarely on the shoulders of Ganga Prakash, who was promoted to general manager (GM) on 15 January 2002. One of the reasons for the promotion was perhaps the letter of recommendation written by the then law minister, Jethmalani, to Finance Minister Yashwant Sinha, which Jethmalani admitted having issued at the request of Anil Gote.

Also, the fact that Telgi could infiltrate India's closely guarded security press so extensively and for so long, reflected the manner in which India's intelligence establishment (both revenue and security intelligence) had been compromised. Investigations revealed that the conspiracy included involvement of several serving and retired officials of ISP-Nashik. Some ex-officials/serving employees of the press had actively helped the gang of counterfeiters procure the technical know-how and various aspects of printing of genuine stamps supplied by ISP-Nashik.

The Special Investigation Team (SIT) set up by the Government of Maharashtra to investigate the counterfeit stamp case concluded that the prime accused A.K.L. Telgi and his associates had managed to obtain printing materials such as negatives and positives of stamps/stamp papers, special kind of paper meant for printing stamps, gummed papers, perforating machines, inks, etc., with the active connivance of ISP officials. Allegedly, ten perforating machines used for the manufacture of stamp paper had been clandestinely removed from ISP premises. In the raids carried out by the Special Investigation Team at the residence of Ganga Prakash, several incriminating documents were found in his possession. Some of his service documents, including a representation for promotion and posting seized from Telgi's bank locker by the Pune Police, provided evidence of closer links between the two. Moreover, in a statement that Ganga Prakash made to the investigating team of the Maharashtra Police, he confessed to his links with Telgi. He revealed that he had met Telgi, along with an ISP official, to seek the latter's intervention in his promotion/transfer case. He also admitted to having initially accepted two costly watches offered by Telgi in one such meeting at Mumbai, which he claimed to have returned to Telgi later.

Ganga Prakash and several other officials at ISP-Nashik conspired with Telgi by not only providing him technical know-how for printing of government stamps and stamp papers but had also handed over-sensitive ISP documents relating to strategy for marketing and distribution of stamp papers. Telgi was allowed access to designs, speciality paper, ink – he even knew of the production schedules. The dandy roll, a security feature used to produce the watermark, was 'given' to Telgi and his associates.

And how was Telgi able to produce duplicate stamps in such large quantities consistently? By using the same offset printing and perforating machines used by ISP-Nashik. ISP had a procedure for disposing retired printing machines by an open tendering and auction process. However, before such an auction, there was an operational imperative to dismantle the machine and remove or destroy the printing plates to prevent misuse. Ganga Prakash was apparently instrumental in delivering used offset printing machines and perforating machines for auction purposes without getting these machines dismantled, thereby facilitating the printing of counterfeit stamp papers using such machines.

From the copies of the tender notices issued by ISP-Nashik for disposal of condemned machines in the year 1998, it was revealed that M/s Unique Enterprises, No. 7, Second Floor, Mithila, Bytco Point, Nashik Road, had been a consistent bidder in all the auctions. Details of condemned machines purchased by M/s Unique Enterprises against these tenders in the year 1998 as well as the dates on which deliveries of these machines were taken by M/s Unique Enterprises and copies of ISP, Nashik Road, delivery documents/ material gate passes, also established that M/s Unique Enterprises was not just the most consistent, but also the most successful bidder in these auctions. M/s Unique Enterprises, purported to have been floated by Telgi, was run by one of Telgi's trusted aides, Jain Kishan Singh (aka Bengali), who appears later in this chronicle.

In his defence, Ganga Prakash appealed that the tender was accepted by a committee of which he was not in charge. Neither was he in charge of the auction process, which was carried out by some other officer. Moreover, M/s Unique Enterprises had bid successfully even before Ganga Prakash was posted at Nashik (in March 1998). Further, since the India Security Press did not market the stamp papers, he couldn't be held responsible for counterfeiting government stamps.

However, Ganga Prakash's pleas of innocence didn't cut ice, given the gravity of his misdemeanours. His aiding and abetting Telgi in the stamp paper scam had a direct bearing on the nation's financial security and economy since it had not only compromised on security but had also resulted in causing revenue loss of unprecedented scale both to the Central government, as well as some of the state governments. In view of the subversive activities indulged in by Ganga Prakash, it was decided to initiate disciplinary proceedings against him. The appalling situation at ISP-Nashik leading to a large-scale organized racket in fake/counterfeit stamp papers as well as the large value of fake stamp papers/stamps seized by different state police authorities across the country worth nearly Rs 3,500 crore proved the enormity of the racket.

The government was forced to crack the whip. The proposal to dismiss Ganga Prakash from service was recommended by the finance minister. His case was submitted for consideration of the committee of advisers, led by the home secretary with secretary (personnel), secretary (legal affairs), finance secretary and director, Intelligence Bureau as members. It was decided that Ganga Prakash was not fit to be retained in government service. The recommendation of the committee of advisers was approved by the finance minister as minister in-charge of the administrative ministry, ultimately approved by the prime minister.

By an official order dated 24 April 2003, Ganga Prakash was transferred to the Security Printing Press-Hyderabad, where he took up responsibility on 3 May 2003. Apparently, investigators wanted him out of the way – and far from the incriminated premises of ISP-Nashik, while they ferreted for more clues. Ganga Prasad was suspended from his duties vide another order on 16 July 2003. He was arrested by the CBI in connection with the scam on 19 December 2003. By an order dated 1 April 2004, he was terminated under Article 311(2)(c) of the Constitution of India, a little more than a year before he was due to retire from his services on 31 May 2005. It is interesting that in the subsequent legal recourse by Ganga Prakash to clear his name and challenge his dismissal from duty, he referred to the appreciation of his work by the Chief Electoral Officer and even his promotion to general manager.

Ganga Prakash also attempted to use the judicial delays and provisions of the law to have the case against him dismissed. The Delhi High Court had set aside the order of his termination vide judgment/order dated 1 November 2010, i.e., after more than six years from the date that the power under Article 311(2)(c) of the Constitution was exercised. Ganga Prakash, in the meanwhile, had retired from service on 31 May 2005. Departmental proceedings could not have been initiated against the petitioner after the order of the Delhi High Court dated 1 November 2010, as there was gap of more than four years. The limitation period of four years, as stipulated in Rule 9(2)(b)(ii) of the Central Civil Services Pension Rules, came in the way. The court dismissed Ganga Prakash's appeal on 19 October 2005, stating that it was clear that he was never exonerated on merit but rather due to the Law of Limitations. The court also observed that this had allowed a tainted official to be promoted from a deputy general manager to a general manager and enabled him to draw severance benefits at a higher pay grade. (Original Application-O.A. No. 1130/2004 refers.)

There were also allegations that Railway Protection Force (RPF) personnel had helped Telgi by stealing stamp papers while they were being transported from ISP and selling them to Abdul Karim Telgi. In 2003, seven RPF personnel were charged with pilfering stamp papers worth Rs 23 crore by breaking the locks on railway wagons. A CBI charge sheet of 2005 had made A.K.L. Telgi the eighth accused. The seven RPF personnel were able to secure bail and after Telgi's death in 2017, the case against them was dismissed for lack of evidence (*The Times of India*, 31 December 2018).

With his death, the cases against Telgi lost steam. Given people's short memory and India's propensity for newer scams, the Telgi story too was swept away from public consciousness.

7

The Business Booms

The counterfeits were made on official hardware. The ability to procure usable machines from India Security Press, along with all necessary inks, bond papers, dyes, plates, production schedules, et al ensured that Telgi was able to forge replicas of the authorised ones, right to the exact texture, feel and look. Telgi allegedly built and rented godowns to store the large number of stamp and stamp papers that were being produced with the presses procured from ISP. The replicas of the originals that Telgi was able to print gave his business a fillip and he virtually had a free run between 1998 and 2001, when he was arrested. Even thereafter, he was able to conduct his business from prison as the prison guards proved to be equally corruptible. During the golden run of over three years, the counterfeit stamp business grew by leaps and bounds and the scamster was able to expand his business in over eighteen cities in India, the principal states being Maharashtra, Karnataka, Gujarat, Andhra Pradesh, Madhya Pradesh, Delhi, Goa, Bihar, West Bengal. Though his dubious business came to light everywhere, he escaped by paying bribes.

Indore, located 190 km from Bhopal, the capital city of Madhya Pradesh, is the most populous and the largest city in the state. It serves as the headquarters of both Indore District and Indore Division. It was thus a natural operation centre for Telgi in the state. In 2000, Telgi along with Abdul Gafur Mujahid, Sohail Khan, Shabbir Ahmed Sheikh, Jagjeevan Yadav, Mansoor and Ashfaq Mulla established M/s Malwa Enterprises for the sale and distribution of counterfeit government stamps and stamp papers. The template differed little from similar outfits that now dotted the most important states in India. The front men were Abdul Gafur Mujahid and Sohail Khan, the latter as the owner of M/s Malwa Enterprises. Abdul Gafur Mujahid wasn't a resident of Indore, but stayed at Hotel Chandralok near Sarwate Bus Stand during his visits to Indore. Sohail Khan, who was earlier working in Delhi on the payroll of Abdul Karim Telgi, was sent to Indore and appointed as proprietor and in-charge of M/s Malwa Enterprises. Abdul Gafur Mujahid arranged for the office premises at City Centre, a prominent commercial centre on M.G. Road, Indore, on lease. He also took up a chamber in Trade Centre, Indore, for commercial purposes along with a residential premise at Regency Spring Building, in Chandralok Colony on rent. These premises were used as residences of Sohail Khan and his associates. Additionally, Abdul Gafur Muhajid also applied for and secured two landline telephones connections each for the City Centre and the Trade Centre offices.

Sohail Khan, in turn, also hired premises at Giriraj Apartments, Indore, on rent for running another office of Malwa Enterprises. On 28 January 2000 and 1 February 2000, Abdul Gafur Mujahid published advertisements in the Hindi daily newspaper *Dainik Bhaskar* seeking to employ local persons in different capacities in Malwa Enterprises. Abdul Gafur Mujahid and Shabbir Ahmed Sheikh interviewed local persons, who applied in response to the advertisement. They recruited boys and girls, who were imparted training to work as marketing executives and telephone operators for Malwa Enterprises.

Sohail Khan opened a current account on 27 March 2000 for M/s Malwa Enterprises at the State Bank of Indore (then a subsidiary of the State Bank of India [SBI]), Y.N. Road Branch, Indore, to give financial legitimacy to the operation. As with the other business models of Telgi, the syndicate required a licenced stamp vendor to front the nefarious designs of Malwa Enterprises. Jagjeevan Yadav fronted the racket by furnishing a photostat copy of his stamp vendor licence as document of proof in the bank. This was used as evidence of authenticity of the business of Malwa Enterprises. Clearly, A.K.L. Telgi wanted to control the operation with the help of his own people or those he trusted and yet use the licence of others to further his business. The fake stamp baron wanted 'outsiders' to take the risks but not control his trade.

Abdul Gafur Mujahid, Shabbir Ahmed Sheikh and Sohail Khan told the marketing executives that they were working for a big firm having its offices at various places across India. They also assured the executives that M/s Malwa Enterprises was an approved vending company under the requisite laws, and it was selling stamps in the name of Jagjeevan Yadav, a licenced stamp vendor, authorised to sell special adhesive stamps, insurance policy stamps, revenue stamps and non-judicial stamp papers of various denominations.

The photocopy of the licence of Jagjeevan Yadav was also provided to the marketing executives to convince financial institutions that the business of Malwa Enterprises was legitimate. It is strange that most institutions who were approached by the marketing executives of Malwa Enterprises didn't question the locus standi of Jagjeevan Yadav. The most basic question was not asked: Given that Jagjeevan Yadav was not the proprietor of the firm, why was his licence being used by the executives?

Perhaps the discounts provided by Malwa Enterprises were too attractive to pass up and many thought that they had kept themselves covered when they made payments to Jagjeevan Yadav, rather than Malwa Enterprises or Sohail Khan, the proprietor of the firm.

One such example was United India Insurance Co. at Indore, which issued cheques in the name of Jagjeevan Yadav for purchase of stamps from Malwa Enterprises. Jagjeevan Yadav deposited the said cheques in his own account at the State Bank of Indore, Court

Compound Branch and Mill Area Branch, and also withdrew the amount, thereby establishing his role in the conspiracy.

While Abdul Gafur Mujahid, who was posted at the office of Malwa Enterprises at 418, City Centre, Indore, updated A.K.L. Telgi about sales performance of Malwa Enterprises, Sohail Khan was in charge of all the local staff working there. His duty was to supervise all their activities, including the collection of orders for sale of stamps obtained by various marketing executives from different banks/ financial institutions. The sale proceeds of these stamps received in the form of various cheques/DDs/cash used to be deposited by Sohail Khan in the current account held by him as the proprietor of Malwa Enterprises in State Bank of Indore, Y.N. Road Branch, unless of course, the payment was made to Jagjeevan Yadav.

The account of Sohail Khan as proprietor of the firm was operational till 28 September 2000 and a total amount of Rs 35,80,000 was deposited through cheques, demand drafts, cash, and an amount of Rs 35,30,000 was withdrawn from the said account by various cheques issued by Sohail Khan.

Shabbir Ahmed Sheikh was the go-between A.K.L. Telgi and the operations of Malwa Enterprises. He visited Indore frequently from Mumbai to supply fake stamps in Indore and to collect the proceeds from the sale of fake stamps from Sohail Khan. Initially, the fake stamps were couriered to Malwa Enterprises from the office of M/s Metro Exports, A.K.L. Telgi's firm in Mumbai through Flyking Courier Services, Mumbai. Subsequently, Shabbir Ahmed Sheikh personally ferried the fake stamps to Indore. Ashfaq Mulla and Mansoor Bacholikar, both from A.K.L. Telgi's native village, were deployed in Indore and worked as per directions of Sohail Khan. Their duties were to put the fake stamps in envelopes and hand them to Sohail Khan at the Trade Centre office of Malwa Enterprises. The business thrived on a nimble network of operatives and couriers to make detection difficult.

The mastermind, flush with cash, jet-setted in style. A.K.L. Telgi flew to Indore periodically, using his favourite carrier Jet Airways, travelling business class. He stayed in posh hotels like Hotel Shrimaya and Hotel Sayaji. During these visits, he dropped in at the twin offices of Malwa Enterprises on various occasions, and exhorted the local staff, along with Sohail Khan and Abdul Gafur Mujahid, to increase the sale of stamps. He promised higher sales-linked incentives and enhanced salaries for the performers.

The operations of Malwa Enterprises came to light with the registration of a criminal case at the Tukoganj Police Station in Indore based on an FIR lodged by the branch manager, Bank of India, Simrol Branch, Indore. The bank used to purchase special adhesive stamps from the treasury. In June 2002, the branch manager was contacted by employees of M/s Malwa Enterprises, who advised that Sohail Khan, Abdul Gafur Mujahid, Karim and Ashfaq were the owners of the firm and that their firm could supply stamps and stamp papers directly to the branch itself and the firm had licence to sell such stamps in the name of Jagjeevan Yadav. The branch manager was shown a Xerox copy of the licence of Jagjeevan Yadav. The bank purchased 260 special adhesive stamps of Rs 50 denomination each and four non-judicial stamp papers of Rs 1,000 denomination each and one non-judicial stamp of Rs 5,000 denomination.

When the branch manager heard that fake stamps were being sold in Indore, he tried to contact M/s Malwa Enterprises, but no one was available. The stamps so purchased were shown to the district registrar, who declared them fake. A complaint was duly lodged by the branch manager, triggering the investigation.

Telgi's manufacturing hubs where the printing and perforating machines along with other necessary inks, dyes, plates, bond papers, etc., were housed included M/s Unique Enterprises in Nashik, M/s Mudran Offset Printers in Mumbai and another unit in Pune. In the investigations throughout India conducted by the CBI in the various fake stamp cases, huge quantities of counterfeit stamps, printing machines and perforating machines were recovered. The recovery was the largest for the case registered at the Bund Garden Police Station, Pune. During the investigation, fake stamps supplied by M/s Malwa Enterprises were seized and sent to the Indian Security Press, Nashik, for their opinion. Authorities at ISP mentioned that the stamps were not only forged but were similar to the stamps seized in Crime No. 135/2002 at the Bund Garden Police Station, Pune. They, thus, concluded that the same machinery was used for counterfeiting government stamps sold at Indore.

Abdul Gafur Mujahid passed away during the investigations. Charge sheets were filed against A.K.L. Telgi, Sohail Khan, Shabbir Ahmed Sheikh, Jagjeevan Yadav, Mansoor Bacholikar and Ashfaq Mulla. They were arraigned to face trial for the offences punishable under various sections of the IPC, Indian Stamps Act 1899 and Madhya Pradesh Stamp Rules 1942. Ashfaq Mulla and Mansoor Bacholikar turned approvers and were pardoned, but their evidence made the case against the others accused almost watertight. During the trial, Jagjeevan Yadav died and prosecution against him abated. A.K.L. Telgi, Sohail Khan and Shabbir Ahmed Sheikh were sentenced and fined.

Judgments were passed in 2005 and the criminal appeals heard in 2014 (Criminal Appeal No. 58/2010 [Arising Out of S.T. No. 109/2005], Criminal Appeal No. 150/2010 [Arising Out of S.T. No. 109/2005]; Criminal Appeal No. 148/2010 [Arising Out of S.T. No. 108/2005]; and Criminal Appeal No. 57/2010 [Arising Out of S.T. No. 108/2005] and final judgment passed on 3 April 2014.

The name of Abdul Gafur Mujahid also appears in another case of M/s Prime Services in New Delhi (Criminal Appeal No: 21/2012 judged on 10 October 2012). Though the case had been decided against Telgi and his accomplices earlier, this appeal was made by his counsel seeking leniency in the sentence on account of his failing health and multiple diseases in prison. The appeal was denied.

A.K.L. Telgi along with Abdul Gafur Mujahid, Anand Thorat, Sachin Munna and Ashfaq Mulla had floated a company by the name of M/s Prime Services with its office at Devika Tower, Nehru Place, New Delhi, during 1997-98 for illegal trading in counterfeit stamps/non-judicial stamp papers in various parts of Delhi and adjoining areas. Allegedly, the lease for the premises was executed by Mujahid on the instructions of Telgi. Mujahid opened a current account No. 10731 in the name of M/s Prime Services with the Punjab National

Bank, New Friends Colony, New Delhi, in the year 1998, wherein the sale proceeds from counterfeit stamps worth Rs 70 lakh were deposited by way of cheques issued by the buyers. It has been alleged that another office of Prime Services was opened at New Friends Colony, where Thorat was in charge. Thorat and Mulla later withdrew most of the money from the aforesaid account of 'Prime Services.' Based on a complaint of one A.K. Bass, investigation officer, on 29 March 2004, the case was registered.

Along with C.S. Balaji, Telgi also set up M/s Sagayam Enterprises in Chennai at Purasawalkam High Road, Kellys. Based on the CBI's composite charge sheet on 26 July 2005 in Special Case No 2 of 2003 against Telgi and sixty-five others, in which Telgi ultimately pleaded guilty, both Telgi and Balaji were sentenced on 26 August 2007. An appeal was filed by both (Criminal Appeal Nos.436 and 766 of 2008), which was decided on 8 April 2010, wherein a part remission was made as charges were reduced from manufacture/preparation and distribution to one of distribution alone, as counterfeit stamps were not manufactured in Chennai but brought in from Nashik and Mumbai.

8

Competition and Complicity

Telgi had by now templated his business model. The Bhopal and Bengaluru blueprints were replicated in many commercial and state capitals across the country. He would find a corruptible person in a target city with a valid vendor licence, build a proprietary firm or a partnership with his own key persons heading it and handling operations. The involvement of the said vendor would be limited to providing a copy of the licence as proof of business and collecting payments made directly to him. Supply of stamps would be handled by Telgi's trusted persons carrying them from the 'production centres' of Nashik, Pune and Mumbai. And in case of detection and arrests, the local allies would take the rap while A.K.L. Telgi and his gang would escape by greasing the right palms.

Telgi realised that organic growth by a smattering of these small firms across the country was not viable in the long run and would stretch him thin. Trust and secrecy were key in these operations, and the members in his close circle, on whom he could depend, few. It was impossible to expect that his coterie would be adequate to criss-cross the length and breadth of the country to oversee his prospering business. He thought of an alternative model to grow his business.

So, while his marketing executives targeted large corporations, banks and bulk purchasers, he began to lure the thousands of independent stamp vendors to stock and sell his counterfeit stamps at higher commissions, rather than the 2 to 3 per cent they earned when they obtained their stocks from the government treasury.

Large corporations such as the Life Insurance Corporation or Indian Oil would be approached by Telgi's executives with lucrative discounts of up to 5 per cent, almost double what most stamp vendors offered (*Frontline*, 10 February 2006). Additionally, the clerks tasked with the purchases of stamps didn't need to run around to procure the stamps as Telgi's sales staff would deliver these to their offices. Most dealing officers and clerks at the large corporations succumbed to the temptation, bought the stamps in bulk and, of course, kept quiet. Telgi flourished, while the government lost crores of rupees in revenue.

As a report in *India Today*, dated 10 March 2003, observed, "Only the state treasury was allowed to sell non-judicial stamp papers of values above Rs 500. But Telgi's vendors sold these in bulk to people, who were ignorant about this rule," just as they were about the need to buy adhesive stamps from authorised offices.

There were, however, two developments of significance. The first was the direct complicity of the police and the keepers of law. They now wanted a share of the commissions in the business and not just bribes 'to look the other way'. The second was the establishment of smaller 'clones' of Telgi, who wanted to emulate him and profit from the well-spread and established business of counterfeit stamps, but whom Telgi would try and marginalise by using his connections. A case in point was M/s Blue Star Services in New Delhi. Narender Singh, proprietor of Blue Star Services, along with Prahlad Singh, Hemant Dubey of Mumbai and others were running a parallel network of fake stamps in Delhi.

During 1991-2001, Police Inspector Puran Singh was posted in the District Crime Cell (South District) Delhi. He was the investigating officer of a case (FIR No. 803/99), involving the sale of fake stamps leading to loss of government revenue. During the investigation of this case, he came in touch with A.K.L. Telgi. According to the CBI (which reopened this case along with many others involving Telgi), Inspector Puran Singh, along with Sub-inspector Gaurav Aggarwal, Head Constable Om Prakash and constables Ratan Singh and Sanjay Bajad helped A.K.L. Telgi sell counterfeit stamps and stamp papers to business houses, while ensuring that Telgi was deliberately kept out of the purview of investigation and didn't face the heat. Besides favouring Telgi, when one Anand, wanted in case FIR No. 803/99, was arrested, Inspector Singh allegedly abused his position and did not investigate or file a charge sheet against him.

Ranbaxy Laboratories Ltd (M/s Ranbaxy) were using foreign bill stamps, which were required to be affixed on their export and import documents. The company, which earlier purchased foreign bill stamps from the post office, bought foreign stamps from M/s Capital Services (a firm run via proxy by Telgi through Patil and Hafiz), M/s Unique Consultants (another firm run by Telgi by proxy through his men) and M/s Blue Star Services, payments for which were made through cheques.

Ranjan Paul, an employee of M/s Ranbaxy, who appeared as prosecution witness (PW number 11) and who maintained the stock position records of foreign bill stamps for the company between 24 November 2000 and 6 December 2000, stated that M/s Ranbaxy received foreign bill stamps worth Rs 1 lakh from M/s Blue Star Services. The available stock position on 4 December 2000 was Rs 4,900. They then bought foreign bill stamps for Rs 1.5 lakh from M/s Unique Consultant on 5 December 2000. The available stock position on 6 December 2000 was Rs 47,100. The stamps purchased from M/s Unique Consultants were, reportedly, sent to Hong Kong and Shanghai Banking Corporation (HSBC) along with the documents. Inspector Singh visited HSBC, Connaught Place, New Delhi on 6 December 2000 in connection with the investigation of case FIR No. 803/99. He checked and declared the foreign bill stamps and allied documents presented by Ranbaxy Laboratories Ltd bogus and issued instructions to HSBC to keep the same in safe custody but did not investigate the matter further.

On 7 December 2000, he visited the office of Ranbaxy Laboratories Ltd, Devika Tower, Nehru Place, New Delhi, and checked the available stock of foreign bill stamps. Ranjan Paul said they had purchased stamps from Blue Star Services. Inspector Singh examined the remaining stock of Rs 37,500 (375 stamps of Rs 100 denomination each) in the presence of Ranjan Paul and his senior manager S. Vishwanathan and declared them fake. He seized the same and duly prepared the seizure memo. After seizure, Inspector Singh advised Ranjan Paul that he wanted to nab the delivery boy red-handed, and requested Ranjan Paul to place fresh order for supply of stamps from M/s Blue Star Services. Ranjan Paul accordingly ordered stamps for a total value of Rs 1 lakh over the telephone in the presence of S. Vishwanathan and Inspector Singh. Prahlad Singh of M/s Blue Star Services promised supply the next day (8 December 2000) as he didn't have sufficient stock at that time.

As per the stock records, on 7 December 2000, the available stock of foreign bill stamps worth Rs 37,500 which Inspector Singh seized could include a maximum Rs 4,900 worth of stamps supplied by M/s Blue Star Services (since after 4 December 2000 purchases had not been made from M/s Blue Star Services till the order which reached them on 8 December 2000). The remaining would have to pertain to supplies by M/s Unique Consultants, Telgi's firm! This matter was glossed over and allegedly the stock records presented as evidence were changed, too.

On 8 December 2000, Inspector Singh arrested, without following due legal procedure, Prahlad Singh who delivered the stamps from M/s Blue Star Services. During investigations, fake stamps worth Rs 18,48,300 were seized from the locations disclosed by Prahlad Singh. Prahlad Singh said the fake stamps were being supplied by one Hemant Dubey, son of Surya Kant Dubey, of Mumbai. On his arrest and interrogation, Narender Singh, the proprietor of M/s Blue Star Services, disclosed that his firm dealt in the supply of stamp for the purposes of share transfer, insurance, etc., and that the said stamps were supplied by Hemant Surya Kant Dubey, Subhash and one Ms Rupali of Mumbai. Inspector Singh lodged a case, FIR No. 878/00, at the Kalkaji Police Station, New Delhi, against Narender Singh. Further, during investigations, Inspector Singh and Gaurav Aggarwal illegally prepared seizure memos and recorded false statement, etc., turning the spotlight away from Telgi and facilitating the expansion of his racket of counterfeit stamps. Hemant Dubey was arrested by the Crime Branch, Mumbai, on 21 May 2001 (FIR No. 131/01).

Narender Singh surrendered before the court on January 2001 in connection with the investigation related to case FIR No. 878/00. His police remand was taken by Inspector Singh, and he was shifted to Mumbai for investigation. Om Prakash, Ratan Singh and Sanjay Bajad also accompanied Inspector Singh. The police custody was to expire on 10 January 2001, but it appears that a transit remand till 12 January 2001 from the Mumbai court was obtained, though the police team brought Narender Singh back to Delhi on 10 January 2001.

Further, Narender Singh, while still in police custody, was taken to Corporation Bank, CGO Complex Branch, Lodhi Road, New Delhi on 11 January 2001 where he withdrew a total sum of Rs 8,55,000 and the amount was distributed among all the conniving policemen. According to the case details, Inspector Singh received Rs 2,95,000 as personal gratification. However, the daily diary entry did not reveal this transgression. The money was paid voluntarily by Narender Singh so that M/s Blue Star Services was spared and not indicted in said case FIR No. 878/00 (PS Kalkaji). Additionally, Narender Singh was given full liberty, was permitted to move freely and even to stay at his residence during the same period of police custody. These facts were revealed when Narender Singh moved an application on 11 August 2004, praying that he wanted to disclose certain facts, and made a confessional statement.

The CBI's investigation further revealed that Inspector Singh, while investigating the case FIR No. 878/00 (PS Kalkaji), New Delhi, had visited Chennai along with A.K.L. Telgi and issued false/fictitious house/office search memos for M/s Marina Services, one of Telgi's firms, and in respect of the residential premises of Nizamuddin, proprietor of Marina Services and a close associate of Telgi, on whose licence Telgi was dealing in fake stamps. Further investigations were conducted in Chennai and the same revealed that certain search memos were issued by Inspector Singh under his seal and signatures, in respect of the business establishments of Telgi, indicating that Singh searched the said premises. No fake stamps were, however, found on the premises, but only genuine ones.

This effectively gave a clean chit to Telgi's firms such as Marina Services and Shara Enterprises, and it was affirmed that they were dealing in genuine stamps only.

The CBI further discovered that in fact no searches on the said premises were ever conducted by Inspector Singh and the memos were prepared by him under his seal and signatures, in pursuance of the conspiracy hatched by him, along with A.K.L. Telgi and others, with a view to facilitate the sale/expansion of the latter's fake stamp business in Chennai and in other parts of Tamil Nadu. These memos issued by Inspector Singh were frequently used by the marketing executives of M/s Marina Services and Shara Enterprises, owned by Telgi, to obtain orders of stamps from LIC and other clients by showing the same as endorsements/ certificates to the effect that they were dealing in genuine stamps.

Copies of two such false /fictitious house/office search memos were available on record (Crime Report RC No.02/2004, EOU-VII), seized from the office of Marina Services/Shara Enterprises. A copy of one such false/fictitious house/office search memos was handed to the investigating officer by M. Mohana Peruman, Manager (Claims), LIC of India, Divisional Office, Sellur, Madurai.

The investigations also revealed that the above said two house search memos and house/office search memo did not find any mention in the case diary file of FIR No. 878/00 (PS Kalkaji), New Delhi, investigated by Inspector Singh.

The three search memos – for Marina Services at their address in Sindoor Shopping Centre, Anna Nagar West, Chennai; for the residential premises of Nizamuddin, proprietor of Marina Services, Anna Nagar, Chennai; and for M/s Shara Enterprises

– were prepared by Inspector Singh at the behest of Telgi when Inspector Singh had accompanied Telgi on his visit to Chennai. In meetings with his close business associates, Telgi apparently boasted that the said memos had been obtained from Inspector Singh by paying him huge sums of money and that they should be leveraged to enhance the sale of fake stamps and to source orders from behemoths, including LIC, a potential client for insurance policy stamps.

The investigation in FIR No. 878/2000 brought to light facts pertaining to the preparation of fabricated documents and fake seizures by Inspector Singh and his team members. The demands for bribe made by Inspector Singh from those who figured in the counterfeit cases being investigated by him were also revealed. A separate case was registered based on the revelations against Inspector Singh, Gaurav Aggarwal, A.K.L. Telgi, Om Prakash, Ram Ratan Singh, and Sanjay Bajad on 20 February 2004. Inspector Puran Singh was arrested on 21 February 2004.

A charge sheet was also filed against Narender Singh and Prahlad Singh on 1 February 2005 in the court of the learned Metropolitan Magistrate Special Cases, Patiala House, New Delhi. During the investigation, further samples of fake stamps were seized, which were examined by the India Security Press in Nashik. An investigation pertaining to the accused, Narender Singh and M/s Blue Star Services, New Delhi, Hemant Dubey of Bombay was also conducted, and a supplementary charge sheet filed. Investigations revealed that Inspector Singh, along with a few others, was able to implicate and ensnare the business rivals of Telgi in false cases. Telgi had used the police establishment efficaciously to push the frontiers of his fake stamp syndicate.

Stamps worth lakhs of rupees were supplied by M/s Blue Star Services to different companies of Delhi and Noida, etc., which were later surrendered/seized by CBI (Crime Report RC 1/2004-EOU V and RC 2/2004-EOU V). The same were taken on record and sent to ISP-Nashik for examination, which revealed them as counterfeit. Many rivals of Telgi, who had managed to evade arrests, were emboldened by the arrest and incarceration of A.K.L. Telgi in 2001, to resurrect their respective businesses. This allowed the crime to fester well after Telgi's imprisonment, though Telgi managed to run his own business from prison for a long time.

In a strange twist to this case (and perhaps others which involved business rivals of Telgi), an advocate, Deepak Anand, had filed a writ petition, W.P. (C) No. 3903/2011, as a Public Interest Litigation (PIL) seeking a direction from the Ministry of Home Affairs, Government of India, to constitute an independent SIT or a Special Task Force (STF) for fair, unbiased, impartial, and proper investigation of case FIR No. 878/2000 (PS Kalkaji), New Delhi, and to expose the fake stamps scams, and book all the persons involved in the crime. Mr Anand's contention was that:

i. Though the accused in the FIR had disclosed getting fake stamps from Hemant Dubey of Mumbai, after the CBI took over investigation of the case, the agency surprisingly not only gave a clean chit to Hemant Dubey but also cited him as a prosecution witness in the charge sheet.
ii. From what emerged in the investigation, it was evident that apart from the 'Telgi Scam', there was another fake stamp scam, which ran parallel to the 'Telgi Scam'.
iii. Though the fake stamp scam of Abdul Karim Telgi had come to an end, the parallel scam of Hemant Dubey and others was yet to be unearthed.

The CBI – Respondent 2 in the case, along with the Union of India – was, however, able to successfully defend its position stating that the contention in the petition that the fake stamps recovered were printed by Hemant Dubey was devoid of any merits. The role of Hemant Dubey was probed, but except the allegations of accused Narender Singh nothing substantial came on record. Thus, according to the CBI, there was no ground for prosecuting Hemant Dubey. Further, the CBI argued that the petition had been filed at the behest of the accused persons (A.K.L. Telgi and others) in an attempt to scuttle/delay the progress of the trial against Telgi and his fellow criminals. The petition was dismissed forthwith.

***

The CBI's position on Hemant Dubey (not that he was totally blameless) had its antecedents in two cases of significance. The first related to CBI's Case No.RC-6/2004/ E.O.U.-VII -New Delhi, corresponding to Crime No.123/2000 registered at Satpur Police Station, Nashik.

According to the original case details, a posse of policemen, headed by Inspector Anil Muralidhar Deshmukh of the Nashik Crime Branch, while patrolling the city on 10 October 2000, allegedly spotted a white Maruti Van parked near Mauli Petrol Pump, Nashik-Trimbak Road. Suspicious of the four persons in the vehicle, namely, Sachin Gotiram Zhaveri, Raju Tukaram Satpute, Ajay Shivaji Dhisale and Jitu Premchand Harvani, they searched the vehicle and recovered a plastic bag containing twenty sheets (each sheet with 180 insurance stamps of Rs 500 denomination), amounting to Rs 18 lakh.

Upon interrogation, Dhisale admitted to working as a driver for one Jai Kishan Singh (aka Bengali referred to henceforth), who had kept a suitcase with Dhisale advising him that it contained office papers. The police team searched the residential premises of Bengali at the Maharashtra Housing Colony, Satpur, in the presence of Savita, his wife. The raid yielded about forty sheets of insurance stamps of denomination of Rs 20 and Rs 1,000 (each sheet containing 180 stamps) amounting to Rs 36.72 lakh.

All those apprehended were arrested by the Crime Branch, Nashik, on the same day i.e., 10 October 2000, and produced before the Court of the Judicial Magistrate, the next day. Their police custody remand was sought along with permission to investigate the offence under Section 124 of the Bombay Police Act. The custody was denied. The seized insurance stamps were sent to the Indian Security Press, Nashik, and the expert opinion confirmed that the stamps were counterfeit. This led to the registration of Crime No. 123/2000 against all those arrested. Police Sub-inspector R.M. Pawar, one of the policemen in the team, who had apprehended the culprits, was entrusted with the investigation of the case and on 31 December 2000, he filed the charge sheet (C.C.No.31/2000). Bengali, who was shown as absconding, was arrested on 25 January 2001, after obtaining his transfer from Tihar Jail, Delhi, where he was lodged in Crime No.678/2000 of Kalkaji Police Station, New Delhi. Sub-inspector Pawar took police custody of Bengali.

In his recorded statement, Bengali disclosed that Hemant Dubey, Subhash Bhai, and Shiv Shankar Singh were the persons responsible for the printing, perforation and circulation of the stamps in Nashik. Pawar filed supplementary charge sheets on 8 May 2001 against Bengali and the persons named by him, who were, however, shown as untraceable. Hemant Dubey was arrested on 7 June 2001 from Thane, though he was discharged for lack of evidence on 9 August 2001.

On 11 February 2003, this case was transferred to N.B. Tambade, deputy commissioner of police, Nashik, by the order of commissioner of police, Nashik. Accused Shiv Shankar Singh and one Sirajuddin Nasipudi were arrested on 19 March 2003 and 28 March 2003, respectively. The supplementary charge sheet filed against these two persons included the names of A.K.L. Telgi, Mahiram, Bharti, Madhu and Umesh Nayak. This was the first instance in the case that Telgi's name had cropped up in three years. This case was also amongst those to be transferred later to the CBI on 15 March 2004. During the investigation, MCOCA provisions were invoked on 30 September 2004 by the order of deputy inspector general, Economic Offences-III, CBI, New Delhi. The case was transferred to R.K. Shukla, deputy superintendent of police, CBI, New Delhi.

Investigation by the CBI changed the entire complexion of the case. It was revealed that the Crime Branch, Nashik, had seized fake insurance stamps worth Rs 54.72 lakh from the accused Raju Satpute, on 8 October 2000, when he was sitting in the Maruti Van on the Mumbai-Nashik Highway near Sachin Hotel and the story of the discovery of the vehicle two days later, on 10 October 2000, near Mauli Petrol Pump near Nashik-Trimbak Road was false. This was corroborated by Assistant Sub-inspector Gosavi, who was also a part of the police team which had made the seizure. The accused, Sachin Gotiram, was driving the vehicle. According to the CBI investigation, in October 2000, Inspector Anil Deshmukh was in-charge of the Crime Branch, Nashik, where Sub-inspector Pawar too was posted. Investigation of the case was entrusted to Pawar after its registration on 12 October 2000. Allegedly, the stamps in question were taken out by Dhisale, driver of Bengali, in a suitcase which was kept in a different flat in the Maharashtra Housing Colony, Satpur, by Bengali. This apartment was owned and possessed by Dhisale, and Bengali had handed over the suitcase for safe custody. Subsequently, Dhisale gave the suitcase to Raju Satpute for sale of stamps. Satpute, with the help of Jitu Harwani, arranged for sale of the insurance stamps at Nashik.

False panchnamas were allegedly prepared by officers of the crime branch, including Pawar, to show the seizure at a different place and a different date i.e., 10 October 2000. The police officers also showed a false recovery from a different house – that of Bengali in the same Maharashtra Housing Colony. When Savita Singh, Bengali's wife, was arrested and brought to the Crime Branch, she revealed in her statement to Deshmukh and Pawar that her husband was in the stamp business at Nashik on behalf of A.K.L. Telgi, who was staying in Mumbai.

During the search conducted in the office of M/s Unique Enterprises (the same entity which had secured the printing presses at the India Security Press auctions), Bitco Point, Nashik Road, belonging to Bengali, on 17 November 2000, Pawar seized two receipt books and an office file containing details of the machineries purchased in an auction from ISP, Nashik, by Bengali. The diary also revealed Bengali's business links with A.K.L. Telgi. On the same day, the statement of Rajaram Bhaguji Jadhav, the owner of the office premises of M/s Unique Enterprises, was recorded by Pawar. Jadhav told him that the office belonged to A.K.L. Telgi, and that Bengali was looking after Telgi's business from this office.

Investigating officer Pawar, under the supervision of inspector Deshmukh, deliberately and in consideration of pecuniary advantages, ignored vital facts and testimonies of important witnesses. The disclosure statements recorded by the police officers focused on implicating rival stamp vendors of Telgi, and other lesser-known persons, namely, Hemant Dubey, Shiv Shankar Singh and Subhash Bhai in this case knowingly and wilfully to divert the line of investigation away from the organized crime syndicate of A.K.L. Telgi for monetary consideration.

Bengali was taken to Rajni Industries, located at G-74, MIDC Ambad, Nashik, where he confirmed that perforation work on the stamps was done on the machines installed there. Sub-inspector Pawar deliberately omitted to bring on record the vital fact that both Bengali and Shiv Shankar Singh worked for A.K.L. Telgi, as was revealed by the chowkidar and local tea vendor of Rajni Industries.

Hemant Dubey was arrested by Pawar on 7 June 2001 and taken on police remand. On 8 August 2001, Pawar, with the knowledge of Inspector Deshmukh, filed a discharge application in the Court of the Judicial Magistrate at Nashik on the ground that there was no evidence against Dubey. He was discharged by the court on 9 August 2001. Pawar received pecuniary advantage of Rs 9.5 lakh on different occasions from the family of Hemant Dubey for his staff and self, including Deshmukh, to ensure that Dubey was comfortable in custody, and finally to secure his discharge in this case. Rupali's (Hemant Dubey's wife) statement confirmed this. Hemant Dubey's statement recorded on 3 July 2004 alleged that although he was in custody of Thane Police, the team of Nashik Police came seeking his custody on a transfer warrant. He knew that there was a case pending against him at Nashik, which he was not involved in, and that the Nashik case was being investigated by Pawar. He also alleged that Pawar had sought money from his wife Rupali. According to Hemant Dubey, he was taken to Telgi's office in Mumbai. In Mumbai, Pawar allegedly also informed Dubey that Telgi's wife had tried to bribe him.

These statements recorded show that both Inspector Deshmukh and Sub-inspector Pawar were aware of Telgi's organised crime syndicate and that stamps were being perforated and transported from Nashik. They also knew of the activities being carried out on the premises, belonging to Bengali and Telgi, and that the stamps and stamp papers were not genuine. This case revealed the complicity of the police, wherein not only were false persons (Telgi's competitors) implicated, but they also had to pay heavy bribes to secure their release!

On 11 June 2001, Pawar, during his investigation in Mumbai, arrested Sirajuddin Nasipudi and questioned him. Although the queries revealed that Nasipudi was looking after the work of transport of A.K.L. Telgi in Mumbai and Nashik, he was brought to Nashik and then let off apparently at the behest of Telgi, who paid Rs 7 lakh to Pawar. This was another example of allowing a close member of Telgi's crime syndicate to go scot-free in exchange for monetary consideration. The investigation further revealed that the stamps were printed by AKL Telgi in Mumbai and transported to Nashik, initially in Bengali's car and later by transport managed by Sirajuddin Nasipudi, for perforation at Rajni Industries. Shiv Shankar Singh, along with Madhu, Lakhi, Mahiram and Umesh Nayak, would do the perforation work on the instructions of Bengali. Allegedly, after the registration of crime No.123/2000, Bengali negotiated the settlement of the case against A.K.L. Telgi and himself with Inspector Deshmukh and Sub-inspector Pawar and paid Rs 10 lakh. However, Bengali was arrested while A.K.L. Telgi did not figure as accused anywhere in the investigation conducted by Crime Branch, Nashik.

This case validates that Telgi's interests enjoyed the protection of senior police officials who manipulated case records. Their role in undertaking superficial searches and extorting money rather than finding the original source of printing of the counterfeit stamps was also established.

Following a departmental inquiry, Deshmukh was arrested on 8 October 2004. He applied for bail vide Criminal Miscellaneous Application No.16 of 2004, which was rejected by the special judge, MCOCA court, Pune, in an order dated 29 November 2004, following which he preferred bail application in this case (CBI's Case No.R.C.-6/2004/ E.O.U.-VII). Deshmukh's lawyer argued that MCOCA provisions were not applicable as the whole case was one of dereliction of duty rather than criminal involvement. The court did not find merit in this as it was established by the statements of Prakash Ramdas Kale (Bengali's acquaintance) that the police had sought Rs 15 lakh for Savita's release and 'settlement of the case', which was negotiated down to Rs 10 lakh, and the money was paid by Telgi in Mumbai to Kale, and one Suresh Vavre. The CBI didn't find Savita Singh complicit and she was discharged in the case. The lawyer's argument that Inspector Anil Deshmukh was also a venerated officer and a recipient of President's Medal didn't hold water and the bail application was rejected.

The second case that influenced CBI's position on Hemant Dubey was Crime No. 131/2001 of Police Station, Thane Nagar, Maharashtra, against Sandeep Krishna Kandar, George Thomas and others, which was another example of police complicity and deflection of the crime away from A.K.L. Telgi. The case was registered as RC.10/2004/EOU-IV/New Delhi, when it was transferred to the CBI vide the Supreme Court order of 15 March 2004. The case pertained to the seizure of counterfeit revenue stamps and share transfer stamps worth Rs 51,390 from one Sandeep Krishna Kandar, resident of Charlie Pereira Chawl, in Andheri, in front of Khandelwal Sweets, Station Road, Thane, on 16 May 2001 at 21.40 hours.

After investigation, the Crime Branch submitted its final report against Sandeep and two others, namely, Hemant Dubey and George Thomas, on 12 June 2002, vide Criminal Case- CC No. 211/2002. Supplementary charge sheets were additionally submitted against Shabeer Mushtaq Ahmed and Shankar Gannappa on 25 March 2003, and against Shiv Shankar Kamleshwar Singh on 3 April 2003. The Thane Crime Branch also arrested M.D. Jadhav, Jacob Chako, Sheikh Mohamed Hussein Sheikh, Sirajuddin Nasipudi, Feroze Abdul Rehman Sheikh and Mohd. Yousuf Singutti, when it handed the case over to the CBI.

The CBI investigation, undertaken by Deputy Superintendent of Police S. Balasubramony, on 2 April 2004 revealed serious infraction on the part of the Thane Police led by Sub-inspector Hitendra Manohar Vichare (Applicant in Criminal Application-CA No. 1048 of 2005 and CA No. 1666 of 2005) and Inspector Dattatraya Krishnaji Ghule (Applicant in CA No. 1202/2005). The duo had challenged the order passed by the trial court (special judge under MCOC Act, Pune) permitting further 'continued detention'. Their application was dismissed on 13 April 2005 on the grounds that Sub-inspector Vichare and Inspector Ghule had knowingly aided and abetted A.K.L. Telgi's crime syndicate and allowed the perpetration of its unlawful activities for more than a year till they were arrested in the Bund Garden Case on 8 October 2004.

The probe by the CBI hinted that something was irregular in the past probe by the Thane Police, principally because the source of stamps found in possession of Sandeep Kandar on 16 May 2001 and that of the stamps recovered from his residence were never investigated. These stamps were forged and resembled the make of stamps seized in the Bund Garden case (principal accused A.K.L. Telgi) and therefore the source should have been the same for these stamps. When queried, the Thane Police were vague. They said that Sandeep used to purchase from two or three vendors and sell it to Shabbir. They failed to explain why Shabbir Mushtaq Ahmed Sheikh, a key Telgi associate dealing in the manufacture and sale of forged stamps, should purchase stamps from a small-time vendor like Sandeep Kandar.

Statement of witnesses further conclusively proved that Shabbir Ahmed was in custody of the Thane Police during the period 16 May 2001 to 20 May 2001. However, the records of station diary collected from the Thane Police Station did not show the arrest of Shabbir, which meant that he was kept in illegal custody and then allowed to escape (he was later taken into custody in the Bund Garden case). Further, evidence collected on Shabbir's role contradicted what was explained by the Thane Police. Shabbir was the main person who had supplied the stamps to Sandeep Kander, which were seized by the Thane Police. Shabbir met Sandeep posing as one Madhav, who worked for Hemant Dubey, a wanted accused. So, the spotlight of the investigation was deftly shifted from Shabbir to Hemant Dubey, who was later arrested by Sub-inspector Vichare.

Sub-inspector Vichare was thus charged for allowing Shabbir to escape, for booking persons not connected with the crime and for showing forged recovery from them. The role of Inspector Ghule was also similar to that of Vichare. He became associated with the case after the arrest of Sandeep Kandar. He had played an active role in the arrest of Hemant Dubey and George Hiwale and showed forged recoveries from them through false panchnamas – document bearing the details of the crime dated 23 May 2001 and 24 May 2001 as well as a forged disclosure dated 24 May 2001. The panchnamas showing the arrests of Hemant Dubey and George Hiwale, and the recoveries were proved to have been manipulated by the officers of the Crime Branch handling the case. George Hiwale was picked up on 22 May 2001 from his office in Worli with stock of fake stamps, for which no panchnama was made. The arrest and the recovery from vendors George Hiwale and Hemant Dubey were proved false since no recovery was made from them.

The evidence collected during further investigations conducted by the CBI clearly established that Vichare and Ghule of the Thane Crime Branch misused their official position for pecuniary gains by diverting the investigation of the case from the actual culprits and foisting a false case on two persons not involved in the case, namely Hemant Dubey and George Hiwale. They also diverted the recoveries made from the actual culprits to the account of Hemant and George, who were falsely implicated in the case. They allowed a crucial Telgi aide, namely, Shabbir Mushtaq Ahmed Sheikh, to escape from police custody by not showing his arrest in the initial stages of the case. Both Vichare and Ghule were released on bail and sureties in February 2007. Media reports called them 'Telgi's agents' (Rediff.com News, 11 February 2007).

Importantly, ample evidence indicated that the business of fake stamps continued well after the incarceration of Telgi, most of those accused and his accomplices. Whether these were by his rivals or by those he had groomed remain a matter of much debate even today. Telgi's words – as the prime accused in the multi-crore fake stamp paper scam to his interrogators of the Stamp Investigation Team (STAMPIT) at the Central Prison in Bengaluru when he was arrested in 2001 – seem almost prophetic. "I challenge you; you can't stamp out fake stamp paper, it has been going on since pre-Independence days. Mine is only one of the gangs and it is not the biggest" (*Frontline*, 2 January 2004). And it's not just the developments in the Bengaluru City Market case, when the CBI took over investigation, that stands testimony to this.

As recent as 11 October 2020, *Deccan Herald* reported that the Bengaluru Police had busted a fake stamp racket similar to the Telgi scam and arrested four people. This scam had been masterminded by Hussain Modi Babu, who had earned the moniker of 'Chhota Telgi'. A total of 443 fake stamps valued at Rs 2.7 crore had been recovered from him. The scam came to light after S.J. Park Police, based on a tip, arrested Babu as well as Harish, a court typist, on S.P. Road, central Bengaluru, on 3 October 2020. Babu's arrest led to the arrest of two women brokers as well, who purchased fake stamp papers from the duo and sold them to the public. They were identified as Shawar alias Seema, and Najma Fathima, both from Bapuji Nagar. Shawar had dropped out of a B. Com degree course and began to work as a typist at Kandaya Bhavan, which houses several state governmental offices and commercial establishments on K.G. Road in Bengaluru. Najma, who studied till Class 7, had been working as a broker in Kandaya Bhavan for thirteen years.

The police raided Babu's home in Viveknagar and seized fake stamp papers of face values ranging from Rs 10 to Rs 25,000. Fake franked sheets, seals of various sub-registrar offices, a computer, printers and A4 papers with watermarks – which had been used to prepare backdated general power of attorney (GPA) documents – were also seized. This was another example of the loss of governmental revenue despite the many steps that had been taken by India after the Telgi scam to plug the leakage and improve the security surrounding the production, procurement and sale of stamps and stamp papers.

However, it would be incorrect to ascribe all and every lawkeeper as corrupt. Police action by those incorruptible and determined, aided by their internally shared intelligence in the fake stamp paper scam perpetrated by A.K.L. Telgi across India, would finally bring the scamster down.

9

A Murder Too!

Telgi was brutal not just about business competition. He was ruthless about disloyal employees, as the heinous murder of Christopher Bhatti bears out.

Arun Hurli, Christopher's brother-in-law, had introduced the twenty-three-year-old Christopher to their neighbour A.K.L. Telgi in 2000. Telgi offered Christopher a job, but owing to a fallout, things soured between them, and Christopher left Telgi's employment. Telgi then called Christopher to Mumbai in 2001 to resolve the dispute and Arun accompanied Christopher (*The Mumbai Mirror*, 2 December 2007).

It appears that Christopher, who also worked as Telgi's driver initially, became involved in the scam and started vending fake stamp papers in Chennai, along with another aide, Suraj Butki. They decamped with Rs 1,80,000 from Telgi's Chennai office (some reports list the amount as Rs 2,50,000) and staged it as a robbery. Christopher failed to return the money he had stolen from Telgi and went into hiding. According to reports, Telgi sent his men to flush Christopher out of his hiding in his hometown in Karnataka. Telgi's henchmen brought Christopher back to Mumbai from his hometown on the pretext of wishing to settle the matter.

In August 2001, when Christopher reached Telgi's apartment at Cuffe Parade in Mumbai, Telgi and his associates tortured Christopher. He was attacked and beaten up savagely with hockey sticks. "Telgi assaulted Christopher in front of his brother-in-law, Arun Hurli," Sub-inspector Anil Mahabole, who was part of the SIT that investigated the murder case, said. During the assault, Christopher sustained serious injuries to his head. His leg fractured and began to bleed. "Telgi asked his men to bring bandage rolls and a wooden support, which they tied around Christopher's leg," Mahabole said. According to Mahabole, Christopher later died of shock. By that time, Hurli had been asked to leave. The body was then allegedly taken in a car to Dharavi and dumped in the Mahim creek near Shahu Nagar on the night of 27 August 2001. After killing him, Telgi called his family to say that Christopher had run away.

"Next day, the police recovered the body, but could not identify it," Dr Harish Pathak, associate professor, Forensic Science Department, Sion Hospital, told the *Mumbai Mirror*. "The body had almost two dozen cigarette burn marks, signs of assault and a fractured leg." Since the body could not be identified, it was disposed of. A case was registered at the Shahu Nagar Police Station (CR No.123 of 2001), and his clothes and photographs were retained for identification.

The murder came to light after nine months when the Pune Police began investigating the fake stamp papers scam. The Pune Police arrested Telgi's associates, who confessed to Christopher's murder. Investigations of the murder case were handed over to the Cuffe Parade police (since the incident occurred in Telgi's house) and then to the Mumbai Crime Branch. Assistant Police Inspector Dilip Kamath, who was subsequently arrested in the fake stamps scam, was assigned to probe the murder. He arrested Telgi on 27 October 2002 and filed a charge sheet. Significantly, the Christopher murder case was the reason why the Maharashtra Police sought Telgi's custody from Karnataka (Telgi was lodged at the Bengaluru Central Prison, then).

When a SIT led by former Director-General of Police S.S. Puri was set up to reinvestigate the stamp scam, the Christopher murder case was also investigated afresh. "We found that the case was not investigated properly and there was not much proof to substantiate that the body recovered from Mahim creek was that of Christopher," Sub-inspector Mahabole said. The Special Investigation Team and forensic expert Dr Harish Pathak felt there was no option but to conduct a DNA test. "More than two-and-a-half years after the murder took place, we summoned an expert from Kolkata's Forensic Science Laboratory (FSL) and opened Telgi's flat in Cuffe Parade to check if there were any bloodstains," Mahabole added.

"The expert found three to four stains in Telgi's house, and one in Telgi's car, but they were too small for collecting DNA samples," Dr Pathak told the *Mumbai Mirror*. As the police had not found significant bloodstains in the car, the court released the car on a bond of Rs 25,000. As the owner of the car, Telgi, however, was convicted. When the SIT felt it had lost all hope, Sub-inspector Mahabole and Dr Pathak realised that the unidentified body had a bandage wrapped around its leg and the piece of the bandage was still in custody of the Crime Branch.

That piece of the tell-tale bandage which A.K.L. Telgi's men had tied around the fractured leg of his injured driver, Christopher Bhatti, ultimately turned out to be Telgi's nemesis, giving the special CBI court crucial proof to accuse him in the killing. "The bandage was blood-soaked, and it had sufficient dried blood to help us collect DNA samples. We then matched the sample with Christopher's mother, father and brother, and all the samples matched," Dr Harish Pathak told the *Mumbai Mirror*. "The DNA report was critical in the investigation, in the subsequent trial and in the statements of Christopher's family members. Suraj Butki helped us collect strong scientific and circumstantial evidence against the accused," Mahabole added (*Mumbai Mirror*, 2 December 2007).

On 29 November 2007, six years after the death of Christopher Bhatti, the special CBI court convicted Telgi and four others under the Indian Penal Code Section 304 Part II (culpable homicide not amounting to murder). Telgi was also fined Rs 3 lakh, failing which he would have to serve another year in prison. The jail term did not run concurrent with the imprisonment under the stamp paper scam case. The four others convicted in the case were Mohamad Ghas Shigvi, Sajid Khan, Maqdoom Tadkod and Kalim Bandaawaz, who were each sentenced to seven years of rigorous imprisonment, along with fine of Rs 20,000 each. The prosecution failed to prove in the court that Telgi and the others should be booked under Indian Penal Code 302 (murder). As Telgi entered the court (via videoconferencing), he requested the presiding judge, U.D. Salvi, for a lenient punishment on the ground that he was HIV-positive. All the accused, including Telgi, pleaded not guilty.

Christopher's family welcomed the court verdict. "Justice is finally done after six years. The court has punished Telgi for killing my son," said sixty-four-year-old Chennaya Bhatti, Christopher's father. Chennaya, a resident of Dandeli in Karnataka, had expected Christopher, the only educated one among the five siblings, to take care of the family. "I thought he would support the family, but he was killed. Later, police told us that Telgi had murdered him." Saroja, sixty, Christopher's mother, lamented, "He [Christopher] was well-known in the area for playing the tabla. He also used to send us Rs 2,000 every month for household expenses. We never met Telgi, nor did he ever visit us. Christopher's father used to work in a paper mill. He retired five years ago. But after our son's death, he still goes to work as a part-time loader as he is the only earning member in the family. My elder son, Chemaya, is mentally unstable and can't work. The court should have given harsher punishment to my son's killer" (*Mumbai Mirror*, 2 December 2007).

10

Other Business Interests

Arising from the developments of the raid in Shalimar Hotel, Bengaluru, in the City Market case (CR No109 of 1997) where fake stamps worth Rs 300,000 and government seals were seized from rooms 104 and 101, the CBI reopened the investigations after the transfer of the cases from the SIT in March 2004. During the investigation, searches were conducted in M/s Srinivasa Printing Press, Lala Kaman Street, at Bellary, owned by P. Munria and M/s Janatha Offset Printers, Goodshed Road, in Bengaluru, owned by K.A. Raghavendra Prasad. One bundle of stamp papers of the denomination of Rs 5,000 (twenty-four sheets, valued at Rs 1,20,000), Rs 2,000 (eighteen sheets, valued at Rs 36,000) and Rs 100 (425 sheets valued at Rs 42,500) were seized from the office room of M/s Janatha Offset Printers and the total value of the stamp papers was assessed at Rs 1,98,500. The CBI also recovered and seized six sheets having three watermarks, "GOVERNMENT OF INDIA-BHARAT SARKAR (IN HINDI), around the Ashoka Chakra, without the stamp crest impressions.

Simultaneously, in the raid conducted at Manovarthpet, Bangalore, at the residence of M. Ramachandra, an employee of M/s

Janatha Offset Printers, one bundle of printed fake stamp papers with 2110 sheets of papers with stamp impressions of Rs 5,000, Rs 2,000 and Rs 100 denominations along with watermarks of the Ashoka Chakra were seized. Each sheet, valued at Rs 7,100, yielded a total value of Rs 1,49,81,000. Each sheet appeared to have undergone a meticulous 'quality check' and was found to have engravings of 'colour OK' written in erasable pencil upon it.

A search was also conducted at the residence of Raghavendra Prasad on Reservoir Street, Basavangudi, Bengaluru, and eighteen positives (transparencies) having impression of 'INDIA NON-JUDICIAL' for printing stamp paper of various denominations were seized from the almirah in Prasad's bedroom. This included four positives for printing Rs 5,000 denomination, eight positives for printing Rs 2,000 denomination, three positives for printing Rs 500 denomination, and three positives for printing Rs 100 denominations. The total value of the fake stamp seized from both the premises was Rs 1,51,79,500, indicating that most of the inventory and stores were kept safe, away from the office premises.

It was also a grim validation that even though the mastermind A.K.L. Telgi was in prison, the business of fake stamps was booming. M/s Janatha Offset Printers was earlier known as M/s Janata Printery and was owned by one Purpili Nagaraja, who was running his business at a loss and couldn't even recover the cost of the HMT printing machine he had purchased in 1998. He sold the printing press to Raghavendra Prasad, an acquaintance, for Rs 750,000, who managed to turn it hugely profitable, thanks to the business of counterfeit stamps sponsored by A.K.L. Telgi.

Along with the raids on the premises of M/s Janatha Offset Printers and the residences of Raghavendra and Ramachandra, a search was conducted at the premises of Munna, an employee of Srinivasa Printing Press at Bellary. Two tracing papers containing inscriptions of the Government of Andhra Pradesh, Commercial Taxes Department, one half sheet of white paper and one tracing paper containing writings 'Government of India' (both in English and in Hindi) and one engraver of aluminium metal were seized. In both the printing presses therefore, the inventory and stores appeared to be in custody of the owners and trusted employees. Thereafter, the seized materials were examined in the India Security Press, Nashik, and opinion was sought regarding the genuineness of the said stamp papers. Vaddepalli Shridhar, senior vigilance assistant in Hindustan Aeronautics Limited (HAL), Bengaluru, accompanied the CBI for these searches.

The experts of the India Security Press opined that the stamp papers seized from the premises of M/s Janatha Offset Printers, Bengaluru, and the stamp papers seized from the residential premises of M. Ramachandra were not genuine stamp papers and were not printed by them. The positives/transparencies seized from the residential premises of K.A. Raghavendra Prasad, the proprietor of M/s Janatha Offset Printers, were used to print fake non-judicial stamps of the denominations of Rs 5,000, Rs 2,000 and Rs 100, on sheets seized from the premises of Janatha Offset Printers and of M. Ramachandra. They further opined that the watermarks on the stamp papers were not genuine. The tracing paper seized from the premises of Munna matched those of the imitation watermarks printed on the stamp papers seized from the premises of M/s Janatha Offset Printers, and of M. Ramachandra.

Shashikanth Barde, an officer of the India Security Press, Nashik, who retired as assistant works manager after working there for several years, upon the request of the CBI, examined the printing machine seized from the premises of M/s Janatha Offset Printers in Bengaluru on 20 August 2004. This was an HMT INVICTA 36-R OMIR type machine bearing Sl. No. 3845, having feeder board size of 66 × 77 centimetres and plate size of 92 × 77 centimetres. He also examined stamp papers sent by the investigating officer and after comparing them with genuine stamp papers and other materials, he provided his professional opinion on 13 September 2004 that the referred stamp papers were forged. He said that there appeared to be an attempt to rewrite the lettering pattern of the watermark and the wheel with intent to reproduce the replica of the same. Further, having examined the seized positive images of stamp papers of Rs

2,000 and those of stamp papers of Rs 500 (eight positives and three positives respectively), he confirmed that these had been used for printing the counterfeit stamps. Further, in his professional opinion, the printing machine on the premises of M/s Janatha Offset Printers that had been examined by him, could print the description of the stamp papers concerned in the case.

M/s Srinivasa Printing Press, Bellary, in connivance with M/s Janatha Offset Printers, Bengaluru, were indulging in printing and supply of fake stamps and stamp papers, for sale, circulation and use in Karnataka and Andhra Pradesh. They were suppliers of fake stamps/stamp papers inter-alia to M/s Citizen Enterprises, Bengaluru, which was managed by Abdul Rahim Telgi, brother of A.K.L. Telgi. M/s Srinivasa Printing Press was used for the purpose of printing watermarks on stationery, necessary before the printing of the crest impressions of various denominations could be done. After completion of the above process, the papers were brought to Bengaluru for using the positives to print crest impressions of various denominations, colour the bond papers and cut/size them at M/s Janatha Offset Printers.

Bhaskar, an erstwhile employee of M/s Janatha Offset Printers, stated in the court that when he was employed there, he was responsible for preparing the plates by using the positives, and thereafter they were used for printing; the number of plates required dependent on the number of colours. He had taken the job on a part-time basis when he was in college. He attended college in the morning and worked in the press in the afternoon. Raghavendra Prasad was the custodian of the positives for making the various denominations and gave them to Bhaskar to prepare the plates. Bhaskar and other employees were told that they were for orders from the government. Very often, the orders would be rushed, and the explanation provided was that the urgency was for meeting delivery deadlines from the government. However, the printing would not be done till the next day or even the third. Sometimes, Bhaskar would find that the printing had been completed overnight. After printing, the sheets would be cut and sized, and Ramachandra performed the role of the cutter. Bhaskar also deposed that according to his understanding, the printed materials were shifted to Ramachandra's premises owing to a dispute between Raghavendra and the owner of the premises where the machinery and inventory of M/s Janatha Offset Printers were housed.

Muniswamy, an operator in M/s Janatha Offset Printers, who was paid a monthly salary of Rs 3,000, deposed that he would print bond papers (stamp papers) for government orders as requested by Raghavendra, who would instruct him to mix colours to get a particular combination, while printing the stamp papers. Though he was able to identify the seized HMT printing machine in court as the one he had worked with, he was unaware of the source of the positives/transparencies. Clearly, employees performing the various tasks in the press were segregated and their work timings staggered so that they wouldn't meet one another.

The above case was investigated by T.V. Joy, an inspector in the CBI, Bengaluru (Security and Frauds), and the seizures of incriminating evidence was made by him. He was assisted by Anil Kumar Ohri, superintendent of police, CBI, Delhi, who registered an FIR (Crime Report-R.C. 2/2004) based on the original crime No. 109/1997 of City Market PS, Bengaluru City, on 23 March 2004, and submitted his report to the court in view of the orders of the Supreme Court of India. K. Hari Om Prakash, another inspector in the CBI, also investigated the case.

And how did A.K.L. Telgi spend his ill-gotten wealth? There is ample evidence that in addition to investment in real estate (he had allegedly invested in over thirty-five properties), he was totally besotted by Bollywood. Through Sana Movie International, a company that he named after his daughter Sana, he tried his hand at film production. The movie *Bechainee*, produced at a budget of Rs 40 lakh in the year 2000, failed at the box office and though Telgi suffered substantial losses, he made sure that his name appeared on the film credits and the posters which read: 'Sana Movie International presents *Bechainee*, Produced by Abdul Karim.'

Undeterred with his losses in film production, Telgi set up Sana Film Distributors to try his hand at film distribution. The movie *Jis Desh Mein Ganga Rehta Hai*, starring Govinda and directed by Mahesh Manjrekar in 2000, was a remake of the 1972 Marathi film, *Ekta Jeev Sadashiv*, and the 1974 Kannada film *Bangaraada Panjara*. The movie was also remade in 2003 in Bengali as *Mayer Anchal*. Though all the regional versions of the film did excellent business, *Jis Desh Mein Ganga Rehta Hai* failed at the box office, and Telgi, who had bought the distribution rights for Karnataka and Maharashtra, suffered losses. Telgi took up the distribution rights for another Govinda-starrer, *Akhiyon Se Goli Mare*, in 2002, which, too, sank without a trace. Telgi's passion for films had burnt a deep hole in his pocket.

Telgi's starry-eyed fascination for tinsel town found another expression. In his book *Telgi Scam: Reporter Ki Dairy*, Sanjay Singh mentions that in 1996, Telgi apparently blew Rs 80 lakh in a night, in a bar, on a provocative bar dancer, Muskan. Later, he took the dancer to Rajasthan and bought a mansion for her there. S. Hussain Zaidi and Brijesh Singh's *Dangerous Minds: Eight Riveting Profiles of Homegrown Terrorists* expounds in detail Telgi's obsession for bar dancers who were lookalikes of famous Bollywood heroines. He would frequent Topaz Bar in South Mumbai, which would hire dancers who were lookalikes of Bollywood heroines. The bar apparently had a common dance floor for regular customers, exclusive ones for the rich and even private chambers for the affluent and the well-heeled seeking privacy. On New Year's Eve in 2000, Telgi, along with an aide, who carried hard cash in a bag, apparently spent a sum of nearly a crore (as per reports by the Mumbai Police and *The Times of India*, the sum was Rs 93 lakh), though the figure was whittled down to a more modest Rs 35 lakh in the CBI's supplementary charge sheet years later.

When he was a special correspondent for *Mid-Day*, Mumbai, Hussain Zaidi interview the woman on whom the largesse was bestowed by Telgi. The lady, who preferred to be called Madhuri (after actor Madhuri Dixit, whom she allegedly resembled), referred to Telgi as 'Karim Sahab', and said that Telgi was a gentleman who never took advantage nor used obscene language in the presence of women. He was, however, obsessed with the divas of Bollywood and fantasized about them. Zaidi writes, "When he failed to gain access to the real Bollywood stars, he settled for the clones, who were on display at various bars. Over time, it seemed that Telgi had a fetish for the fakes – from actresses to stamp papers, his fixation was the counterfeit."

While his foray in films ended in disastrous losses, if A.K.L. Telgi is to be believed, he did engage in the clean business of vending white kerosene, which yielded him better returns than his dirty business in fake stamps! Perhaps, that was true only if the comparison was being made with his 'recorded' transactions in stamp vending. It was only natural that Telgi's business transactions would come under the Income Tax scanner, which sold some of his properties in Bengaluru to realise their tax dues. An article in *The Hindu*, dated 8 November 2010, refers to his statement made to the IT department and the Karnataka High Court, before which he had filed an appeal.

Telgi claimed that during 2003, he was in the business of selling white kerosene, apart from marketing stamp papers and that while his total earnings from stamp papers and franking totalled Rs 5,15,625, that from the kerosene business stood at Rs 33,20,000, in his total declared income for 2003-04 at Rs 38,35,625 (*The Hindu*, 8 November 2010). According to Telgi, he would earn an attractive commission of Rs 2 per litre of kerosene sold. Contesting the tax dues computed by the IT department at Rs 4,09,87,500, for the same year, Telgi said that despite filing all his income details, the assessing officer, had issued notices to him, while he was in the Bengaluru Central Prison.

"I went on appeal before the IT Tribunal, but it dismissed my application and upheld the addition of Rs 6,38,79,688 under various sections of the Act for various years," he said. Despite Telgi's notoriety, according to him, it was only in March 2004 that the income tax department first examined his income records. The examination, he said, was permitted by the special court, which had been set up by the Karnataka state government to hear cases relating to the stamp paper scam. The IT department studied his returns from 1995 to 2003, years in which Telgi had filed incomes ranging from Rs 20 to 30 lakh per year. "The department," he said, "wanted an explanation for an undisclosed income of Rs 4.55 crore, deposited in three bank accounts in Mumbai, as well as those about the immovable properties worth Rs. 3.75 crore in my name" (*The Hindu*, 8 November 2010).

The most incontrovertible evidence of Telgi comingling his tainted stamp scam money with his legitimate business (also strengthening the postulation that these were being used to 'front' the proceeds of his illegitimate business) is provided in the case papers Shamshad Ahmad versus State of Karnataka Upparpet Police Station (PS) Bengaluru (Criminal Appeal 708/2010 decided 8 August 2017).

Ahmad owned a space in a property named 5th Avenue on Brigade Road, Bengaluru, which had been leased to one Subhan for running a coffee shop. In June-July 2000, Subhan advised that A.K.L. Telgi was interested in buying the property and the consideration was agreed at Rs 50 lakh. A.K.L. Telgi paid an advance of Rs 25 lakh and when Ahmad sent the sale papers to Telgi, and before the balance could be paid, the scam erupted, and the sale wasn't concluded. When the court asked Ahmad to deposit the Rs 25 lakh as it was money from Telgi's corrupt business, the explanation offered was that these sums were from Telgi's clean business and thus couldn't be attached as 'tainted property'. Upon investigation, it was found that Metro Corporation (allegedly Telgi's 'clean' company) ran its business in Bengaluru from 27 August 1998 to mid-2000. The reported turnover return for the year 1998-99 (27 August 1998-31 March 1999) was Rs 5,39,925 and that for the fiscal 1999-2000 was Rs 9,51,464, totalling a little under Rs 15 lakh.

It was thus not possible for the advance of Rs 25 lakh to be made from Telgi's clean business. More importantly, the payment of Rs 25 lakh did not come from the account of Metro Corporation, but from that of M/s Sri Sai with Vysya Bank (account no. 7309) by the issuance of five cheques. M/s Sri Sai was one of the firms set up by Telgi for the distribution and sale of fake stamps.

Additionally, the investigation revealed that Telgi had purchased other properties in Bengaluru – Azad Plaza and Azad Point – for Rs 65 lakh. For this, Rs 30 lakh had been paid from current account no. 6175 of Metro Corporation with Amanath Co-operative Bank and Rs 20 lakh from current account no. 1862 of Metro Corporation with Canara Bank. Telgi had also bought a property at 50/10, Police Road, in the year 2000 with a DD issued for Rs 27.5 lakh from the same account with Amanath Co-operative Bank. Deposit trail in the account with Amanath Co-operative Bank reflected gross deposits of Rs 71.06 lakh and withdrawal of Rs 69.71 lakh between the period 23 September 1998 and 30 June 2000. Deposit figures of nearly five times the reported sales turnover figure of Metro Corporation for the same period could only have one explanation: tainted funds were mixed with proceeds from the clean kerosene business.

Evidence of Telgi's involvement in other businesses such as spices, pulses and dyestuff exists. Manoj Ramesh Mehta, Telgi's business associate, was arrested by Bund Garden Police Station on 11 June 2003 in connection with C.R. No. 135 of 2002 for offences punishable under MCOCA. C.R. No 135 culminated in Special Case No. 2 of 2003 before the special judge, MCOCA, Pune, in which Mehta applied for bail. His bail was rejected on 10 January 2006. Mehta then appealed to the Mumbai High Court, which, too, was rejected on 27 January 2007, as was his Criminal Appeal 1868 of 2008 in the Supreme Court on 25 November 2008.

According to case proceedings, Telgi's company, Metro Corporation, was set up at Kemps Corner, Mumbai, in 1993-94. It was engaged in the business of import and export of spices and pulses through the State Trading Corporation (STC). Mehta ostensibly assisted in the booking the consignments, which were routed through the STC. Telgi opened a bank account (No. 17240) with Bank of Madurai in the name of Metro Corporation. Cash amounting to Rs 8,33,000 was deposited in this account. Mehta issued cheques totalling Rs 19,99,500, which were credited to this account. There was, however, no corresponding transaction between Mehta and Telgi to justify this credit to Metro Corporation's account. Telgi had also established another firm, Metro Exports, to deal in export and import of dyestuff. The account of Metro Exports was established with UCO Bank, Colaba.

An amount of nearly Rs 48 lakh was deposited in this account without corresponding transaction. Allegedly, these were proceeds from the sale of fake stamps and stamp papers, which were mixed with bona fide transactions.

There were other inexplicable transactions too. Credits came into Mehta's account for the purposes of making payments for imports through STC, on behalf of Telgi. A deal was made for the import of pulses and demand drafts purchased/issued from the said credits with STC as beneficiary. Later, however, the deal was cancelled and STC informed. The corresponding DDs, too, were cancelled. Yet, the funds were not returned to Telgi's company account. If Mehta was indeed a commission agent, he would normally not accept money for the principal transaction as an agent is only interested in his commission. The main payments and refunds for cancellations of deals thereof should have been from the account of the principal importer, Metro Corporation. However, not only did Mehta accept large sums of money, but the amounts were retained in his bank account after the cancellation of the deal. Money was not returned after deducting usual commission and other charges. There was also prima facie evidence that purchase of printing machines for Telgi's illegal activities were also routed through Mehta's accounts.

Further seizure and study of Telgi's accounts revealed that a sizable amount of the money was diverted to bank accounts for import of naptha, which was later used for the clandestine business of adulteration of petrol and diesel for which Telgi was found guilty and sentenced on 4 February 2013 for seven years by a special CBI court (Zee News, 4 February 2013). Telgi accepted these charges in December 2012. Allegedly, the adulterated petrol and the diesel were supplied to petrol pumps in Maharashtra. There were fourteen accused in this case, including a company, Thane Polyorganics. The adulteration case was busted by the CBI with raids on Telgi's front company and other places.

On 10 March 2004, thirty-one oil tankers in Mumbai and five in Chennai were seized and there were allegations of involvement of senior personnel in public sector oil companies of having secretly diverted raw materials to Telgi's companies. Some of the oil tankers didn't have seals and contained adulterated petroleum products (*The Times of India*, 11 March 2004). The name of Antim Totla, too, surfaced in this connection (*The Times of India*, 19 December 2003), though he denied all allegations when questioned by the Mumbai SIT. Totla was a Jalgaon-based multi-millionaire, who owned Progressive Petroleum Company Ltd, and was one of India's largest naptha importers. In addition to the alleged links with Telgi, he also had political connections of significance.

The allegations in the Mehta nexus ran deeper. During the period that A.K.L. Telgi was in Central Prison, Bengaluru, the tapping of telephone conversations revealed that Manoj Ramesh Mehta was camping at Hotel Pride in Pune. On 7 June 2002, A.K.L. Telgi sent Rs 5 lakh through his nephew Tabrez Ahmed (Abdul Rahim Telgi's son) to Mehta. An attempt to sabotage the investigation in the Bund Garden case, which was registered on 7 June 2002, was made by bribing a senior police officer, ACP Mohd. Chand Mulani (an accused in the case, A-61), who was closely associated with the investigation. An amount of Rs 15 lakh was allegedly paid to Mulani through Abdul Rashid S. Kulkarni, Telgi's lawyer (accused A-49). Similarly, as per the charge sheet, huge amounts were paid to scuttle the investigation in Mumbai cases against the members of Telgi's organised crime syndicate, with Assistant Police Inspector Dilip P. Kamat (accused A-44) being a beneficiary.

That A.K.L. Telgi was involved in businesses outside counterfeit stamps was also corroborated by Rehan Baig, who surrendered before STAMPIT chief R. Srikumar in Bengaluru on 20 December 2003. Rehan's name had been linked to Telgi's since November 2001 when Telgi was arrested. Soon after, Rehan, a doctor by profession, left for Saudi Arabia. He returned to Bengaluru early in 2003 when his father died. The STAMPIT questioned him about his involvement and impounded his passport, which prevented Rehan from returning to Saudi Arabia.

Rehan confirmed that he was dealing with Telgi, selling provisions such as oil, dal and rice to Telgi's company, Metro

Corporation. "When I met him, I had no idea he was running a fake stamp paper racket. Only after his involvement in the racket became public, I came to know about Karim's true picture. I fell into Telgi's trap, without knowing that he was involved in the fake stamp business. Had I known him fully, I would not have ventured into any kind of association with him," Rehan averred. He also denied allegations that he had rented out his premises to Telgi to operate in Bangalore. Rehan denied that he and his brother Roshan, a cabinet minister in Karnataka, were involved in the racket and that was the reason that he had voluntarily surrendered so that he could offer his version to the authorities.

According to a report in the *Frontline*, dated 2 January 2004, however, it appears that Rehan Baig did indeed declare to the commercial tax officer, vide a letter, that he had rented a space in his premises in Brigade Road in Bengaluru to "his family friend Abdul Karim Telgi of Metro Corporation for marketing purposes without any rent and security deposit". The Bharatiya Janata Party and the Janata Dal (Secular) released copies of this letter on 6 March 2000, for political mileage against the ruling Congress. Rehan's brother Roshan Baig was a member of the Karnataka Legislative Assembly and a member of the Congress party during 1994-2019, the period covering the Telgi scam.

Rehan was later arrested in connection with the Upparpet case, in which the Upparpet police had seized nearly Rs 10 crore worth of fake stamps in Bengaluru city in November 2000. On the preliminary charges against Rehan, Srikumar said, "Rehan has been maintaining that he was involved in the kerosene business with Telgi, and the company was called Metro Corporation. At times, he said he was a partner, at others, an agent and manager of the company. We found that the Metro Corporation had links with the fake stamp paper business and Rehan has been arrested."

The Rehan-Telgi connection supposedly ran deeper, and Rehan was perhaps responsible for Telgi's arrest and jail term in Bengaluru in 2001, changing the course of the stamp scam story.

PART III

THE LAW CATCHES UP … OR DOES IT?

11

The Upparpet Case and Telgi's Arrest

A name which seldom figures in any discussion about Telgi and the fake stamp scam is that of Jayant M. Tinaikar, whose crusade against the scamster has not been as well recognised or rewarded as it should have been. Tinaikar and Telgi were brought up in Khanapur, where Tinaikar was better off and ran a family-managed hotel, while Telgi sold fruits on the footpaths, leading a hand-to-mouth existence.

Telgi disappeared suddenly and returned a few years later. He aroused Tinaikar's suspicion when he began acquiring immovable properties at a premium. Tinaikar sensed that there was something amiss in Telgi's sudden affluence and began his crusade, relentlessly pursuing the truth. According to *Daijiworld Media Network (24 May 2012)*, "For seven years starting from 1996, he knocked on all the doors of authorities, and even wrote to the President of India, but he did not receive any response." Supposedly, he even met the then Opposition leader B.S. Yediyurappa in Bengaluru and handed over hundreds of incriminating documents as proof. The government eventually mounted pressure on the police.

In a report dated 7 November 2008, the *Bangalore Mirror* said that it was Tinaikar who had tipped the then director general of police,

Bengaluru, H.T. Sangliana, late in October 2001 about Telgi's visit to Khwaja Bande Nawaz, a shrine in Ajmer, days before Sangliana was to assume office as police commissioner of Bengaluru. This led to Telgi's arrest. Tinaikar continued with his battle, spending his own money, and almost became bankrupt at the end of his crusade. In return for his efforts, saving several hundred crores of state revenue, braving threats to his life, all he received was a paltry sum of Rs 2,000 from the government. Tinaikar refused to accept the money.

On 19 August 2000, G.A. Bawa, the then assistant commissioner of police, Chickpet Police Sub-Division, Bengaluru, along with his officers, apprehended Badruddin and Vittal Maruthi Sungar in front of the erstwhile Kapali Talkies, on Subedar Chatram Road, Bengaluru. They had received a call (that was traced to a public phone booth in Seshadripuram in West Bengaluru) that "thousands of fake stamp papers were being sold there". They seized fake stamps of different denominations totalling Rs 53,12,400 and other articles from the duo. A case was registered (Crime No. 545 of 2000) at the Upparpet Police Station, Bengaluru City, for offences punishable under various relevant sections of the IPC.

During the investigation, H.J. Mariswamy Gowda, the then police inspector, Upparpet Police Station, arrested thirteen people. Raids were conducted in Vasanth Nagar (premises of Telgi's company M/s Sri Sai) and R.T. Nagar, the latter yielding a rich haul of fake stamps valued at Rs 8,63,57,927, cash worth Rs 34,13,000 and other incriminating material used for printing, franking and embossing stamp marks. According to the expert opinion of the prosecution witness (PW 228) R.K. Srivatsav of the India Security Press, Nashik, the stamps were counterfeit.

Corroborative evidence by prosecution witnesses Smt. Siddananjamma (PW 59), Prabhakar (PW 160) and Puttasiddaiah (PW 128), directors of the Treasury, indicated that the instruments seized from the aforesaid premises were not genuine. Smt. Siddananjamma further advised that the seized documents that were franked were not genuine either. Franking of the documents was always carried out by the Sub-Registrar, Franking Cell,

Gandhinagar, Bengaluru, but the documents seized had not been franked at the Gandhinagar cell.

Charge sheets were filed against a total of eighteen accused before the 9th Additional Chief Metropolitan Magistrate Court, Bengaluru City, in Criminal Case No. 20577 of 2000 for various offences under the IPC. As the interrogations had revealed the name of Abdul Karim Telgi, he was made an accused in the case as well, though he was still at large. According to reports in the *Frontline*, dated 2 January 2004, of the twenty-eight persons against whom as many as seven charge sheets were filed, eight, including the mastermind Telgi, were absconding.

The operation in which Telgi was eventually captured on 7 November 2001 was quite dramatic. Bawa and his men camped in Ajmer for almost a week, but Telgi, who apparently suspected that the police were closing in on him, remained elusive. G.A. Bawa recalls, "After the case was registered in 2000, we had seized stamp papers worth nearly Rs 10 crore and Rs 37 lakh in cash. Our search for Telgi had begun. In fact, the previous city police commissioner, Madiyal, had also given out cash incentives to informants to gather inputs about Telgi. In 2001, Sangliana shared the phone number of an informant with me. It took 2-3 months for me to get him on call as he was reluctant to share information. In August that year, the informant called me to say that Telgi was attending a marriage in Ajmer, Rajasthan, and was travelling by train. We reached by air and with the help of the railway police, we searched for him, but in vain. We bought some Pathan costumes and attended the marriage which Telgi was supposed to attend, but we could not find him. We searched the lodges, too. After a few days of search, we wanted to return. One day, I got an alert that he was coming to a dargah. I went there disguised as a Pathan businessman and a local police sub-inspector kept me company. About 150 people were at the dargah. The police officer with me was scared about the consequences if we arrested him. But I decided that it was now or never. I saw a man who was kissing the door of the dargah. I remembered the face as he had been previously arrested by the Andhra Police. I followed him as he entered the dargah and sat with a group of people. He deliberately sat in the middle of the crowd to evade detection. After nearly an hour, he appeared relaxed. I approached him and called out, 'Lala' (a name Telgi was called by his friends). He thought I was a business associate and came near me. I just put my hand around his shoulders and asked him to come with me. As we came out, he recognised me as a police officer and asked me not to arrest him in public view. I made him sit in his car and took him to the inspection bungalow. Later, we took him to his room in the lodge, where he was staying. We recovered valuables; a suitcase full of fake stamp papers worth Rs 35 lakh including cash, an old tape recorder and Hindi film song cassettes. We then brought him to Bengaluru." (The reports that appeared in the *The Indian Express* as well as *Bangalore Mirror* about his arrest were in conflict about the timeline as well as who received the tip about Ajmer, but it did result in the arrest that precipitated Telgi's decline.)

Sangliana, by his order dated 22 November 2001, entrusted further investigation of the case to the then assistant commissioner of police, Bengaluru City, S.K. Hegde. Given the inter-state ramifications of the case and allegations of the involvement of police officials and politicians, Sangliana had initially favoured a probe by the CBI. According to a report in the *Frontline*, dated 30 January 2004, after Telgi's arrest in November 2001, Sangliana had interrogated him and had submitted to the state government a detailed eighteen-page report on Telgi's activities, the names of his associates and supporters. Allegedly, the government chose not to act on the report.

The Congress government in Karnataka headed by S.M. Krishna, vide a government order dated 25 January 2002, constituted the Stamp Investigation Team (STAMPIT) and handed over the probe to it. The team was headed by a crack officer R. Sri Kumar, additional director general of police, who had worked for the CBI for eleven years and was on the team that had probed the assassination of former prime minister Rajiv Gandhi. This decision was pushed through by the government despite a three-day gridlock in the state legislature owing to the Opposition protesting the investigations through the STAMPIT and demanding a CBI probe in the matter.

When team STAMPIT took over the investigation, eighty-six days had already lapsed since Telgi's arrest. As per rules, if a charge sheet was not filed before a court within ninety days of arrest, the accused was eligible to get bail. "We had hardly investigated the case and we were left with no options but to file a charge sheet with the information provided by the local police," Sri Kumar said. (*The Quint*, 25 October 2017.)

Once the charge sheet was filed, Telgi was sent to judicial custody, which meant the investigators/police couldn't question him. The team moved the court to get permission to question Telgi in prison. "It was only weeks later that the team got the permission," Sri Kumar added.

According to a *Frontline* report dated 13 August 2004, the political opposition in Karnataka continued clamouring for Roshan Baig's ouster owing to his brother Rehan's business connections with Telgi. Roshan Baig had however staunchly maintained that he was in no way involved in the stamp scam. The pressure on the Congress for Baig's resignation persisted despite Rehan's surrender before the STAMPIT on 20 December 2003 (he was charged with managing Metro Corporation, Telgi's front organisation, and of aiding A.K.L. Telgi, the prime accused).

It was a widely held belief that Telgi was supported by many in both the police force and by those in political power in Karnataka. Many, especially the BJP leaders in the Opposition, believed that the Congress government's disinclination to hand over the investigation to the CBI stemmed from this tacit support extended to the scamster. This was also why, it was alleged, the government had chosen to overlook the advice of the former director general of police, Sangliana, who headed the investigations that led to Telgi's arrest and who favoured that the CBI take over the proceedings against Telgi. The Krishna (Congress) government defended its decision on the ground that the state's police force was "doing a good job of unearthing the scam" and that the then Atal Bihari Vajpayee-led BJP government at the Centre could use the investigation for its own political ends. The STAMPIT, which spearheaded the investigation for over two years, filed thirteen charge sheets against sixteen accused and arrested fifty-nine of those accused. A special fast track court to try the cases was also constituted.

Despite the brouhaha over the Baig brothers' proximity to Telgi, the success of the Bengaluru Police's bust of A.K.L. Telgi's multi-crore fake stamp paper ring has been attributed to a considerable degree to the squabble between Telgi and his Metro Corporation partner Rehan Baig. CBI investigations revealed that a rift between Rehan Baig and Telgi had led to the registration of the Upparpet case in August 2000. The information at the disposal of the police about Telgi's operations in Bengaluru, including details of the storage of fake stamps, probably came from the Baig camp. Police records stated that the Upparpet police apprehended two of Telgi's gang members, Badruddin and Vittal Maruthi, on Subedar Chatram Road on 19 August 2000. However, Badruddin said during investigation that he was not arrested from Subedar Chatram Road on 19 August 2000 but was summoned to the Upparpet Police Station and placed under arrest.

The CBI believed that the seizures had been made possible by the schism in the Telgi-Baig association. The partnership between A.K.L. Telgi and Rehan Baig which began in April 1997, when Roshan Baig was home minister, developed cracks in February 1999 and fractured during February-March 2000. The exact reason for the collapse of the ties – stitched after Rehan Baig helped Telgi break the law to pull his brother Abdul Rahim Telgi out of the City Market police lockup in 1997 – is not quite known. During interrogation by the previous investigators following his arrest in November 2001, Telgi revealed that he had been cheated to the tune of nearly Rs 55 lakh by his partner Rehan Baig. When he (Telgi) tried to recover this amount, differences cropped up, Telgi told the STAMPIT. A second theory propagated as the reason for the rift was Telgi's growing contacts with businessmen in Bengaluru, contrary to the wishes of the Baig camp. A third theory was that Rehan Baig, a qualified doctor, was miffed with Telgi for not appointing him as the head of Telgi's Sana Hospital in Bengaluru, a project named after his daughter.

When the ties soured, Telgi cut off his business links with Rehan Baig. It is believed that after the partnership collapsed completely, the Baig camp decided, sometime in 2000, to get even with Telgi by exposing his fake stamp business. Telgi himself reportedly indicated immediately after his arrest that he had been fixed following the souring of ties with Baig. The CBI believed that information regarding Telgi's gang members and the location of fake stamps which Rehan Baig was privy to was given to the police as a fallout of this rivalry in August 2000. The agency also had reason to believe that the actual raids were conducted before 19 August 2000 and that the Upparpet Police were carefully chosen to carry out the raids though much of the stamps were stored in the R.T. Nagar area.

Notwithstanding the political noise over the handling of the case to the STAMPIT rather than the CBI, clearly, the law enforcers of Karnataka did a better job than their compatriots earlier in Maharashtra, where Telgi had begun his trade in fake stamps as early as 1994 but was not imprisoned.

Following his arrest in the Upparpet case and the allegations of his involvement in large-scale manufacture, sale and circulation of fake stamps, A.K.L. Telgi was lodged in Central Prison, Parappana Agrahara, Bengaluru, as an under trial prisoner (UTP No.4148.)

His jail term appeared to do little to discourage his illegal activities. Sale and circulation of fake stamps continued unabated in different parts of the country such as Delhi, Chandigarh, Chennai, Trichy and Hyderabad. It was clear that Telgi was able to continue his links with his associates across various locations, either personally in prison when they visited him or by contacting them on their mobile phones. The investigators gathered information to the effect that his associates, Badruddin and Rafi Ahmed, were regularly visiting Bengaluru Central Prison on some pretext or the other to meet Telgi.

The STAMPIT obtained necessary permission from the competent authority under Section 5(2) of the Indian Telegraph Act, 1885, for intercepting clandestine communications between Telgi and his associates, so that they could tap his phones. The telephonic surveillance was mounted on various mobile numbers being used by Telgi and his associates. The audiocassettes containing the conversation, together with the specimen voice samples of Telgi and his associates, were sent to the Central Forensic Science Laboratory, New Delhi, where it was confirmed that the voices were those of Telgi and his men.

The pressure on Badruddin led to the recovery of the mobile phones (Samsung and Nokia) on 18 October 2020. Telgi was initially using a Nokia handset, but after he got a Samsung handset, he handed over the Nokia phone to Badruddin. During investigation, it was revealed that Telgi was exclusively using four mobile numbers from these handsets.

The accused were frequently changing SIM cards, resulting in change of mobile numbers. According to Sri Kumar's interview in *The Quint*, on 27 October 2017, "We began tracking the phone calls to gather evidence. However, he (Telgi) always had the knowledge that we were tracking him. Whenever we identified a mobile number he was using, he would change it." By changing mobile numbers, Telgi exploited police procedures to his advantage. "Every time, we had to intercept a mobile phone number, we had to get permission and the process took several days. He was aware of this loophole and kept changing the mobile numbers, so we couldn't track his communications," Sri Kumar pointed out. According to another report in *Frontline*, dated 2 January 2004, "The interception of telephone calls – 1,300 calls in Urdu, Hindi, English, Kannada, and Marathi – provided the STAMPIT with over hundred hours of recorded conversation on 54 tapes." These tapes were later called for by the Bombay High Court.

The analysis of the intercepted conversations between Telgi and his associates revealed that Telgi was monitoring and instructing his associates on ways to circulate fake stamps across the country despite his confinement in prison. It also came to light that Telgi was given the status of a special security prisoner in prison, and Badruddin and Rafi Ahmed met him regularly.

12

Business as Usual, from Jail

Confinement in prison, in a strange way, became Telgi's safe business bet. Following the lead obtained from the conversations being tracked between Telgi and his associates, arrests were made. Their interrogation led to the seizure of large volumes of fake stamp papers, seals and allied materials from different parts of the country. Stamps worth more than Rs 165 crore were seized from many locations.

Of the various operations, the ones in Hyderabad and Chennai yielded fake stamps worth nearly Rs 154 crore. Details for these are hereunder:

1. Telgi's organized crime syndicate engaged in sale and circulation of fake stamps operated in the state of Andhra Pradesh (currently Telangana and Andhra Pradesh), principally from the city of Hyderabad. The firms, M/s Sams Services and M/s Star Services, were in business since 2001. Syed Hameeduddin, an active member of the criminal syndicate, used the licence issued to another person and circulated fake stamps illegally. Khadersha Mohammed

Yousuf Singoti (aka Sajju), who worked with Telgi in Mumbai, confessed that he had handed over the stock of fake stamps to Syed Hameeduddin and Mohd Abdul Waheed Quadri, his accomplice, as many as ten to twelve times at Metro Exports office of Telgi, and at the Gulf Hotel, in Mumbai.

Mohd Abdul Waheed Quadri, a staff at M/s Star Services, in his confessional statement stated that Hameeduddin removed stock of stamps from the premises of M/s Star Services, when the police raided premises of M/s Sams Services. As per the confessional statement of Telgi's key aide Badruddin, Hameeduddin arranged the office space of M/s Star Services at Model House, Punjagutta, Hyderabad, in October 2001. He also arranged residential accommodation for the representatives of M/s Star Services at the Begumpet locality in June 2002. A lease agreement was signed by him in the false name of Aqueel Patel at a monthly rent of Rs 7,500. An advance of Rs 30,000 was also paid.

According to the charge sheet, Hameeduddin also rented Flat No G-4 in Asha Residency, Bazarghat, Hyderabad, from one Mohd Shafeeq for Rs 1,800 a month. Fake stamps of various denominations to the tune of Rs 3.67 crore were recovered from here on 29 June 2002, according to the report in Crime No. 73 of 2002 of P.S. Dharavi Crime Branch, Mumbai. The SIT, Hyderabad, filed a case (Crime No. 1 of 2003) against those accused under various sections of IPC, Indian Stamp Act, 1899, and Section 3 of Andhra Pradesh Control of Organised Crime Act, 2001 (APCOCA). Hameeduddin was eventually arrested on 7 April 2004. His subsequent pleas for bail/release (Criminal Petition. No. 6086 of 2004 and 667 of 2005) were rejected.

This was one of the cases transferred to the CBI from the state government, and was registered as RC No. 4(E)/2004/CBI/EOW-1/DLI. The CBI after investigation filed a charge sheet and the case was taken on file and registered as Criminal Case No. 4 of 2004 for trial of cases under APCOCA-cum-I

Additional Metropolitan Sessions Judge, Hyderabad. Syed Hameeduddin's name appeared in another large seizure amounting to Rs 830 crore, but this case was linked by the Mumbai Police to case CR 73 of 2002 of Dharavi, Mumbai, with ulterior motives.

2. One of the accused whom Telgi contacted from prison was Nizamuddin, the proprietor of M/s Marina Services Chennai, who was selling fake stamps at the instance of Telgi during 2001-2002. Nizamuddin opened a current account with Punjab National Bank, Anna Nagar Branch, Chennai, where cheques received for the sale of stamps were credited.

   Based on the voluntary statement of one accused in the case (duly recorded by M.K. Ganapathy, investigating officer), counterfeit stamps worth Rs 150,49,59,000 were recovered from House No. 51, Jayamahal Street, Sham Park View Apartments, Shenoy Nagar, Chennai. Prosecution Witness Sri Balasubramanyam (PW-55) and Gnanam (PW-57) also confirmed that the house from which the counterfeit stamp papers were recovered also yielded various seals of the bank and treasury, which were used in the process of validation and circulation of the stamp papers. These were also seized.

3. The evidence of M.K. Ganapathy disclosed that on comparison of the sample seals of the treasury and banks, the seized seals were found to be fake and counterfeit. This was confirmed by Syed Azgar Imam (PW-115), scientific officer of the Forensic Science Laboratory. During recovery of the counterfeit stamps, two typed unregistered stamp papers, containing the signature and seal of Nizamuddin, were also recovered by the investigating agency, which made Nizamuddin complicit. Intercepted calls and incriminating conversations also established Nizamuddin's guilt. Criminal Appeal No. 1190 of 2010 filed by Nizamuddin on 14 September 2010 against various cases against him was eventually dismissed on 31 July 2017.

After Telgi's imprisonment, based on the investigation report of the STAMPIT and revelations, various charges under the IPC, Karnataka Stamps Act, 1957, and Karnataka Control of Organised Crimes Act, 2000 (KCOC Act) against thirty-three persons were framed. Crime No. 1100/2002 was registered at Madiwala Police Station, Bengaluru, on 16 January 2002. This case, too, was among the forty-eight transferred to the CBI by the Supreme Court on 15 March 2004.

Clearly, the impunity with which Telgi conducted operations whilst in prison (Telgi was lodged in the Central Prison, Bengaluru, till 25 October 2002 before being temporarily shifted to Mumbai) was only possible with insider collusion. The two held responsible were P.N. Jayasimha (senior superintendent of Central Prison, Bengaluru) and Nanjappa (working as assistant superintendent of Central Prison, Bengaluru). They were impleaded as accused Nos. 32 and 33 under supplementary charge sheet filed in Crime No. 1100/2002 alleging that they had committed offences punishable under the POCA, 1988, and sections of KCOC Act.

When A.K.L. Telgi was arrested on 7 November 2001 and lodged in Central Prison as an under-trial, Jayasimha and Nanjappa colluded with him and, in violation of the prison rules and regulations, permitted and facilitated his use of mobile phone(s) for unlawful activities and also allowed him to host a party on the jail premises in exchange for illegal gratification. They also assisted in the visits of several of Telgi's accomplices, specifically Badruddin and Rafi Ahmed, in the special room, where Telgi was accommodated.

The trial court was of the view (despite the depositions of the witnesses) that though certain aberrations had taken place in the prison, the accused public servants were only discharging their official duties in good faith. This, they felt, was on account of the necessity to provide certain facilities to Telgi due to his status as a high-security prisoner and the fact that he suffered from severe ailments. Hence their acts of commission or omission couldn't be made culpable under various sections of POCA.

Details are available from the court proceedings of Criminal Appeal No. 87 of 2011 (decided on 3 August 2017), where the state of Karnataka challenged this stand of the trial court, inter-alia, against acquittal of certain accused (including Jayasimha and Nanjappa). It was revealed that at the behest of Jayasimha and Nanjappa, Telgi was accommodated in one of the rooms attached to the hospital, and not in the main prison. This room, measuring 10ft x 10ft on the premises of the prison hospital, was intentionally converted/modified to facilitate Telgi to continue his fake stamp racket. The windows of the room had been covered with cardboard and curtains so that Telgi's voice would not be audible outside the room when he spoke on his mobile phone.

Further, both Jayasimha and Nanjappa deliberately disregarded the directions of their superiors and instructed their subordinates to take care of Telgi's security. It was specifically alleged that on several occasions, Telgi would have closed-door meetings with the duo, and they would prevent their subordinates from checking Telgi's room. Despite the complaint lodged by the warden, the two accused did not take steps to either replace the wooden door of the room or reinforce it to enhance the flimsy security that it offered for such a high-profile criminal.

When Mohan Kumar (a subordinate working in the Bengaluru Central Prison, who appeared as Prosecution Witness 32) tried to remove the curtain fixed to the window, Jayasimha and Nanjappa shifted Mohan Kumar from duty. Also, they did not take any action even though a mobile phone was found in the cell of Telgi by the executive jailor (appeared as PW-34). They allowed Badruddin and Rafi Ahmed to meet Telgi without making any entry in the visitors' book. Further, it was alleged that accused Jayasimha accepted gratification of Rs one lakh through Badruddin as well as a refrigerator, uniform, shoes, etc., in lieu of providing luxuries to Telgi in captivity.

Though Jayasimha and Nanjappa were arrested on 9 December 2003, Jayasimha moved an application for bail before the Special Court (S.C. 353/2004), which was rejected on 28 October 2005. He then filed Criminal Petition No. 285 of 2006 before the high court seeking bail, which too was rejected on 25 August 2006. The high court, however, allowed Jayasimha to move a similar application in the month of January 2007, if the trial was not concluded by then. Accordingly, as the trial was not concluded, Jayasimha moved the high court again vide Criminal Petition No.196/2007, which was dismissed on 27 February 2007 inter-alia on the ground that Jayasimha could indulge in tampering with the witnesses if released on bail.

Though Jayasimha was arrested in December 2003, charges were framed only in August 2006, and it was stated that 256 witnesses were examined and cited. However, by August 2007, Jayasimha had already been imprisoned for about three years and nine months. Since Nanjappa, too, had served similar time and had been released on 17 April 2007 – Criminal Appeal No. 574/2007 arising out of Special Leave Petition (Criminal) No. 6030/2006 – Jayasimha's appeal (Criminal Appeal 1275/ 2007) was allowed in the court, and he was released on bail and sureties.

Not just the jail authorities, but there were allegations that doctors, too, aided the stamp scamster. The investigation team (STAMPIT) chanced upon a conversation between one Dr Agnihotri and Dr K.H. Jnanendrappa (in charge of the diabetic clinic, Victoria Memorial Hospital, Bengaluru) on 20 September 2002. Since this conversation disclosed the commission of cognizable offence, an information report was prepared on 5 October 2002, and a complaint was registered by the Madiwala Police in Crime No. 1100 of 2002. Based on various evidence presented, the trial court concluded that two doctors from Victoria Medical Hospital – Dr K.H. Jnanendrappa and Dr K.M. Channakeshava (specialist and administrator at the hospital) – had demanded and accepted illegal gratification from an associate of Telgi for issuing two favourable medical certificates, dated 6 June 2002 and 20 September 2002, which enabled Telgi to secure bail from judicial custody while jailed for Case No 545 of 2000.

Charges of issuing false certificates, receiving illegal gratification and abusing the power and position as public servants in the health department of the Government of Karnataka earned both the doctors indictments under the POCA and IPC. After the CBI took over the investigation, on 5 July 2004, V. Nava Raju, the then police inspector, CBI, at Bengaluru (and who appeared as PW 20), operated the computer/monitor and the central processing unit (CPU), wherein the conversations between Dr Agnihotri and other accused were recorded. Further on 14 July 2004, a search at the offices and residences of both the doctors were conducted. Soon after, on 23 July 2004, based on the statement of an attendant, Krishna, working in Victoria Hospital and a prime eyewitness to the doctors having received illegal gratification, the CBI raided the offices and residences of the two government doctors. The bureau arrested Channakeshava, but Jnanendrappa admitted himself to a hospital in Bengaluru. The investigation bureau also questioned Dr Sunil Chavan, medical superintendent of the Central Prison, Bengaluru.

The criminal appeals of all three accused (Telgi-1187/2007, Dr Jnanendrappa-1123/2007 and Dr Channakeshava-1241/2007) against the earlier conviction held against them were eventually heard at the Karnataka High Court on 11 July 2017.

Deepak Kumar Tanwar, the then senior scientific officer, Central Forensic Science Laboratory, New Delhi, who had analysed the voice samples recorded in the audiocassettes with specimen voice samples confirmed that the voice belonged to Dr Jnanendrappa. Notwithstanding this and the evidence of the attendant, Krishna, who apparently saw Rs 50,000 being paid by a 'boy' sent by Telgi, and the statement from the bank manager of Chartered Sahakari Bank, Niyamitha Branch, Koramangala, Bengaluru, that on 30 June 2002, a sum of Rs 50,000 was credited to the joint account of Dr Channakeshava and his wife, the appeals of the three accused were upheld. The court rejected the charges against the doctors and Telgi on account of the following:

a. Five constables had accompanied Telgi when he went to Victoria Hospital for examination and had waited outside the doctor's chamber; thus, the attendant alone 'witnessing' exchange of cash seemed specious.

b. Regarding the said conversation between one Dr Agnihotri and Dr Jnanendrappa, the judge opined that the prosecution/investigating agency had not made any attempt to trace Dr Agnihotri, let alone examine him. Even if it could be accepted that there was a conversation between Dr Agnihotri and Dr Jnanendrappa, it didn't establish conspiracy between Telgi and the two accused doctors. There was no material on record to show that Telgi, at any time, was in contact with either of the accused doctors.
c. The original medical certificates issued by the two doctors were forwarded to the superintendent of the prison. If so, the theory of conspiracy as well as the circumstances pleaded by the prosecution that the said certificates were obtained by the associates of Telgi by paying illegal gratification appeared incorrect. If, in fact, Telgi had secured the certificates, the originals thereof would have been collected either by him or his associates without the knowledge of the prison authorities.
d. It was also confirmed that for about ten days prior to his examination, Telgi was vomiting blood which necessitated the prison authorities (the doctor and medical officer) to send Telgi for medical examination and Telgi never visited them of his own volition. The prosecution witness (PW11) who escorted Telgi to Victoria Hospital categorically stated that Telgi was produced before the superintendent of Victoria Hospital as per the instructions of the superintendent of Central Prison, and did not directly meet the doctors accused.

13

In STAMPIT's Custody

Telgi's history sheet had been unflattering much before his arrest in 2001. He was involved in various crimes pertaining to fake stamp papers earlier than his incarceration in Bengaluru Central Prison for crime number 545/00 (and the case thereafter filed by the STAMPIT, Crime No. 1100/02 on 16 January 2002). He continued his criminal activities even in jail with impunity and this led to several cases being filed against him across India. Hence, he was a criminal wanted by the law simultaneously in different police stations and courts.

In an interview given to the deputy managing editor of Rediff News, George Iype, published on 12 December 2003, R. Sri Kumar, who was heading STAMPIT, said, "It is difficult to estimate the magnitude of the scam. The seizures of fake stamps and stamp papers in the last 18 months is of the order of Rs 3,500 crore. The exact value can be calculated only by the revenue authorities or the accountant-general's office, who watch the revenue collections. The magnitude of the scam could be anything from Rs 3,500 crore to several times the amount." He added, "Cases are registered and Telgi's operations are known in Andhra Pradesh, Delhi, Goa, Gujarat, Karnataka, Kerala, Maharashtra, Madhya Pradesh, Punjab,

Rajasthan, Tamil Nadu, Uttar Pradesh and West Bengal. We suspect Telgi's operations and links in other states like Bihar, Himachal Pradesh, Jharkhand and Orissa."

While imprisoned in Central Prison for Crime No. 545/00, Telgi was produced in court for Crime No. 1100/02 on 25 October 2002. On the very same day, the investigating officer filed a petition seeking police custody of Telgi for interrogation and recovery of incriminating materials in the same Crime No. 1100/02. Telgi's counsel sought time to file objections. Simultaneously, the sessions judge passed an order permitting Telgi to be taken to Mumbai on 28 October 2002 to be produced before the additional chief metropolitan magistrate, III Court, Esplanade, Mumbai, as per the order issued in C.C. No. 200/P/2002, for the Christopher murder case.

On 4 November 2002, when Telgi was still in Mumbai, an order was passed instructing that Telgi be handed to the custody of M.K. Ganapathy, assistant commissioner of police, City Crime Branch, Bangalore, for a period of ten days, commencing from the day on which Telgi would be brought back to Bangalore from Mumbai, on or before 8 November 2002.

However, on the date of passing of this order, the magistrate was aware that Telgi was neither in police custody, nor in judicial custody for crime No. 1100/02 or for crime No. 545/00. Nor was Telgi brought to Bangalore on or before 8 November 2002, but only on 24 January 2003. The shocking events chronicling the developments in Mumbai during the period October 2002 to January 2003 have been discussed later.

On 24 January 2003, the investigating officer, Bengaluru, filed another application under Section 167 CrPC (Code of Criminal Procedure), requesting Telgi's remand in police custody immediately (i.e., from 24 January 2003 itself). This was rejected on 6 February 2003 by the judge in line with the Karnataka Criminal Rules of Practice, on the grounds that the IO had failed to notify the court when Telgi was not brought back from Mumbai to Bengaluru on or before 8 November 2002, vide the order passed on 4 November 2002. The second reason for rejection was that beyond the first fifteen days, an accused could not be remanded in police custody and as per the existing order of 4 November 2002, that period had already lapsed.

Hence, the petition to seek police custody had to be filed again under a different section (Section 482 of the CrPC), for which there was a delay of over two months in securing a governmental sanction. Only on 10 April 2003 did the IO submit a petition which was awarded on 4 August 2003 and Telgi was remanded in police custody, i.e., in the custody of M.K. Ganapathy, for a period of ten days commencing from 6 August 2003. This was an example of how legal/procedural provisions delayed the police investigation process by eight months!

The police custody was granted by the court subject to the following conditions:

a. The investigating officer was directed to take special care of Telgi's fragile health and to consult the concerned medical expert (cardiology) whenever he intended to take Telgi outside Bangalore for the purpose of interrogation during the investigation.
b. The investigating officer was further directed that during the period of police custody, he would get Telgi examined by a medical expert at least once in twenty-four hours or as and when necessary.
c. Telgi would not be subject to any harassment or maltreatment either physical or mental during such custody.
d. Telgi would be at liberty to seek legal consultation from any lawyer of his choice prior to interrogation by the investigating officer during such custody period, either in or outside Bangalore.
e. The investigating officer was forbidden to use any illegal methods of interrogation.
f. The investigating officer was required to produce Telgi before the magistrate concerned before the end of tenth day of police custody from the date of taking him to police custody, i.e., on or before 15August 2003.

This period of police custody of ten days became important as Telgi later alleged that he had been injected with the AIDS virus by the STAMPIT team when they had taken him to hospital for treatment during police custody. When asked about this allegation (in the same Rediff News interview of 12 December 2003), R. Sri Kumar said, "He is trying to create grounds for getting bail on health grounds. This is not borne out by the medical records available. In fact, the Pune Police recovered his medical records showing him as HIV positive before he was arrested by the Bangalore Police in Ajmer in November 2001." According to Sri Kumar, who had interacted with Telgi several times during interrogation, Telgi was a tough nut to crack. "He is shrewd and intelligent and does not easily volunteer information. He speaks little and answers questions with limited details. Instead, he confirms only such information which he finds that he cannot deny if cornered with evidence."

M.T. Nanaiah, Telgi's lawyer, however, had a different story to tell (Rediff.com News, 21 November 2003). "From 6 August 2003 to 15 August 2003, by the order of the high court, Telgi was remanded in police custody for examination. Since he is a chronic diabetic, he was being given insulin and then taken to hospital by the STAMPIT for treatment. So, according to Telgi, the only possibility is that he got infected with AIDS then. He said that the STAMPIT police were responsible for this. Telgi felt that since the STAMPIT had no material to connect him to the scam, they intended to eliminate him by keeping him in custody. Telgi feared for his life not from the world outside, but from the STAMPIT and had filed an application in the court about this too on 11 November 2003. Each time, when he needs medical treatment for ailments he is suffering from, the prosecution says it will file an objection."

Nanaiah further added, "Telgi went to the National Institute of Mental Health and Neuro Sciences (NIMHANS) hospital in Bangalore on 6 November 2003 for medical treatment. He suffers from diabetes and needs insulin injections. While the doctors were doing tests on him, they realized that he was HIV positive.

Immediately, they informed Telgi about it. On 9 November 2003, it was further confirmed by additional tests that he was indeed HIV positive. According to Telgi, he was taken to the Bowring and Lady Curzon Hospital in Bangalore every day by the police, while in custody, for treatment of his diabetes. That's the only possibility where this could have happened. As to who are responsible needs to be investigated by the state. It is too premature to say now whether it is accidental or motivated. According to Telgi, it is motivated. STAMPIT people have instructed the jail authorities not to provide Telgi with the facilities that he was enjoying earlier. The television in his cell has been taken away; under the plea of risk to his life they have posted additional security around him, hampering his movements. They have also put a camera in his room. He doesn't have as much free movement as the other inmates of the jail do. All this, Telgi feels shows that the STAMPIT people want to take out their vengeance on him."

Nanaiah argued that Telgi was arrested two years ago, and hence it was not possible that his HIV illness had remained undetected for so long. He had been taken to the hospital on numerous occasions and several examinations had already been conducted on him. As soon as Telgi was arrested and taken into police custody in early November 2001, he had been ill for about fifteen days and was treated, but HIV could not be traced then.

Telgi's lawyer also complained that Telgi was not getting adequate medical attention for his multiple illnesses like HIV, diabetes, or cardiac problems. He had not been extended any medical facilities, except for access to the rather limited facilities of the jail hospital. Despite court orders, all medical treatment to him had been stopped. Rather, Telgi should have been admitted to some bigger hospital for proper treatment.

Much of Telgi's angst and allegations against the STAMPIT was on account of their disciplined and relentless investigations and their filing of charges against his crimes. Even though Telgi's machinations had started much earlier (in 1994) in Mumbai, he had been escaping the arm of the law, till he was arrested in 2001 by the intrepid efforts of the Bengaluru police. It was the STAMPIT's efforts, thereafter, that started the nationwide hunt for various sites of Telgi's nefarious activities.

Reports in the *Frontline*, dated 2 January 2004, indicate that very early in the investigations, the STAMPIT had tried to engage the public and had created a website in English (www.stampit.info), accessible also in Kannada and Marathi. This carried details of the scam including photographs of the those accused, the cases against them and the status, rough sketches of team members and press releases. Comments and help were sought from the public. Sri Kumar said: "The idea was primarily to get local people to give us information in confidence. We also wanted to make our investigations as transparent as possible since the case was sensitive and had interstate ramifications. While the website was useful in disseminating news on the status of the investigation, confidential information from whistle-blowers was hard to come by. The team received more abuses than intelligence on the website."

A grouse against the STAMPIT was that they hadn't enough to show for political arrests. In an article on 13 August 2004 in *Frontline*, which covered the various allegations made by the retired ACP T.G. Sangram Singh (the police officer involved in the City Market case discussed earlier), the officer also made the serious allegation in the court on 13 July 2004 that STAMPIT officials Sri Kumar and Deputy Inspector General of Police Raghavendra H. Auradhkar were responsible for destroying vital documents and key evidence which linked politicians to the scam before they handed over the case papers to the CBI. Sangram Singh further alleged that as a quid pro quo for the protection provided by Sri Kumar, Krishna and Kharge of the Congress government had promised to make Sri Kumar the police commissioner.

According to a newspaper article in the *Indian Express* on 30 July 2017, an internal report by D. Roopa, Karnataka's deputy inspector general (prisons), which was later leaked to the media, alleged corruption involving Telgi in Bengaluru Central Prison. Roopa's letter to H.N. Sathyanarayana Rao, director general of police (prisons), dated 12 July 2017, alleged that preferential treatment was being accorded to Telgi, which included providing him with prison inmates as personal help and masseurs. According to reports in Rediff News, dated 13 July 2017, Roopa's letter said, "Earlier, he was on wheelchair and the court allowed people for his assistance. But now, when he is fine, why is this continuing? In fact, three or four undertrials are there to serve him, who even gave him hands and feet massage."

The *Indian Express* article also carried the defence of the police officials who were well acquainted with the Karnataka prison system. They maintained that the allegations could be 'misplaced', as the jail manual allowed assistants for prisoners who were evaluated as ill and required support. "There is a lot of small corruption and a definite hierarchy of prisoners. That cannot be completely eradicated," a senior IPS officer, who oversaw different state jails, admitted. "Some things (in DIG Roopa's report) are allowed under prison rules, and many involve complicity of jail officials who depend on prisoners in running day-to-day affairs of different jails, given the staff shortage."

Jail officials often work around rules in an informal way to maintain peace, the officer said. "When high-profile politicians such as (BJP leader and former chief minister) B.S. Yediyurappa, (mining baron and BJP leader) Janardhan Reddy or (former president of the AIADMK and close aide of J. Jayalalithaa) Sasikala, are lodged in VIP cells, jail authorities ensure that they are not locked up with a hardened criminal as a cellmate. They are provided a choice of cellmate(s) or someone, who could help them in jail with everyday activities," the former prison official said. According to a senior IPS officer, much of the allegations of luxuries being granted were 'exaggerations', as the prison system in Karnataka, over the years, had come under heavy scrutiny. "Prisoners (now) have to pay to even breathe in peace; it is a perk to be just left alone by jailors and other prisoners," the officer said. "It is a closed system, and those in jail, including officials, rule the roost."

While D. Roopa's letter alleged that Sasikala had paid a bribe of Rs 2 crore to the director general of police (prisons) for largesse such as a separate kitchen, police sources refuted the allegation of a separate kitchen though they did admit that perhaps certain concessions had been made, such as allowing the jail kitchen to remain open beyond 5 p.m. to provide hot food to Sasikala and keeping a couple of empty cells in the women prisoner's barracks as a security measure. A senior official added another reason for the empty cells. Many inmates had been moved to a special women's jail built in Tumkur. But, the official said, "There is no way air-conditioning can be provided in a prison cell, as was allegedly done in Sasikala's cell. Televisions are allowed, and there are often fights in common viewing areas over which channels to watch."

D Roopa's report prompted the chief minister of Karnataka, Siddaramaiah, to order a high-level inquiry, though her superior, H.N. Sathyanarayana Rao, denied having received such a report. Significantly, as per a CNN-News 18 report of 17 July 2017, "Deputy Inspector General (Prisons) D. Roopa was transferred to the traffic wing days after submitting the controversial report which alleged that V.K. Sasikala and Abdul Karim Telgi were being given 'preferential treatment' in Bengaluru Central Jail."

The controversial report and its media leak erupted into a major controversy, with Siddaramaiah asking Roopa to explain her conduct and saying that it was 'absolutely against the rule book'. Denying that D. Roopa's transfer to the traffic wing was a 'punishment' transfer, D.K. Shivakumar, Karnataka power minister, told CNN-News18, "We have some rules. An investigation is on. No officer is allowed to go to the media. A fair investigation will be conducted."

14

We Go Back a Long Way...

Before we turn the spotlight on the significant and shocking developments in Maharashtra in the Telgi story, we will dispense with the 'connection in high places' that Telgi was able to muster in Andhra Pradesh, where some of his operations have already been discussed in a previous chapter. Telgi's headway in this state has an interesting background.

Details from Criminal Appeal 1286 of 2006 (decided on 8 December 2006) filed by Chenna Boyanna Krishna Yadav reveals that Krishna Yadav, an advocate by profession, was elected as a member of the legislative assembly of the state of Andhra Pradesh in 1994. Till the year 1998, he was a minister in the Andhra Pradesh government and in 1999, he was again elected as a member of the legislative assembly. He held several portfolios as a minister between October 1999 and November 2001.

During investigation, and the ensuing search on 11 January 2003, the SIT, Mumbai Police, discovered a micro-audiocassette in one of the premises occupied by Telgi. This contained recording of alleged conversations between Krishna Yadav and Telgi. The cassette was dated 16 January 1998. An analysis by the Forensic Laboratory opined that the voice samples belonged to Krishna Yadav, and that he was involved in the kidnapping of two employees of Telgi, namely, Abdul Wahid and Sadashiva, in 1998. Yadav allegedly demanded a ransom of Rs 2 crore from Telgi for their release. A deal was struck and as a result thereof, Krishna Yadav came closer to Telgi. Their friendship grew.

Thereafter, Krishna Yadav allegedly rendered active support and help to Telgi in his unlawful activities in Andhra Pradesh, relating to the printing and the sale of counterfeit stamps and other documents. It was alleged that Yadav received huge amounts of money from Telgi's organised crime syndicate in return for using his political clout to provide protection and turn a blind eye to Telgi's activities. Evidence of such business in Andhra Pradesh under the names of M/s Sams Services and M/s Star Services have already been discussed in an earlier chapter.

Though investigations were initiated by the SIT, later, the case, along with forty-seven others, was transferred by the Supreme Court to the CBI. A case was registered against Krishna Yadav under various sections of the IPC, MCOCA, provisions of the Bombay Stamps Act, 1958, and POCA. Krishna Yadav was arrested on 6 September 2003 and remanded in police custody before being transferred to judicial custody on 26 September 2003. The charge sheet was filed on 29 December 2003. Subsequently, some more charge sheets were filed and finally a supplementary charge sheet was filed by the CBI on 26 July 2005. All these charge sheets were consolidated into one.

Two applications for bail by Krishna Yadav (on 6 August 2004 and 19 February 2005) were rejected in the Mumbai High Court. The Supreme Court finally granted bail on 8 December 2006 in Criminal Appeal 1286 of 2006 on the principal premise that while the alleged taped conversation may prove Krishna Yadav's acquaintance with Telgi, but (in absence of other evidence) was insufficient to prove the former's direct role in the aiding and abetment of Telgi's organised crime.

The Bund Garden case and its positive developments in Maharashtra (discussed later) marked a watershed in the Telgi chronicles. Perhaps the 'awakening' of the Maharashtra Police was spurred by the positive action of their Karnataka counterpart. However, the embedded scourge of corruption continued to fester even after this case, echoing in similar incidents of aiding and abetting that had allowed Telgi to operate unfettered since the 1990s. Examples from the cases of Gokul Bhagaji Patil, Babanrao Tukaram Ranjane and Vashishtha Rambhau Andhale stand testimony to how Telgi's operations were facilitated by official collusion.

Gokul Bhagaji Patil, was posted as a senior police inspector at Mira Road Police Station, Thane District, Maharashtra, during the period 2 June 1999 to 13 May 2000. On or about 15 August 1999, based on some information received by Mira Road Police Station about the printing of fake revenue and postal stamps by a gang, raids were conducted at certain places and some persons arrested. A crime report (C.R. No. 274 of 1999) was duly filed under various sections of the IPC, along with Section 55 of the Indian Postal Act 1898.

An inquiry was conducted by the then additional superintendent of police, Thane (Rural), on the investigations (in C.R. No. 274 of 1999) carried out by Patil and his team. It was revealed that although the printing press – situated at Mulund and Bora Bazar, Mumbai – where counterfeit stamps and stamp papers were being printed had been identified, Patil and his junior, Sub-inspector Kakade (since demised), in charge of the case, had neither sealed the said premises nor seized the machines. They thus ensured that A.K.L. Telgi, the kingpin of the operation as well as the prime accused, was not arrested and remained at large, till he was arrested by the Karnataka Police. Patil also failed in his duties as the counterfeit stamps seized in the case were not sent for examination to the Indian Security Press.

Patil abused his position as a public servant, and knowingly and intentionally, aided and abetted the activities of Telgi's organised crime syndicate till 7 June 2002, for nearly three years. He was thus charged for offences committed and punishable under sections of MCOCA.

Based on these investigations, Patil's name figured in the Bund Garden case too (C.R. No. 135 of 2002). Patil, who by then had been promoted as the assistant commissioner of police was arrested on 18 October 2003 by the SIT and remanded in judicial custody. His immediate bail application was dismissed, though he was released on 8 December 2006 on a personal bond of Rs 2 lakh with two sureties after spending three years in judicial custody (Criminal Appeal 1287 of 2006).

Another accused (A-62) in the same Bund Garden case was Babanrao Tukaram Ranjane, who was arrested on 8 December 2003. Ranjane was, at the relevant time, the deputy superintendent of stamps. According to the supplementary charge sheet, Ranjane was aware of the activities of A.K.L. Telgi since December 1998 and was rendering help and support to the latter. He had deliberately not acted against one licenced stamp vendor, Madhav M.D., who was a close associate of Telgi, and who was actively involved in Telgi's business. Ranjane had also failed to initiate legal action in the case of stamps issued by Sanjay Sharma, who was also a member of Telgi's crime syndicate. Ranjane was aware of Telgi's association with Madhav M.D. and Sanjay Sharma and yet took no action despite specific directions from his superiors. Ranjane's application for bail was initially rejected. He appealed again (Criminal Appeal 640 of 2006) in the Supreme Court and was granted bail on 12 May 2006, after spending two years and three months in judicial custody.

Police Inspector Vashishtha Rambhau Andhale, who was posted at District Crime Branch (DCB), Crime Investigation Department (CID) Unit VIII, Dharavi, Mumbai, led the raiding party consisting of various police officers including Assistant Police Inspector Dilip Kamat in the Fort area, Mumbai, on 16 December 1998. Zameer Ahmed Gulab Sanadi and Tabrez Ahmed Abdul Rahim Telgi were arrested, and counterfeit government stamps and stamp papers were seized from them. Based on a complaint lodged by Sub-inspector Dilip Pandurang Shinde, C.R. No. 78 of 1998 was registered on 17 December 1998 against Zameer Sanadi, Tabrez Ahmed Abdul Rahim Telgi and one Murgoad. The investigation was entrusted to Kamat.

According to the statement on record dated 27 February 2004 by Sub-inspector Nandkishore Kondalkar, who worked at the same unit as Andhale, on 16 December 1998 at the instance of Andhale and Kamat, a trap was laid, and accused Tabrez Telgi and Zameer Sanadi were arrested with fake stamps. According to Kondalkar, he came to know that on 18 December 1998, Telgi was brought to DCB CID Unit VIII at the instance of Andhale after Tabrez Ahmed Abdul Rahim Telgi, the nephew of A.K.L. Telgi, disclosed details of the unlawful activities of his uncle. There, Telgi had met inspector Andhale and Kamat. Sub-inspector Shinde, who was attached to the same unit and had lodged an FIR on 17 December 1998, in his statement dated 27 February 2004, corroborated Kondalkar's statement.

Rasna Ankalesaria, who had worked as a receptionist in A.K.L. Telgi's office at Fort, in her statement dated 22 February 2003 claimed that Inspector Andhale was a close friend of Telgi. Immediately after Tabrez Telgi and Zameer Sanadi were arrested, Telgi was called to the office. These facts established that Andhale had knowledge about the involvement of Zameer Sanadi and Telgi in the circulation and sale of counterfeit government stamps and stamp papers as early as 17 December 1998.

Later, when Andhale was in charge of the Sahara Airport Crime Branch Unit, Mumbai, simultaneous raids were conducted on 20 May 2002. The raid on the offices of Mark Enterprises, Jaitun Building, in Andheri was led by Andhale and that on the office of S.S. Services at Fort, Mumbai, by Inspector Darekar. These two offices were headed by Zameer Sanadi and Firoz Abdul Rehman Shaikh respectively. Large quantities of counterfeit government stamps and stamp papers were found on both the premises. Inspector Andhale brought Zameer Sanadi, along with other staff, and the recovered stamps and stamp papers to the Sahar Airport Unit. Similarly, Darekar, too, brought Firoz Shaikh along with the staff and recovered evidence to the same office and presented them to Andhale.

Inspector Andhale allegedly accepted Rs 15 lakh on 20 May 2002 from one Khadersha Mohammed Yousuf Singoti (aka Sajju), another accused (A-8). Zameer Sanadi and Firoz Shaikh were allowed to go scot-free, along with their entire stock of the counterfeit stamps and stamp papers. Andhale neither registered a criminal case nor did he seize and take charge of the said counterfeit goods. These facts were corroborated by the statement of Sajju recorded under MCOCA provisions by Vineet Vinayak, superintendent of police, CBI, New Delhi. According to Sajju's statement, he had received a call from Telgi in Bengaluru (Telgi was lodged in Bengaluru Central Jail). Allegedly, Telgi had instructed Sajju to collect Rs 15 lakh from one Badami, go opposite Sahar Airport and hand over the cash to Andhale. According to Sajju, he had followed those instructions. The diary of Khalid Abdul Sattar Badami, another accused, showed disbursements of Rs 10 lakh to Sajju on 20 May 2002 and a further sum of Rs 5 lakh on 21 May 2002.

Staff members of the two offices raided, too, admitted the aforesaid facts in their statements. Investigation revealed that the account of M/s Mark Enterprises, Jaitun Building, was operated by Shabbir Shaikh, another accused (A-25), at the HDFC Bank in Andheri. The account of S.S. Services, Fort, was maintained at the erstwhile ABN-Amro bank by accused Shaikh Mohd Ashraf K. Musabha Shaikh (A-28). Both these accounts show the deposit of a large number of cheques, issued by buyers of counterfeit government stamps and stamp papers. The telephone number of Inspector Andhale also figured in the diary maintained by Rasna Ankalesaria, Telgi's office assistant. Several other accused such as Laxman Maruti Tirveer (A-47), Zameer Sanadi (A-34) and Tabrez Ahmed Abdul Rahim Telgi (A-64) also deposed against Andhale in their confessional statements.

Allegedly, during the period December 1993 to January 2003 – even well after 21 February 1999, when the MCOCA came into force, thus bringing all unlawful activities of the syndicate under its purview – Inspector Andhale, along with others, was party to the continuing unlawful activities, carrying on various illegal acts in an organised manner as a member of Telgi's organised crime syndicate. The phrase organised crime syndicate finds a definition under MCOCA and has been used in many of Telgi's case proceedings and pronouncements. Inspector Andhale and others, working as public servants, rendered help and support to the organised crime syndicate and 'dishonestly and intentionally' falsified records, thus diluting the enormity of the crime and suppressing the offence. Their failure to intentionally apprehend the criminals saved the perpetrators of the syndicate from legal punishment, allowed the syndicate to flourish, causing losses to the national exchequer. Towards this, they also accepted illegal gratification from the syndicate.

Inspector Andhale was suspended from duty, arrested on 18 October 2003 and charge sheeted as accused (A-55) in MCOCA Special Case 2 of 2003, commonly known as Telgi Stamp Case of Bund Garden Police Station, Pune. However, on 26 June 2007, a MCOCA Special Court, Pune, discharged him. The CBI appealed under Section 12 of the MCOCA, against the order (Appeal 763 of 2007). Interestingly, two judges heard the appeal and delivered separate judgments on 27 February 2008. While Justice Dr Radhakrishnan concurred with the MCOCA Special Court and confirmed the discharge of Inspector Andhale, Justice (Smt.) Roshan Dalvi directed the MCOCA Special Court to frame charges against Andhale and proceed with the trial in accordance with the law.

In view of the difference of opinion under Section 392 of CrPC, the appeal was placed before Judge Ranjana Desai J., who set aside the judgment/order of 26 June 2007 passed in MCOCA Special Case No. 2 of 2003 and directed the special judge to frame the charge and proceed against inspector Andhale.

15

The Bund Garden Case

Perhaps the most significant development, discussed earlier in snatches, which precipitated the rapid chain of events in Maharashtra, was the Bund Garden case. Several big names were implicated, sending ripples of fear in the police rank and file.

Ranjitsing Brahmajeetsing Sharma (R.S. Sharma) was the commissioner of police, Pune, from 30 April 2000, and the commissioner of police, Mumbai, from 1 January 2003 to 30 November 2003. On 7 June 2002, Sharma received information that on that very day, three persons in a silver-coloured Indica car bearing registration number 10H-04-A1200 were travelling from Mumbai towards S.T. Stand near Pune Railway Station with fake stamp paper. He conveyed the message telephonically to the Bund Garden Police Station. The vehicle was intercepted by officials of the police station on the same day and the three men, along with fake stamps worth about Rs 200 crore, were arrested. Those arrested included Mukadam Hussain Mohd Sub Tadkod, the driver of the vehicle, Shankar Rajaram Ganappa, and Mohd Moulali Gaus Siggve.

A First Information Report (FIR) was lodged by Inspector Kale and was recorded by Senior Inspector Prakash Deshmukh of the

Bund Garden Police Station. An offence vide Crime No. 135/2002 was registered to probe the delivery of the consignment. Extensive investigations were launched. Several places were raided and huge quantities of stamps and printing machinery worth Rs 21,28,47,63,824 were seized.

Initially, the investigations were conducted by Deshmukh, under the day-to-day direct supervision of Additional Commissioner of Police (Crime) S.M. Mushrif, who oversaw the operations of the Crime Branch, Pune. Mushrif reported to Maheshgauri, the joint commissioner of police. Several teams, comprising various officers, investigated this crime. Records disclosed that Mushrif had divided the investigation and connected work among four teams, namely, (i) appraisal of seized papers/documents; (ii) examination of computer records and decoding; (iii) investigation; and iv) fieldwork. The team tasked with fieldwork included assistant commissioner of police (Crime Branch), Pune, Mohammad Chand Mulani, and other officers. Commissioner Sharma was the overall in-charge.

Considering the spread and magnitude of the fake stamp trade, a proposal to invoke the provisions of MCOCA was forwarded by Deshmukh on 9 July 2002. This was followed by another appeal on 26 August 2002 to Maheshgauri as the statutory period of ninety days within which the charge sheet was required to be filed was due to expire on 3 September 2002. Maheshgauri granted approval to invoke MCOCA on 3 September 2002 but only for two of the accused, Telgi and Shabir Shaikh. The first charge sheet was filed against all the twenty-three accused on 3 September 2002. The crime was attributed to an organised crime syndicate, run by A.K.L. Telgi. The criminal activities of this syndicate, it was stated, began several years ago; they expanded across several states in India and as many as twenty-seven cases were registered against Telgi and his associates in the country.

Deputy Commissioner of Police (DCP) Jai Jadhav took over the investigation of Crime No. 135/2002 on 6 September 2002 under the SIT constituted for the purpose and reported to Deputy Inspector General of Police S.K. Jaiswal. Importantly, Mushrif, who was supervising the investigation, levelled serious allegations against senior police officers, including Commissioner Sharma, in his letters dated 16 October 2002 and 23 October 2002, inter-alia addressed to the additional chief secretary, Government of Maharashtra.

To make in-depth investigations, follow up on the bogus stamp case on a priority basis, and to probe the charges made by Mushrif, the state of Maharashtra constituted a SIT by a government resolution dated 2 November 2002. This was headed by S.K. Jaiswal. He was to be assisted by a deputy commissioner of police, an assistant commissioner of police, and three inspectors. The composition of the team was to be decided by the director general of police. The infrastructural support in terms of manpower, vehicles and communication, etc., was the responsibility of the Pune City Police. The team was to report to A.K. Agarwal, additional director general of police, CID, Pune.

In response to a proposal by Deputy Commissioner of Police Wakade, Jaiswal, the head of the SIT, granted an approval to invoke MCOCA provisions against all the accused in the case on 22 November 2002. A supplementary charge sheet was filed on 25 November 2002. The investigation team submitted one more original charge sheet before the special judge, Pune, under MCOCA, Special Case No. 2/2003, on 27 March 2003. Supplementary charge sheets were filed by the SIT on 15 September 2003 and 3 February 2004. When this case, along with several others was transferred by the Supreme Court to the CBI on 15 March 2004, the bureau scrutinised the role of all the accused persons and filed a composite charge sheet on 26 July 2005.

With the charge sheets, the skeletons began tumbling out of the closet as the keepers of the law and public servants complicit with Telgi fell into the dragnet of the investigation. In addition to the names of Deputy Superintendent of Stamps Babanrao Tukaram Ranjane (accused A-62) and police officials Gokul Bhagaji Patil (A-56) and Vashishtha Rambhau Andhale (A-55), discussed in the previous chapter, senior members of the police came under the glare of the probe by the SIT (and later by the CBI). The police officers included

Assistant Police Inspector Dilip Kamat (A-44), Inspector Dattatraya Y. Dal (A-50), Assistant Commissioner Mohammad Chand Mulani (A-61), Deputy Commissioner of Police Pradeep B. Sawant (A-65), Joint Commissioner of Police Shridhar Sumant Vagal (A-59), and Commissioner R.S. Sharma (A-60). For some of the accused police officers mentioned here, the charges extended beyond Pune, to the events which transpired in Mumbai, post the Bund Garden case, when Telgi was transferred from Bengaluru in October 2002. Hence, some of these names and their involvement in the scam will be discussed in the next chapter.

ACP Mulani, who was associated with the investigation of the case since the day the FIR was registered on 7 June 2002 to the date of the filing of the first charge sheet on 3 September 2002, retired on 31 August 2003. Based on his alleged involvement, according to findings by the SIT, he was arrested on 4 December 2003 and arraigned as an accused (A-61) in the supplementary charge sheet of 3 February 2004 with various charges under MCOCA and POCA.

It appears from the details available from ACP Mulani's appeal in the Supreme Court (Criminal Appeal 977 of 2006), decided on 18 September 2006, that he met Telgi through Telgi's lawyer Abdul Rashid Kulkarni. As mentioned earlier, Kulkarni was an accused himself (A-49) for having helped Telgi with financial transactions in the scam. Mulani was instrumental in ensuring that some persons involved in the crime were not shown as accused in the first charge sheet filed on 3 September 2002. In *Telgi Scam: Reporter ki Diary*, Sanjay Singh mentions: "Five wanted accused mysteriously disappeared from the charge sheet and the names of six new persons were put in. They were never mentioned earlier in the investigation or the case diary. These six persons included Telgi's wife Shahida, his daughter Sana and ailing brother Abdul Rahim.'

He further writes, "Mushrif alleged that Prakash Deshmukh and Muhammad Mulani were manipulating and tampering with the investigation. The trio (Telgi's family) was included in the charge sheet to extract bribe from Telgi and would be released thereafter for 'lack of evidence'. He also alleged that although he was the investigating and the monitoring officer, his junior officers disobeyed and took orders directly from Sharma. Mushrif alleged that Sharma was protecting his juniors."

ACP Mulani allegedly received Rs 15 lakh from Kulkarni, as part payment towards a sum of Rs 3 crore agreed as illegal gratification to arrange for the deletion of Telgi's kin (wife, daughter and brother) from the charge sheet, and to ensure that they were not arrested. Significantly, one of the names deleted from the charge sheet of 3 September 2002 was that of Sirajuddin Kamalsab Nasipudi, Telgi's associate. During ACP Mulani's association with this case, counterfeit stamps worth Rs 1500 crore were recovered on 14 June 2002 from a godown at Bhiwandi, taken on rent by Nasipudi. The deletion of Nasipudi's name from the charge sheet cast a shadow on ACP Mulani.

In his defence, Mulani pointed out that he was part of the fieldwork team and not directly involved in the investigation. Nor was he part of the team that conducted the Bhiwandi raid. The decision on who should be made accused primarily rested with the deputy commissioner of police (Zone II), subject to the final decision of the additional commissioner, in consultation with the senior police prosecutor. It was not Mulani's remit to show Nasipudi as an absconding accused in the first charge sheet.

The 22 November 2002 statement of Mushrif, however, weighed heavily against Mulani. Mushrif claimed that Telgi had told him that Mulani and Deshmukh, two senior officers, had threatened that unless he paid them Rs 3 crore, they would arrest his wife, daughter and sick brother. As Telgi was in custody, his counsel A.R. Kulkarni, through whom the demand was made, negotiated the payment. Telgi had already paid Rs 15 lakh. Mulani and Deshmukh had assured his counsel that after the receipt of the balance, the names of the said family members of Telgi would be deleted from the charge sheet.

In his statement recorded on 11 September 2003, Vijay Gunjal (a member of the SIT) stated that he had accompanied advocate A.R. Kulkarni in August 2002, when he had gone to meet Mulani.

Kulkarni subsequently told Vijay that he had given Rs 15 lakh to Mulani, which too, went against the tainted assistant commissioner.

The Mumbai High Court, however, observed, "It cannot be said that it was the applicant (Mulani) who was insisting that the wife, daughter and brother of Telgi shall be kept out of the charge sheet as the Apex Court (in 2005 [5] SCC 294) has already noted that it was Shri Mushrif who was the superior officer of the applicant who was desirous of keeping the said three persons out of the charge sheet."

An important aside of the charges against Mulani, yet one relied upon by the prosecution, was the statement by Adhip Chaudhary, additional chief secretary, Karnataka. He had said that just before a meeting of the senior officers of Karnataka and Maharashtra on 24 July 2002, the head of STAMPIT, Sri Kumar, had warned him to be a little cautious about one of the members of the Maharashtra team, namely, Mulani, as the Karnataka Police had received information about his involvement while intercepting messages when they were tapping Telgi's phones.

Mulani's arrest on 2 December 2003 shook the Pune Police. According to a report in *The Times of India* on 6 December 2003, Mulani enjoyed a good reputation owing to his flamboyance and ability to stand up to his seniors. He was seen as accessible, hardworking and capable. Many thus begrudged his arrest and felt that he had been falsely implicated and was the 'fall guy' owing to his differences with Mushrif. That Mulani had been suspended on 24 August 2003, just seven days short of his retirement, too rankled. "Why spare Mushrif?" Mulani's counsel, Inderjit Gill, asked the court after Telgi's arrest. "Additional Commissioner of Police (Crime) S.M. Mushrif had an hour-long meeting with Telgi. After the meeting, Mushrif gave a letter to the then police commissioner R.S. Sharma, saying that Telgi's wife, daughter and brother should not be included in the charge sheet," he said. "Why is he being spared?"

Mulani's bail was rejected twice, on 1 July 2004 by the special judge, Pune, and then by the Mumbai High Court on 20 October 2005. It was finally granted by the Supreme Court on 18 September 2006 after Mulani had already spent two years and nine months in prison.

The biggest arrest, that of R.S. Sharma, serving then as commissioner of police, Mumbai, happened on 1 December 2003. The charges against Sharma were serious (his CA 572 of 2004 decided on 16 July 2004). Sharma was removed from his post on 18 November 2003 after an SIT report pointed out lapses on his part in the investigation into the racket. Sharma was then moved as an additional director general of police (administration) in the state police headquarters. On 24 November 2003, he was appointed as the chief security officer of the Maharashtra State Road Transport Corporation and the charge sheet was served upon him on 25 November 2003. The Maharashtra government also instituted a departmental inquiry against him and charged him for contravening the All-India Service (Conduct) Rules by not maintaining absolute integrity and devotion to his duties. He was arrested the day after he superannuated on 30 November 2003.

Sharma knew of Mulani's dubious past since 1996 when a complaint about corruption was made against Mulani, who was then a senior inspector at the Dongri Police Station in Mumbai. A copy of the complaint was also received by Sharma, who was then working as the joint commissioner of police, Mumbai. The said complaint was forwarded by Sharma to the Anti-Corruption Bureau, Mumbai, and bore his signature. In the affidavit dated 29 October 2002 filed by Sharma in his capacity as the commissioner of police, Pune, before the Maharashtra State Administrative Tribunal (MAT), he had categorically affirmed that the conduct of Mulani was found to be highly suspicious in the murder case of one Faizulla Khan.

Yet on 6 September 2002, when the Bund Garden investigations were handed over to Deputy Commissioner of Police Jai Jadhav and new teams for the investigation were being formed, Sharma included Mulani's name in the 'investigation' team despite being specifically requested otherwise by Jadhav. Commissioner Sharma insisted on Mulani's inclusion on the pretext that Deshmukh was too overburdened with his duties as in-charge of Bund Garden Police Station, and it was only ACP Mulani who knew all the facts about the case. Sharma's counsel rebutted saying Mulani had in fact been included in the fieldwork team by Mushrif for the purpose of 'tracing and arresting accused persons', which did not come within the purview of the 'investigation of the offence' or 'interrogation of the accused'. Also, the director general of police had certified Mulani as an excellent officer in 2003. Upon invocation of MCOCA, when Jai Jadhav was appointed as the investigating officer and had sought options for names for inclusion in the team, Mulani's name was suggested. Jai Jadhav and Mushrif could have excluded Mulani if they so wished, it was argued.

Ashok Basak, additional chief secretary (Home), Maharashtra, had informed Sharma on 6 September 2002 about Mulani being in telephonic contact with Telgi (who was then lodged in the Central Prison at Bangalore) and about his suspicious role in the fake stamp case. This information was passed on to Basak by Adhip Chaudhary. Commissioner Sharma had assured Basak that he would remove Mulani from the investigation, but never did.

Mulani was transferred to Jat taluka in Sangli district by a government order dated 4 September 2002, which was received in Pune on 6 September 2002. This transfer order was not served till Mulani had obtained a stay against the transfer from the Maharashtra State Administrative Tribunal. Not only was Mulani allowed to continue working on C.R. No. 135/2002, but he was also sent to Bengaluru on 18 September 2002 alone, without the investigating officer of the case. Mulani was also allowed to be associated with the Bund Garden case till 30 September 2002 when he was transferred to the Special Branch. The only explanation Sharma's counsel offered in defence of the above lapses was that he (Sharma) wanted to examine and analyse the legal aspects of the Maharashtra Administrative Tribunal's orders and the procedural delays in both instances of serving the notice and Mulani's protracted involvement with the case was on account of the annual Ganpati festival, which was scheduled from 10 September 2002 till 21 September 2002.

On 10 October 2002, certain names were recommended for awards in connection with the investigation of C.R. No. 135/2002. Although Mulani's name was not listed initially, it was specifically added by Sharma in his own handwriting. Mulani's proximity with Sharma was also evidenced from the fact that Sharma had visited Bengaluru twice, on 9 July 2002 and 23 July 2002. On both occasions, he was accompanied by Mulani. On the second visit, Basak also accompanied Sharma.

A complaint of corruption dated 15 July 2002 from the president of a citizen's forum in Pune, against Mulani, received by Sharma on 31 August 2002, wasn't actioned. The Government of Maharashtra had constituted a Special Task Force (STF) to inquire into all the pending cases relating to counterfeit stamps in Maharashtra and Sharma was appointed as the chairman to head the taskforce. Not a single meeting of this taskforce was convened by Sharma.

According to the reference statement of the director general of police, Maharashtra, S.C. Malhotra, Sharma did not ensure filing of a properly reasoned charge sheet in C.R. No. 135/2002 P.S. Bund Garden and did not ensure the timely application of MCOCA to the whole case. Kishore Jadhav, then DCP Zone II, Pune, also alleged in his reference statement that Sharma had hurried through the filing of the charge sheet.

It was also alleged that Sharma had a closed-door meeting with A.K.L. Telgi in isolation, without the other high-ranking officers (statements of Assistant Commissioner Supriya Patil, DCP (H.Q.) Vasant Koregaonkar, and Deputy Commissioner Jai Jadhav). Vasant Koregaonkar's statement also mentions that Sharma knew Telgi even when he was posted in Mumbai earlier.

Commissioner Sharma's application for bail was refused by the special court on 19 January 2004, and then by the Mumbai High Court on 16 July 2004. He was granted interim bail in November 2004, a status continued by the Supreme Court, vide their order on 7 April 2005 (in Criminal Appeal 523 of 2005). Commissioner Sharma was eventually exonerated. It was indeed ironic that the person who had followed up on the information received and initiated police action in the Bund Garden case was himself entrapped by subsequent developments.

16

Murky Mumbai

In an earlier chapter we discussed the reason for Telgi's travel from Bengaluru to Mumbai on 28 October 2002. The Mumbai Police had applied for Telgi's custody to enable them to conduct the necessary investigation in the Christopher murder case. Though this permission was valid only till 8 November 2002, as we have already seen, Telgi wasn't sent back to Bengaluru before 24 January 2003. The reason for this appears deliberate and diabolical. Between this period, i.e., 28 October 2002 and 24 January 2003, for all intents and purposes, Telgi was a free man and not in the custody of Mumbai Police.

The following events have been gleaned from the case numbers provided in parenthesis. Given the cross references they bear, an itemised validation for the events, unless specifically alluded to, has not been provided. (Referenced: Criminal Application 572 of 2004 decided in the Mumbai High Court on 16 July 2004 [R.S. Sharma], Criminal Appeal 523 of 2005 decided in the Supreme Court on 7 April 2005 [R.S. Sharma], Criminal Appeal 764 of 2004 decided in the Mumbai High Court on 14 July 1010 [P.B. Sawant], Criminal Appeal 411 of 2007 decided in the Supreme Court on 22 March 2007 [Shridhar Sumant Vagal].)

An order of 6 July 2002 was signed by Deputy Commissioner of Police P.B. Sawant stating that under instructions from Joint Commissioner of Police Shridhar Sumant Vagal (to whom he reported), the Christopher murder case (C.R. No. 123 of 2001 registered at Shahu Nagar Police Station) was transferred to the Crime Branch, Unit V, Dharavi. This was strange, for as early as 15 February 2002 this case was fully detected and the involvement of Telgi established. Vagal (A-59), in violation of norms, directed the transfer of this case to the Crime Branch. Thereafter, once Telgi's custody was secured from Karnataka, he was shown as arrested in the Christopher murder case on 28 October 2002. He was in the custody of the Crime Branch till 11 November 2002.

Assistant Police Inspector Kamat (A-44), who was attached to the same Crime Branch where the Christopher case was transferred, was the investigating officer of C.R. No. 78 of 1998. Despite this knowledge, Telgi was not arrested till his custody was obtained by Crime Branch, Dharavi. He was belatedly shown arrested in C.R. No. 78 of 1998 on 11 November 2002. Sawant, as a supervisory officer, did not inquire why Telgi was not arrested earlier in this case. The onus on Sawant was greater for, as the deputy commissioner of police, he had to supervise all the cases of the Crime Branch. However, he allegedly abused his position to help Telgi's syndicate through Kamat and Senior Inspector Dattatraya Dal.

Telgi continued to be in the custody of Crime Branch in that case (C.R. No. 78 of 1998) from 11 November 2002 to 25 November 2002. Surprisingly, on 22 November 2002, Vagal issued an order transferring seven cases registered at different police stations pertaining to counterfeit stamps and stamp papers in which Telgi was involved, to the Crime Branch. The order had been signed and endorsed by Sawant as well. These cases were:

1. MRA Marg Police Station Crime Report (C.R. No. 355 of 1995)
2. General Branch CID (C.R. No. 41 of 1995)
3. Colaba Police Station (C.R. No. 302 of 1995)

4. Cuffe Parade Police Station (C.R. No. 382 of 1995)
5. DCB CID, Unit V (C.R. No. 78 of 1998)
6. Dadar Police Station (C.R. No. 287 of 2002)
7. MRA Marg Police Station (C.R. No. 79 of 2002)

Allegedly, there was an ulterior motive behind Vagal transferring these cases to the Crime Branch. This was done to retain the custody of Telgi with the Crime Branch for a long period of time (with police custody moving for the next case as soon as one expired), disallowing other police stations from obtaining custody. The transfers allegedly protected Telgi. The accusation against Vagal was that since a great many officer of the Crime Branch were compromised, he should have entrusted the cases to the Economic Offences Wing, rather than to the Crime Branch, Unit V, Dharavi. Also, the transfers were done without the approval of the police commissioner.

Vagal was a member of the Special Task Force formed by the government and had directed Inspector Bhat of the MCOCA Cell to scrutinize the case papers of Telgi and submit a report. However, before Bhat submitted the reports (on 28 November 2002 and 6 December 2002), Vagal hastily transferred the cases to the Crime Branch, Unit V.

While in the custody of the Crime Branch, Telgi was neither seriously interrogated nor kept in lock-up. He was allowed to visit places of his choice and made frequent trips to his residence at 7, Cuffe Parade, Colaba, Mumbai. There were also reports that the police had 'put him up at Hotel Apsara in Kurla for nearly 30 days'. (*The Times of India*, 24 October 2003.) Allegedly, Sawant, had full knowledge of these events.

On 9 January 2003, R. Sri Kumar, who was heading the STAMPIT, visited Mumbai to discuss the Bund Garden case with the Mumbai Police. Along with Jaiswal, the head of the SIT, he visited several places in Mumbai, where raids were conducted. On the same day, they visited 7, Cuffe Parade, Colaba, Telgi's flat. Jaiswal wrote in his report that he was astonished to find the arrested accused Telgi, who was in police custody, enjoying tea and biscuits. Jaiswal found signs of 'regular inhabitation' in the flat. One constable was found sleeping. Other constables were in plainclothes. The belongings of the accused were neatly laid out in the almirah, and the bed showed signs of regular usage. A mobile phone was on the premises apparently to allow Constable Pise to contact Dattatraya Dal.

The exposed policemen tried to create an impression that they were waiting to arrest another accused, Tabrez Telgi. But this did not pass muster. According to Jaiswal, there was no doubt that A.K.L. Telgi had been taken to the flat to enable him to enjoy 'luxurious normal living' while in police custody with full connivance of the police personnel. In his report dated 10 January 2003, addressed to additional chief secretary (home), Government of Maharashtra, Basak, a copy of which was addressed to the director general of police and the commissioner of police, Mumbai, Jaiswal furnished a detailed account of the activity he came across in the flat, and strongly recommended action against the guilty officers, including Kamat.

The report was a sad reflection on the credibility of the Crime Branch. Jaiswal confirmed that he had warned Sawant on telephone on 3 January 2003 that Telgi was being provided all creature comforts while in police custody by officers of the Crime Branch. Sawant had assured that he would ascertain the veracity of the facts and initiate action against the errant officials. In his report dated 10 January 2003, Jaiswal said that such action had not been taken.

Sawant's defence was that he had warned the officers concerned to refrain from indulging in such activities. Dal had told him that all this was a ploy and that they were trying to recover a huge stock of fake stamps from A.K.L. Telgi. However, with the developments in the Cuffe Parade flat episode, this excuse appeared specious.

In his book *Telgi Scam: Reporter ki Diary*, author Sanjay Singh writes: "Despite being in police custody for eighty-five days, he wasn't in jail for even a day. Rather, he was kept in his Cuffe Parade apartment, Colaba flat or in Sion's Hotel Shelter. Telgi was constantly provided all the amenities in police custody. The game ended on 9 January 2003, when Maharashtra and Karnataka SIT raided Telgi's house in Cuffe Parade. Jaiswal rejected their defence that they had laid a trap for suspect Tabrez based on the following:

1. The police personnel were sleeping and Dilip Kamat was absent.
2. That Tabrez, a wanted accused, would meet an arrested culprit (Telgi) in his flat was silly.
3. All signs of Telgi's constant stay in the flat were evident.
4. There was no need for the presence of two servants for the trap.
5. Absence of any additional policemen in plainclothes around the building to prevent escape.

"A report was written by Subodh Jaiswal on 10 January 2003. Two important recommendations were made in this report: First, Assistant Inspector Dilip Kamat and the remaining three policemen should be dismissed under section 311(2)(b) of the Constitution to send a strong message to the police force and prevent future misconduct. Second, action to be taken against the investigating officer of the case, Senior Inspector Dattatraya Dal, and DCP Pradeep Sawant, who was responsible for monitoring. This report was sent to the additional chief secretary (home department) of Maharashtra. The then Mumbai Police Commissioner R.S. Sharma (who had taken charge on 1 January 2003 after being transferred from Pune) was also briefed. Following the report, Mumbai Police suspended Assistant Inspector Dilip Kamat and the three policemen and asked Deputy Commissioner of Police Pradeep Sawant to conduct a departmental enquiry into the matter. But when Sawant's name, too, cropped up, the case was handed over to Deputy Commissioner of Police Ankush Shinde. His report/actions subsequently are unknown."

Tabrez Telgi was arrested by the SIT in Mumbai on 4 January 2004. Tabrez had been absconding in the case C.R. No. 78 of 1998.

R.S. Sharma, too, was implicated. On 9 January 2003, the day the charade at Telgi's Cuffe Parade apartment was discovered, both Jaiswal and Sri Kumar met Sharma and informed him about

Telgi being comfortably ensconced in his flat. This was followed up by Jaiswal's report of 10 January 2003 in which Sharma, too, was copied. Sharma had made a noting on this report that Kamat and the erring constables be placed under suspension with immediate effect. However, records show that they were not suspended till 15 January 2003, and no active steps were taken by Sharma to ensure immediate suspension, although this was within his powers.

Sharma's counsel refuted these charges. Sharma had taken charge only on 1 January 2003. M.N. Singh had been the commissioner between October 2002 and December 2002, when Telgi was taken into custody by the police in Mumbai. So, if Telgi was not in custody but staying in his apartment or in a hotel, the onus should have been upon the former commissioner. On 9 January 2003, when Sharma was advised of the developments in Telgi's apartment by Jaiswal, he passed the order of suspension over the telephone. Jaiswal's letter dated 10 January 2003, was received by Sharma's office on 12 January 2003, and on that day itself, an order of suspension was passed. However, the joint commissioner placed Kamat and others on suspension only on 15 January 2003. The delay was seen as less procedural and more for providing time to the accused Kamat and the conniving officers at the Crime Branch to perpetrate the 'fake seizure at Bhiwandi'.

In the same letter, Jaiswal had specifically voiced an apprehension that a big seizure may be concocted to protect the erring police officer, Kamat, and in fact, this fear did come true with the seizure of counterfeit stamps worth about Rs 820 crore by the team led by Kamat, at Bhiwandi. This was also supported by Assistant Commissioner of Police Padwal's statement dated 12 January 2003, alleging a conspiracy by the officials of the Crime Branch in Mumbai to save Kamat.

Further, it was alleged that not only did Sawant allow Kamat to continue with the investigation, but also sought to cover up his misdeeds. A huge stock of counterfeit stamps and stamp papers was seized on 11-12 January 2003 at Vanmala compound godown at Bhiwandi. Telgi was not shown as an accused in this case, rather one Shabbir Ahmed was. This was done apparently to protect Telgi and penalise Shabbir Ahmed as he had confessed in Crime Report C.R. No. 135 of 2002 of the Bund Garden Police Station, accusing A.K.L. Telgi. This case, too, was mired in controversy. Statements of witnesses showed that Sawant was not present in Bhiwandi during this seizure. Nor was he a party to the fabrication of the panchnama. The decision to fabricate the panchnama was allegedly taken by Vagal and Dal, showing Shabbir Ahmed as an associate of Ram Ratan Soni, rather than an associate of Telgi. Allegedly, Vagal received Rs 15 lakh from Telgi for this deflection of blame and various other favours. To add insult to injury, the credit for this seizure was attributed to Kamat, clearly to glorify and save him.

Instead of registering a separate case, the Bhiwandi seizure was linked to Crime Report C.R. No. 73 of 2002 (discussed in the chapter 'Business as Usual, from Jail') registered at Kurla Police Station, wherein one Nandesh and Santosh were arrested. Sawant was aware that the seizures effected in C.R. No. 73 of 2002 were not registered as those pertaining to members of the Telgi gang.

API Kamat visited Bengaluru on 21 July 2002 and on 28 July 2002. His visit outside Maharashtra had to be approved by DCP Sawant who allegedly gave him permission illegally. On 29 June 2002, counterfeit stamps and stamp papers worth Rs 830 crore were seized in Hyderabad. The accused was one Syed Hameeduddin. It was shown that Nandesh and Santosh (arrested in C.R. No. 73 of 2002) had tipped the police about this case. Syed Hameeduddin was brought to Mumbai by Kamat. Though the seized stamps were part of Telgi's operations, it was alleged that Kamat, who was in touch with Telgi during his incarceration in Bangalore, showed it as a seizure pertaining to Syed Hameeduddin to weaken the prosecution case against Telgi and divert the focus away from him.

Sawant also issued a signed press note on 4 September 2002 stating that on 13 July 2002, officers and staff of Unit VI, Crime Branch, laid a trap and nabbed Nandesh and Santosh and seized counterfeit stamps worth Rs 20 lakh from them. In respect of this seizure, C.R. No. 73 of 2002 was registered. The press note further said that during the investigation, Syed Hameeduddin was arrested and counterfeit stamp papers and stamps worth Rs 3,67,78,567 were seized from his Hyderabad residence. Sawant also claimed in the press note that the entire operation was carried out, among others, by Dal and Kamat under the direct supervision of Padwal and Vagal. Thus, he admitted that he had supervised the entire operation. He wrongfully connected the crime of a different state/city (Hyderabad) as a part of C.R. No. 73 of 2002 which was not associated with Telgi's gang.

Further it was alleged that while in custody, Telgi was also assisted in disposing of his properties. The manner in which Sawant had handled the reports against Inspector Andhale (A-55), whose misdeeds have been discussed in the previous chapter, also came under the cloud. The police commissioner received an anonymous complaint in Mumbai on 31 March 2003 against Andhale and his team of officers and Vagal (A-59). The complainant alleged how the staff of Mark Enterprises and S.S. Services, two offices which had been raided, had been rounded up and then released on the payment of bribe, and the matter was hushed up.

On 7 April 2003, Sawant was directed to conduct a probe and submit his report by 15 April 2003 on the foregoing. However, it was alleged that he recorded perfunctory and fabricated statements of the staff members of both Mark Enterprises and S.S. Services, and submitted a report dated 26 April 2003. According to this report, the raids were carried out to nab passport agents from Gujarat, who were forging documents. The police were informed that they were staying in guest houses, which were raided to flush them out. However, these premises turned out to be offices. Nothing was seized from the said places, and nobody was arrested from there.

Further in the report, Sawant commended Inspector Andhale for his effective running of the unit and averred that the allegations made against Andhale were false and baseless. In the report, Sawant stated that he had made inquiries with Inspector Darekar, Assistant Inspectors Patil and Ghosalkar and also with the staff members who were present at those places. Subsequently, the statements of the staff members and the officers recorded by the SIT debunked this report and the real story emerged.

Sawant also wilfully and intentionally neglected the reported unauthorised visit by the accused policeman, Kamat, with Telgi to Khanapur District, Belgaon, and to Goa. Sawant's counsel argued that the records showed that it was Assistant Commissioner Padwal who gave permission to Kamat to accompany Telgi, rather than Sawant. The visit was not unauthorised but conducted on account of C.R. No. 68 of 2002 at Shahu Nagar Police Station and was supported by the statement of Sub-inspector Desai of the Khanapur Police Station.

Telgi was in the custody of the Mumbai Crime Branch, Unit V, from 28 October 2002 to 21 January 2003, though in case C.R. No. 41 of 1995 (one of the seven transferred cases), his police custody was granted till 24 January 2003. In a 'Remand Application' dated 20 January 2003, it was stated that his custody was needed as he was to be put in an identification parade. Yet, on 21 January 2003, his custody was prematurely surrendered to the Government of Karnataka. This was shocking because A.K.L. Telgi was brought to Mumbai by the lifting of a ban imposed on such transfer under Section 268 of the Criminal Procedure Code. The issue of holding Sawant responsible for the early surrender of custody was also argued against by his counsel, since Sub-inspector Mane of Unit V had obtained custody of A.K.L. Telgi from a Karnataka court and Inspector Khade had surrendered it.

Sawant's counsel's defence included the fact that Padwal was to report the progress of investigation, but he hadn't been alerted about Kamat or about Dal, so Sawant couldn't be held responsible. He argued that during the relevant period, Sawant was busy with the investigation of bomb blast cases and had no time to monitor other cases. His office was situated at Crawford Market, whereas the office of Kamat and Dal was in Dharavi. Additionally, old cases of 1995 to 2002 were being cited for which the Crime Branch couldn't be held responsible as it wasn't expected that they would carry a parallel investigation. Sawant was not the investigating officer of those cases nor was he the unit in-charge. Nor could Sawant be personally held responsible for cases which according to routine do not move beyond the assistant commissioner level. Telgi was shown arrested in C.R. No. 135 of 2002 (Bund Garden case) only on 30 September 2002. So, any responsibility before this period couldn't devolve upon Sawant.

Sawant was a much-decorated officer. He was the recipient of the President's Police Medal for Meritorious Service in 2002. He was behind more than 300 encounters in Mumbai during his stint as deputy commissioner of police (Detection, Crime Branch) between 2000 and 2003. It was said that the character of Aamir Khan as Assistant Commissioner of Police Ajay Singh Rathod in the popular Bollywood film *Sarfarosh* (1999) was modelled on Sawant.

Notwithstanding, on account of the lapses enumerated above, Sawant was arrested on 7 January 2004. He was discharged on 26 June 2007 by the MCOCA Special Court, Pune, in the MCOCA Special Case No. 2 of 2003 (Bund Garden case). This was, however, revoked by the Mumbai High Court on 14 July 2010, when the CBI preferred to appeal against the earlier decision (Appeal 764 of 2007) and Sawant faced a similar fate as Inspector Andhale (Appeal 763 of 2007).

Sawant's immediate superior, Vagal, who had served as the joint commissioner of police (Crime), Mumbai, from 21 March 2002 to 17 March 2003, was arrested on 7 November 2003 (A-59). In addition to the allegations outlined earlier, Vagal allegedly fabricated an antedated letter of 10 June 2002, mentioning that action was taken when the commissioner requested him to verify certain addresses in Mumbai where counterfeit stamps were reportedly stored. Also, when large quantities of counterfeit stamps and stamp papers were seized between 8 June 2002 and 15 June 2002 by the Pune Police following the arrests in the Bund Garden case, senior police officers in Mumbai, including Vagal, failed to take immediate follow-up action allegedly with the intention of saving Telgi and his associates.

Additionally, when Senior Inspector I.M. Zahid of Cyber Cell, Mumbai Crime Branch, submitted a report detailing Telgi's crimes, Vagal expressed his displeasure with the inquiry and suppressed the findings/evidence. Interestingly, in December 2002, the SIT investigated whether A.K.L. Telgi was behind the transfer order of Zahid from Mumbai to Gadchiroli. Zahid was investigating a case of fake stamps and stamp papers printed with the help of computers and he had interrogated A.K.L. Telgi, who was in the custody of the Dharavi Crime Branch unit. Telgi feared that he might be booked in a fresh case registered by the cybercrime cell where he had no 'friends'. T.K. Choudhary, who was then the additional director general (administration), and had issued the transfer order for Zahid, was questioned in the matter. The order was subsequently cancelled by M.N. Singh, the police commissioner at the time (*The Times of India* dated 7 December 2003). The SIT even summoned former state Director General of Police Subhash Malhotra to find out the reasons why he had given a clean chit to former Police Commissioner R.S. Sharma in the scam.

Vagal's bail was rejected by the special judge, Pune, on 22 February 2005, and by the Mumbai High Court on 21 July 2006. He was finally released on bail in March 2007 by the Supreme Court. Kamat was arrested on 13 June 2003 and taken into judicial custody by an order dated 10 July 2003. The charge sheet was filed against him on 15 September 2003. His application for bail was rejected by the Special Court (MCOCA Court), Pune, as was his bail application No. 4319 of 2004 before the Mumbai High Court. A special CBI court eventually released him in November 2016. Sawant, Dal and Vagal were later released on bail by the Supreme Court.

17

The Infighting, the Blame Game

As discussed in the chapter 'The Bund Garden Case', the charge sheets filed by the SIT brought the skeletons tumbling out of the closet of the Mumbai Police, and many officers and politicians were arrested. It is important to reiterate that the SIT was constituted not just to provide greater focus to the case, but also to address the open warfare between police officials in Pune, which was proving detrimental to both the investigation and to police morale.

According to an article in *The Times of India* dated 9 November 2003, the 'factional fight' with police officers trading charges with one another had dispirited the force. "The inefficiency of the probe undertaken by the Pune Police first became evident in July 2002, when the Public Accounts Committee (PAC) of the state legislature felt slighted that senior investigating officers failed to turn up for meetings to provide an update on the Telgi probe. When the then Additional Commissioner of Police S.M. Mushrif arrived late for a meeting, the PAC expressed dissatisfaction with the 'status report' presented by him."

In September 2002, while a thirty-member Pune Police team led by Mushrif was continuing its investigation (even before the constitution of the SIT), there were murmurs that investigations should be transferred either to the CBI or to the state CID. In October 2002, when Mushrif made serious allegations against Senior Inspector Prakash Deshmukh and Assistant Commissioner of Police Mulani, of 'managing' the investigation and tampering with evidence, and even charged R.S. Sharma, Pune's police commissioner at the time, of protecting corrupt officials, the rift between the members of the Pune Police force widened.

The charge sheets and the arrests began in July 2003, although the SIT, which had been instituted on 2 November 2002, had completed its investigation in March 2003 and the report submitted sometime in late March 2003/early April 2003. While the dates of some of the arrests have already been mentioned, this chronology is necessary to highlight the calendar-cluster of arrests of politicians, police and government officials in the last few months of 2003 and in the first quarter of 2004.

- On 1 July 2003, Anil Gote, then sitting MLA from Dhule district, Maharashtra.
- On 21 August 2003, Senior Inspector Dattatraya Dal.
- On 6 September 2003, Krishna Yadav, former labour minister of Andhra Pradesh and sitting MLA (Hyderabad).
- On 18 October 2003, Assistant Commissioner of Police Gokul Bhagaji Patil, Inspector Vashishtha Andhale and Sub-inspector Prabhakar Kakade.
- On 7 November 2003, Joint Commissioner of Police Shridhar Vagal.
- On 9 November 2003, Sub-inspector Digambar Wagle and Assistant Inspector Leeladhar Nimade (in Nashik).
- On 10 November 2003, Sub-inspector S.R. Dalvi.
- On 1 December 2003, R.S. Sharma.
- On 2 December 2003, Assistant Commissioner of Police R.B. Yenam and Assistant Commissioner of Police (retired) Mulani (Pune).

- On 8 December 2003, former deputy superintendent of stamps, Ranjane.
- On 10 December 2003, P.N. Jayasimha, former superintendent, Central Prison, Bengaluru, and principal of Prison Training School, Mysore (Karnataka), and Assistant Jail Superintendent Nanjappa.
- On 20 December 2003, Rehan Baig, brother of Karnataka Small Scale Industries Minister Roshan Baig (surrendered to the STAMPIT) and Assistant Police Inspector G.W. Jhadav.
- On 5 January 2004, Stamp Superintendent Ramdas Potale.
- On 7 January 2004, Deputy Commissioner of Police Pradeep Sawant.
- On 2 February 2004, Inspector A. Sonwalkar.
- On 21 February 2004, Inspector Puran Singh (New Delhi).
- On 7 July 2004, Assistant Commissioner of Police (retired) Sangram Singh, suspended Inspector Vali Basha and Sub-inspector V.A. Khan.

Two other developments of significance took place after the SIT team put together its report. The first was its leak to the press/media and the second was the public interest litigation filed by activist Anna Hazare in June 2003, which was perhaps responsible for the momentum seen in the arrests made from the third quarter of 2003.

Jaiswal, who headed the SIT, submitted a 104-page report in which he made several allegations, cited lapses, the slow pace of the probe and the complicity of the police top brass: "After conducting a probe into allegations made by the then Pune Additional Police Commissioner S.M. Mushrif that some of his colleagues had attempted to sabotage the initial investigation into the fake stamps racket, there had been efforts made to get the wife and daughter of Telgi off the hook. Investigations into the multi-crore counterfeit stamps and stamp papers case allegedly involving accused Abdul Karim Telgi had been tardy and knowingly left several loopholes to make the case weak."

A full-length copy of the report available with United News of India (UNI) revealed that the actual investigation process of the case was affected by a breakdown in communication between the then commissioner of police, Pune, R.S. Sharma, and the additional commissioner (Crime), Pune, S.M. Mushrif. There was also a difference of opinion between Sharma and Mushrif over the handling of certain other issues relating to law-and-order matters, the report stated. The Jaiswal committee report said that the shoddy investigation had been further weakened due to groupism among officers, apparently to take credit. "Failure to insist upon the timely application of the Maharashtra Control of Organised Crime Act (MCOCA) provisions to the case by the then Commissioner of Police, Pune (R.S. Sharma), was a strategic error," it said (*Financial Express* dated 18 November 2003).

The key findings of the SIT report as enumerated by author Sanjay Singh (who mentions that he was a recipient of the leaked papers), in his book *Telgi Scam: Reporter ki Diary* were:

"The report by the SIT found Mushrif's allegations correct and made the following observations specific to the persons:

a. Inspector Prakash Deshmukh: Investigating officer. His work shows immoral conduct, inability, negligence and without doubt, dishonesty.
b. Assistant Commissioner of Police Ashok Kamble: Guilty of negligence and incompetence.
c. Assistant Commissioner of Police M.C. Mulani: Most serious. Karnataka Police had a telephone tap between Telgi and Mulani, where Mulani demanded a bribe in crores. He was termed an officer of immoral attitude and misconduct. R.S. Sharma has also described him as an officer of suspicious background.
d. Deputy Commissioner of Police Kishore Jadhav: Responsible for police station investigation. Found to be incapable and ignorant of the law and carried out poor surveillance.
e. Deputy Commissioner of Police Jai Jadhav: Took over the investigation from Police Inspector Prakash Deshmukh in

September 2002. Did not examine Telgi's relationship with the Indian Security Press.

f. Deputy Commissioner of Police Vasant Koregaonkar: found guilty of unnecessary haste to complete the panchnama. Did not follow guidelines. Names of accused not officially put on record.

g. Additional Commissioner S.M. Mushrif said, "I am being deliberately ignored. Many items have been concealed from me. As soon as I realised, I began to keep myself away from the second week of August. Investigating officer Prakash Deshmukh was close to Commissioner Sharma and refused to take my orders. I didn't complain to the Commissioner because it wouldn't have helped."

   The SIT refused to accept this and accused Mushrif of poor monitoring. "He could've done right if he wanted to." The SIT, however, lauded him for raising the irregularities and mentioned that things could have gone awry during the hearing for the rest of the cases in Maharashtra, where Telgi was never arrested, and the police were involved in his escape.

h. Joint Commissioner M.S. Maheshgauri: He was held responsible for the delay in implementing MCOCA.

i. Commissioner R.S. Sharma: He had allowed the situation to worsen and the failure of timely implementation of MCOCA was a strategic error. He knew that Mulani was an officer of suspicious background. The fact that he took Mulani to Bangalore to probe the Telgi scam was incorrect. Putting Mulani's name in the investigation team, too, was incorrect.

   At the end of his report, Jaiswal made the following observations:

i. Inspector Prakash Deshmukh and Assistant Commissioner Mulani to be suspended immediately and a departmental inquiry to be initiated against them for not doing their job.

ii. Assistant Commissioner of Police Ashok Kamble to be given light punishment and sent to a non-executive posting.

iii. Strict action to be taken against Deputy Commissioner of Police Kishore Jadhav for his incorrect working and criminal negligence. To be given non-executive posting and sent to police training institute to learn how to investigate.

iv. Light punishment for Deputy Commissioner of Police Jai Jadhav and Vasant Koregaonkar.

v. Because of the national importance of the case and how the economy of Maharashtra and the country have been compromised in a planned manner, the investigation of the case is important. Therefore, the government must decide on the acts of 'omission and commission' of Commissioner R.S. Sharma and Additional Commissioner S.M. Mushrif.

vi. Police stations cannot function effectively in such cases.

vii. Between 1995 and 2002, twelve cases against Telgi were registered in Maharashtra alone, while fifteen cases were registered across the country. Though Telgi was found to be the main accused in the cases in Mumbai, Nashik, Thane, Kolhapur and Pune, he continued to flourish due to inadequate action, and in most cases in connivance with the stamp department, Mumbai Police, and the local police.

viii. The government unfortunately has been unable to assess how the scam has damaged the economy. The option of the franking machine has also been ineffective as there were cases of fake stamping in Karnataka, despite them having franking machines. Telgi and his associates were able to perpetrate fake franking as well.

ix. Guidelines to be framed to investigate economic offences.

x. The security system of the India Security Press at Nashik is full of loopholes. Appropriate action to be taken so that the Central and Maharashtra governments can avoid such instances of huge revenue losses in the future.

In conclusion, Jaiswal recommended action against senior officials (including Commissioner R.S. Sharma), though he did not spell out what such action should be."

Sanjay Singh also dwells extensively on the Bali report: "Any report as consequential and important as the Jaiswal report would require the opinion of the additional director general of police (Law and Order). Additional Director General of Police (L&O) Om Prakash Bali had also prepared a dossier on the Jaiswal report, supporting its findings, and sent it to the director general of police, Malhotra, but he ignored it. The report was signed by O.P. Bali on 12 April 2003. This meant that not only the Jaiswal report, but also the Bali report, was ignored by Sharma's seniors and the government, and R.S. Sharma was given a clean chit. It is significant that two months later, the state government clarified that Malhotra had not revealed anything about the O.P. Bali report since it was an internal matter of the police department. The suppression of the O.P. Bali report from the media and the public, in the name of privacy, was a deception and underscored the importance of transparency and the Right to Information."

The charges traded between the keepers of the law in the Bund Garden case and the Mumbai developments post Telgi's transfer from Karnataka have been outlined in the last couple of chapters. These charges include the vexatious question of who was responsible for removing the names of the three members of Telgi's family from the charge sheet (Assistant Commissioner of Police Mulani or Additional Commissioner of Police Mushrif?). We have also seen charges being traded between Commissioner Sharma and Deputy Inspector General (and head of SIT) Jaiswal over the delayed action against Assistant Police Inspector Kamat allegedly by Sharma between 9-10 March 2003 and 15 March 2003. The plot became thicker with the 'staged' Bhiwandi seizure of Rs 820 crore in this period. We have had panchnamas allegedly being fudged and the Hyderabad case being linked to case C.R. No. 73 of 2002 in Mumbai to shield Telgi.

Sharma's legal counsel alleged that though the SIT had recommended action against many other tainted police officers like Prakash Deshmukh, Ashok Kamble, Kishore Jadhav, Jai Jadhav and Vasant Koregaonkar on grounds of omission and commission, they were not named as accused in the Bund Garden case (though some of them were suspended). Also, the blame in many cases seemed to lie squarely at the door of senior police officials such as S.M. Mushrif, M.S. Maheshgauri and R.S. Sharma, but only Mushrif and Maheshgauri were cited as witnesses, and thus Sharma was discriminated against.

After being exonerated, Sharma said the judgment highlighted his innocence. He also accused the chief of the SIT, Jaiswal, of jumping the gun and forwarding his report/findings to the O.P. Bali, rather than to Additional Director General A.K. Agarwal, Jaiswal's superior. According to Sharma, Bali bore a grudge against Sharma who had superseded him to the coveted post of the chief of Mumbai Police. "Bali, along with Jaiswal and another senior officer S.S. Puri conducted a trial by the media implicating me in the Telgi scandal," he said (*The Times of India* dated 19 July 2007). The role of S.S. Puri replacing Jaiswal as the head of the SIT is detailed in the next chapter.

It is important to also enumerate the contra-arguments of 'the other camp' on key allegations:

1. Assistant Commissioner of Police Mulani's inclusion: According to Deputy Commissioner of Police Jai Jadhav's (who was handed the responsibility of the Bund Garden case on 4 September 2003) statement, "A meeting had taken place between Commissioner R.S. Sharma, Joint Commissioner Maheshgauri and me to decide which officers should be included in the investigation work. At that time, 'Shri Sharma Saheb' told me that you can choose the officers you want for the investigation. On this, I told him that I did not personally know the officers in Pune. Being in the post of Deputy Commissioner of Police (Departmental Enquiries), I was not conversant with the investigating skill of the officers in Pune city. After I told him so, they finalized the list of the members of the investigation team. In that list, the name of Assistant Commissioner of Police Mulani was first."

   From this statement, it appears that Commissioner Sharma did not suggest the name of Mulani himself. He did so only when prompted by Deputy Commissioner Jadhav, and that, too, in the presence of Joint Commissioner Maheshgauri.

2. ACP Mulani's Bangalore visit: The purpose of such a visit was to have a high-level conference to enable the Government of Maharashtra obtain Telgi's custody. On 9 July 2002 and 23 July 2002, Mulani visited Bangalore with Sharma. On the second visit, the two were accompanied by Basak, the additional chief secretary. On 11 September 2002, Mulani travelled to Bangalore along with Inspector Sampat Kadam as the hearing in Telgi's case was fixed for that day. He is said to have been sent by Additional Commissioner Mushrif, according to the investigation note of Jai Jadhav. Mushrif, on 9 September 2002, had called him to his office and advised him that 12 September 2002 was the date set by the Bengaluru court for the hearing and that the advocate general of Maharashtra, P. Janardanan, and an advocate from Pune, Raman Agrawal (as the special public prosecutor), would be going to Bengaluru for the hearing as well. Mulani and Sampat Kadam were to proceed to Mumbai from where they would accompany P. Janardanan to the Bengaluru court for the hearing. On 18 September 2002, Mulani visited Bangalore in the company of the advocate general of Maharashtra. On this date, the Bengaluru court passed an order under Section 268 of the Code of Criminal Procedure, which later allowed the Mumbai Police to bring Telgi to Mumbai from his imprisonment in Bengaluru in October 2002. As evident from the foregoing, on all occasions, Mulani was accompanied by other officers and had not travelled of his own volition.
3. Commissioner Sharma, in a letter dated 22 November 2002, addressed to the director general of police, had made serious complaints against Mushrif relating to:
    a. The removal of the names of three of Telgi's family members from the charge sheet.
    b. Mushrif writing letters to the investigating officer thereby interfering and obstructing the investigation directly or

indirectly, which were noticed because of the complaints made by the officer.

c. As he was an officer of the rank of deputy inspector general of police, Mushrif was capable of invoking provisions of the MCOCA, but had avoided the same.

d. Mushrif had told the media that the inquiry in this matter should be conducted by director general of police or the Anti-Corruption Bureau. In his letter, Sharma requested that these matters be investigated immediately, and a retired judge of the high court be appointed for the purpose. Hence, not only the allegations made by Mushrif would be enquired into, but the truth about who was trying to indirectly help the kingpin of the racket, by obstructing the investigating right from the beginning, would become clear.

4. The state government through Ashok Basak could also have suspended Mulani. It did not however appear from the records that apart from the fieldwork and searching for the accused, Mulani took any part in the investigation between 6 September 2002 and 30 September 2002.
5. There was no evidence to show that Deputy Commissioner of Police Sawant had any knowledge about the alleged crime committed by Assistant Police Inspector Kamat or Inspector Dal. It was Assistant Commissioner of Police Padwal who was to report the progress of the investigation. Yet he didn't disclose any illegality committed by Kamat. Padwal, in his statement, had stated that he was busy with the bomb blasts case in Mumbai. This applied to Sawant, too. Yet only Sawant was charge-sheeted.
6. There was no substance in the allegation that Sawant permitted A.K.L. Telgi to use his mobile phone while in custody, since there was no material evidence that Sawant was even aware that Telgi was using a mobile phone in custody. Jaiswal, however, in his report of 10 January 2003, while describing his surprise visit to Telgi's Cuffe Parade flat on 9 January

2003, had stated that he had searched the personal belongings of Telgi. Accused Janvekar, in his statement, had said that Telgi possessed a mobile phone. Jaiswal could have seized the mobile phone. He, however, did not take any action against those who were present.

7. Deputy Commissioner of Police Koregaonkar's statement indicated that Shabbir Shaikh had leaked information about one more godown in Dal Mill compound in Bhiwandi and Maqsood had said the key to the said godown was with Khalid. Khalid and Asif were in SIT custody. Jaiswal had in his report said that a large stock of counterfeit stamps lying in a compound were yet to be detected. Yet, the SIT neither made efforts to locate the said godown nor seize the stock.

PART IV

END GAME

18

Anna Hazare's PIL

The Special Investigation Team (Jaiswal) report was forwarded by Subhash Malhotra, director general of police, with his comments to the government on 23 April 2003. Chhagan Bhujbal, deputy chief minister of Maharashtra, called a press conference on 24 April 2003, where he recommended an exoneration for R.S. Sharma as "Sharma, the then Police Commissioner of Pune, where the racket was unravelled, could not be held responsible for any specific acts of commission or omission on the part of the investigating officer and other supervising officers".

He also advised that the report had "recommended action ranging from a reprimand to suspension against seven officers": P.R. Deshmukh (suspension), M.C. Mulani (suspension), Jai Jadhav, Kishor Jadhav, Vasant Koregaonkar, S.M. Mushrif, and Maheshgauri. Bhujbal also said that "he had asked the Director General of Police to seek explanation from officers who faced suspension 'in the interest of fairness and justice'" (Rediff.com News dated 24 April 2003).

Developments in the next few months included the arrest of Telgi's associate Manoj Mehta on 11 June 2003, and the sealing of Telgi's properties by the SIT. Fivc of these were owned by the Telgi and his family, and seventeen were rented. The SIT also moved a special court in Pune for attaching the five properties he owned: the Cuffe Parade apartment, an apartment each at Shirin Manzil and Sunny House, Colaba, a duplex bungalow at Mathurdas Estate and the infamous Alankar lodge (which was not really owned but tenanted under the pagdi system).

Other properties where Telgi operated his racket were also sealed. They included 56 Mint Road, which was Telgi's main office in Mumbai; 22 Sai Vihar Building Fort, where he had his printing press; an office in the Eastern Chambers, Colaba, where he stocked fake stamp papers; godowns at 3rd Pasta Lane, Colaba, and a marketing office in Sunny House, Colaba. The SIT also sealed a factory owned by Telgi, Thane Polyorganics, through a court order. The investigators alleged that all the properties were purchased by Telgi with the money made from selling fake stamps. Telgi's lawyer gave an undertaking in the court that the properties would neither be sold, nor any third-party rights created therein, until the court gave its order. The SIT also asked a special court in Pune to freeze thirty-eight accounts held by Telgi in various banks across the state.

The event which, however, hastened bringing the accused mentioned in the Jaiswal report to book was the filing of a PIL by the social activist Kisan Baburao Hazare (better known as Anna Hazare), on 10 June 2003, in the Mumbai High Court. His case was taken up pro bono by Majeed Memon, a noted criminal lawyer and human rights activist, and P.A. Sebastian, a politician and lawyer. An interesting anecdote was shared by Memon's son Zulfiquar Memon, managing partner MZM Legal, at the weekly meeting of the Rotary Club of Bombay in the last week of September 2019. Speaking to the Rotarians about the nature of white-collar crime (Ref: Rotary Club of Mumbai bulletin *The Gateway* dated 1 October 2019) he said, "I remember the Telgi scam. Classic case! What manipulation! I remember Anna Hazare walking into our office with a one-rupee coin, my father was at his peak as a defence lawyer then. Anna Hazare gave him the rupee and said, 'I want to use your expertise and I want to be a whistle-blower and unearth this scam. It is such a complex scam; it is going to be difficult for people to understand.' It was challenging, we took it up. My father filed the PIL under Anna Hazare's instruction and we unearthed this massive scam."

The PIL, filed as Criminal Writ Petition-WP 865 of 2003, sought to invoke the jurisdiction of the Mumbai High Court under Article 226 of the Constitution. The respondents were the Maharashtra state government, Chhagan Bhujbal, the additional chief secretary (home) and Subhash Malhotra, Maharashtra's director general of police.

In the petition, the following were cited from the report by SIT:

i. The description of "the dubious conduct of the Pune Police in such an important case of counterfeit stamps as an act of collective irresponsibility".
ii. Maharashtra Police had received a communication from the Karnataka government to the effect that while monitoring and recording telephonic conversations of A.K.L. Telgi, the Karnataka Police had received information of Assistant Commissioner of Police Mulani accepting a bribe of Rs 15 lakh from Telgi for the deletion of the names of his wife and certain others from the charge sheet.
iii. The indication of serious irregularities and lapses on the part of the then commissioner of police, Pune, Sharma, in including Assistant Commissioner of Police Mulani in the new investigation team under DCP Jai Jadhav formed in September 2002, despite being aware of his dubious credentials and even after Mulani was transferred by the Maharashtra State Administrative Tribunal vide a government order on 4 September 2002.
iv. Despite the severe indictment of Sharma, on 24 April 2003, the deputy chief minister of Maharashtra held a press conference in connection with the Action Taken Report and gave a clean chit to Sharma. The Action Taken Report published by the deputy chief minister was alleged to be an eyewash, making a scapegoat of lower-ranked officers, while ignoring the illegal acts of high-ranking ones.

v. Despite the allegations levelled by Additional Commissioner of Police Mushrif, also confirmed and reiterated in the Jaiswal report as well as in the noting by Additional Director General (Law and Order) Bali, and an inquiry pending, Sharma was appointed to the coveted post of commissioner of police, Mumbai, w.e.f. 1 January 2003.

The IPL alleged corrupt practices by highly placed Indian Police Service (IPS) officers in Maharashtra, their connivance with criminal activities of a nature and magnitude liable to derail the Indian economy and deprive the public exchequer of thousands of crores of rupees, and the inactivity of the state of Maharashtra. It urged the court to intervene to ensure that the faith of the common man in the administration of justice was not destroyed.

Further the PIL sought:

a. Production of the report submitted by the SIT, headed by S.R. Jaiswal.
b. Production of the Action Taken Report referred by the deputy chief minister of Maharashtra, Chhagan Bhujbal, before the court.
c. A direction to the state of Karnataka to produce the records of the telephone conversations of A.K.L. Telgi, the prime accused in the stamp scam case, which allegedly indicated the receipt of Rs 15 lakh by Assistant Commissioner Mulani.
d. Production before the court of the report submitted by Additional Director General Bali.
e. A direction to the state of Maharashtra to take deterrent punitive action against the guilty police officers in accordance with the recommendations of the SIT report.
f. Initiation of civil and criminal action against those police officers who were indicted in the report.

The court, which had admitted the writ petition in June 2003, issued a notice on 2 July 2003, granting three weeks to the state government to file its reply, based on a request by the advocate general of Maharashtra. By an order dated 6 August 2003, the court also directed Sanjay Barve, additional commissioner of police, Economic Offence Wing (EOW), Mumbai, to file the status report regarding the cases registered in Mumbai against Telgi and his associates from 1995 onwards.

After perusing the affidavits by U.K. Mukhopadhyay, additional chief secretary, Home Department, Government of Maharashtra, Additional Commissioner of Police (Economic Offences) Barve, and Director General Bali, by another order dated 4 September 2003, the Mumbai High Court ordered (key items only):

1. The state of Maharashtra to strengthen the SIT by appointing more officers so that the investigation could be expedited.
2. The SIT to inquire into other Telgi cases referred to in the affidavit of Barve.
3. Such investigation to be conducted under the supervision of S.S. Puri, retired director general of police.
4. The SIT to take appropriate steps/actions for getting transcripts of tape-recorded conversations produced in criminal court in the state of Karnataka.
5. Additional affidavits to be filed stating the steps taken against all the accused in the SIT report.
6. Status report to be submitted within four weeks.

On 24 September 2003, in continuation of the 4 September 2003 order, additional directions were given (key ones):

1. To strengthen the SIT, S.S. Puri to exercise all powers exercisable by a director general of police as if he was in service, including the liberty to appoint such other staff, in addition to the existing staff.
2. S.S. Puri and his team to carry out the investigation of offences and to file appropriate progress report in the court.
3. Allowing the status report (to be submitted within four weeks as per direction of 4 September 2003) to be submitted by 15 October 2003.

In deference to the orders, the Government of Maharashtra, by a resolution passed on 26 September 2003, amended its order of 2 November 2002 on the formation of the SIT. It was changed to comprise Subhodh Jaiswal, who had been originally heading it and was now deputy inspector general, State Reserve Police Force, Mumbai, and additional commissioner, Economic Offences Wing, Barve, and such other staff as decided by S.S. Puri who, for the purposes of the investigation, was reinstated with full powers of an 'in-service' director general of police to head and supervise the SIT.

There were two reasons for S.S. Puri's inclusion (and Jaiswal's replacement as head). The first was the question of suitability of Additional Director General of Police O.P. Bali. Commissioner of Police Sharma had serious reservations about Bali's engagement with the investigations. Cases relating to the fake stamps against Telgi had been registered in Mumbai during Bali's tenure as joint commissioner (Law and Order) from May 1993 to January 1996. So, he could not excuse himself from police inactivity during this period. Commissioner Sharma also contended that though the government resolution dated 2 November 2002 had required the SIT to report to the additional director general of police, CID Pune, A.K. Agarwal, the Jaiswal report "landed into the hands of O.P. Bali, the then additional deputy director general (Law and Order), who had also commented upon the report". Further, Bali was due to retire on 31 October 2003 and hence, handing him the mantle of supervision in September 2003 wouldn't be judicious. Sharma's grievance was also that the Jaiswal report had been leaked to the electronic and print media on 10 April 2003 and brought into serious question the chain of command and responsibility to ensure the report's confidentiality.

The second reason was that if a high-ranking official such as a commissioner of police had to be investigated, the matter could not be entirely left to the investigation of Subodh R. Jaiswal, who held a lower rank, and to that extent the government resolution of 26 September 2003 was correcting its earlier anomaly of 2 November

2002. Hence, a consensus was taken and recorded in the court order of 4 September 2003 that all had agreed that S.S. Puri would supervise the investigation.

Sharma appealed against the court order of 24 September 2003 and the government resolution dated 26 September 2003, but this was turned down (Criminal Application 91 of 2004 in Criminal Writ Petition 865 of 2003 decided on 9 March 2004).

The PIL also highlighted the unsatisfactory performance of the police of the state of Maharashtra since the start of the scam. Telgi's 15 November 1995 filing for anticipatory bail and slipping out of the court room on 1 December 1995 before the bail was rejected came in for sharp criticism from the court as did the ineffective action when Telgi was proclaimed as an offender, thereafter. The court asked what steps the authorities had taken from 1 December 1995 to November 2001, when Telgi was rearrested after considerable delay and, that, too, by the Karnataka force.

According to an article in *The Tribune* dated 13 November 2003, "The Mumbai High Court further agreed to a suggestion by Advocate General Goolam Vahanvati that the SIT report be sent to Chief Minister Sushilkumar Shinde for a decision on the fate of Commissioner of Police Sharma." The court said it would keep in mind that Sharma was due to retire on 30 November 2003 while taking a final decision, though Majeed Memon, counsel for Anna Hazare, had earlier contended that if Sharma had done something wrong while in office, action should be taken before he retired from service. The court gave the Maharashtra government time till 27 November 2003 to decide on action, if any, against the police commissioner.

The Pune bench of the Bombay High Court also granted permission to the SIT to carry out scientific tests on Abdul Karim Telgi, to aid investigation and facilitate the collection of evidence. A polygraph examination was conducted on Telgi on 20 December 2003. Telgi appeared to be concealing relevant information and not truthful about his statement about the involvement of politician and police. He was further subjected to a brain-mapping test on

21 December 2003. He also had to undergo the narco tests on 22 December 2003 (*Frontline*, dated 12 March 2004).

The tests were conducted by the Karnataka Forensic Science Laboratory (KFSL) in Bangalore by Dr Malini, a clinical psychologist. Since 1993, she had worked at NIMHANS as a senior research fellow, under an Indo-US project. While working on the said project, she had conducted narco analysis and brain-mapping tests for various undertrials and suspects who were involved in murders and other organized crimes. She had joined KFSL as assistant director of forensic psychology in July 1999 on an annual renewable contract.

A polygraph or lie detector test attaches a machine to the suspect/perpetrator which records parameters such as blood pressure, pulse rate, respiration and muscle movements. These parameters are monitored for changes or deviations when questions are answered, and the reactions are measured. The brain-mapping test is also called the 'P-300 test' as the machine's sensors (which are attached to the subject's head) monitor the brain's electrical activity and register P 300 waves, which are generated only if the subject has some connection with the stimulus (such as images, sounds or combinations of relevant/irrelevant words).

For the narco analysis or the 'truth serum' tests, doctors or experts mix a few grams of sodium pentothal or sodium amytal in distilled water and administer the same intravenously to the subject. The quantum of the dose is calibrated carefully for the person's sex, age, health and physical condition, and a wrong dose can send the subject into a coma, or even prove fatal. The administered drug depresses the central nervous system, lowers the blood pressure, slows the heart rate, and puts the subject into a hypnotic trance. In such a state, the subject's imagination is arrested/neutralised by making him semi-conscious. Therefore, he cannot lie, as he cannot use his imagination. The answers are believed to be restricted to facts that he is aware of or are spontaneous as a semi-conscious person is unable to manipulate the answers.

However, to conduct these tests, investigators require permission from the court *and* the personal consent of the subject.

These tests against *the will of the accused* would violate Article 20 (3) of the Constitution, the main provision in crime investigation and trial. Article 20 (3) deals with the privilege against self-incrimination, i.e., no person accused of any offence shall be compelled to be a witness against himself. The legal position of applying these tests / techniques as an investigative aid raises genuine issues like encroachment of an individual's rights, liberties, and freedom.

The matter was finally put to rest by a Supreme Court ruling. In May 2010, the Supreme Court held that forcing suspects and witnesses to go through these tests without their consent was unconstitutional and amounted to violation of their right to privacy. The bench stated that while forcible use of these techniques would violate Article 20(3), even in cases where the subject decided to undergo these tests voluntarily, the result themselves could not be admitted as evidence in court. "The subject does not exercise conscious control over the responses during the administration of the test. However, any information or material that is subsequently discovered with the help of *voluntary administered test results* can be admitted, in accordance with Section 27 of the Evidence Act," the bench clarified. However, the determination of the circumstances in which the tests are administered remain a delicate and grey area and most courts are unwilling to admit results as evidence for the purpose of their rulings.

According to senior police officers and forensic experts, however, irrespective of whether the courts recognise these tests, they remain effective tools in developing a line of investigation. Thus, the most pervasive viewpoint of senior police officers and forensic experts is that although tools like polygraph test, narco analysis and brain mapping may not be completely admissible in a court of law, they remain important investigative aids and are of immense value in opening leads or providing clues and connections in investigation.

19

Political Rumblings

The use of drugs on Telgi to extract the truth created a major controversy. Perhaps no other scam till date has sullied the fabric of Maharashtra politics as much as the Telgi scam did. Allegedly, in addition to admitting speed money to top police officials, during the narco tests, Telgi implicated Nationalist Congress Party (NCP) chief Sharad Pawar, then a Union minister, and also Chhagan Bhujbal. Telgi, however, had used the name 'Bhujbal' in his state of stupor, and hence there was a doubt whether it was Chhagan or his nephew Sameer, both of whom were questioned by the SIT in February 2004. However, no material evidence against either of them could be garnered.

Although the narco tests were conducted in December 2003, some media channels aired it years later, on 6 September 2006. The information that the Karnataka Police were also to release conversation tapes between Telgi and Anil Gote, implicating other erstwhile political leaders like Lok Sabha Speaker P.A. Sangma and Vilasrao Deshmukh, chief minister of Maharashtra, added fuel to the fire (*DNA*, 14 August 2006, which also contained excerpts of the alleged conversations between Telgi, Gote and a 'third man'), and opened the proverbial pandora's box. Importantly, Telgi debunked the results of his narco analysis test beamed by television channels as 'false and baseless'. In a three-page letter written to his lawyers Harshad Nimbalkar and Milind Pawar, he denied having met either Sharad Pawar or Chhagan Bhujbal and paying any money to them.

Telgi said in his letter, "This is absolutely false and baseless. I have never stated this in my narco test. This is nothing but a game plan by some political persons to involve them in the fake stamp case." Addressing a press conference, arranged to air Telgi's reaction to the telecast of the purported narco tests, Nimbalkar, who was present with Milind Pawar, said, "Telgi is ready to undergo further scientific tests and even interrogation by any agency anywhere, to clear this issue" (Rediff.com news dated 10 September 2006).

In any event, in his confession to a Pune magistrate on 4 February 2006, Telgi did not name Pawar and Bhujbal, and hence the results of the narco and other tests conducted earlier became irrelevant. The CBI did not implicate these politicians either when they took over the case in March 2004. Their charge sheet included only two politicians, Anil Gote and Krishna Yadav.

However, even before the furore created by the narco tests, political rumblings against the tardy handling of the scam, and specifically against Bhujbal, had started building up since his press conference on the SIT probe and the Action Taken Report of 24 April 2003.

A Rediff.com report of 11 November 2003 said that Opposition leaders in Maharashtra had met Governor Mohammed Fazal on 10 November 2003, demanding "a CBI probe into the multi-crore fake stamp paper scam and immediate removal of Deputy Chief Minister Chhagan Bhujbal for his failure to control corruption in the police force". Though the SIT was 'doing a good job', it had been created under the statutes prevalent in Maharashtra and hence ineffective given that the dragnet of the scam had spread across many states. Opposition leaders opined that it would be appropriate to hand over the probe to a central agency like the CBI.

As a repartee to the Opposition, a week later, Chief Minister Sushilkumar Shinde ruled out handing over of the probe to the CBI. Asserting that the SIT was doing a good job in probing the multi-crore stamp paper racket, he told reporters, "SIT has even arrested an official of the rank of inspector general and interrogated Mumbai Police Commissioner R.S. Sharma. There is no need to take away the case from them." Shinde also pointed out that since the Bombay High Court was supervising the probe, the state government would be unable to take a unilateral decision. Hence, there was little room for the executive to influence the judiciary (Rediff.com news dated 18 November 2003). However, the Maharashtra government eventually had little option but to toe the Supreme Court directive on the transfer of the case from the SIT to the CBI.

Interestingly, the impression that the Mumbai Police was protecting Telgi finds mention in the same article. The Delhi Police had arrested nine people involved in the fake stamp racket and procured a production warrant against the prime accused A.K.L. Telgi and four of his associates from a local court. Apparently, earlier efforts by the Delhi Police to take Telgi into custody had failed after their Maharashtra counterparts resisted by issuing a circular that the accused could not be taken out of the state.

"At that time, he used to receive special treatment at the hands of the Maharashtra Police. But now, the situation has changed, and we hope we will get his custody," the Delhi Police ostensibly said, referring to the fact that Telgi had been finally returned to the custody of the Karnataka Police on 3 January 2003 (against the scheduled return in November 2002). The Crime Branch's Economic Offences Wing of New Delhi had arrested two of Telgi's associates, Sushant Kumar Dass and Lalit Patodi, in the second week of November 2003. Also, in October 2002, seven members of Telgi's syndicate had been arrested, including Lalit Patodi's brother. Recoveries of various stamps and stamp papers including Indian postal stamps, foreign stamps and non-judicial stamp papers valued about Rs 220 crore had been made.

Though the Opposition had been clamouring for his resignation over the mishandling of the stamp scam for months, Chhagan Bhujbal resigned on 24 December 2003. This occurred a few days after Telgi's narco and brain-mapping tests were concluded, and a day after the vandalization of the offices of Alpha Marathi channel, a sister concern of Zee TV, by activists of the Nationalist Congress Party. They were 'protesting' a show aired by the channel the previous night. Bhujbal contended that his resignation had nothing to do with the stamp paper scam. He had resigned because he was 'saddened' that the political vandals who attacked the television office had used his name. Many saw the act of vandalism opportune and an excuse for Bhujbal to vacate the hot seat.

Like its Maharashtra counterpart, the Congress(I) government in Karnataka took the position that they wouldn't abide by any reference made by the Union government forcing it to refer the probe to the CBI. This was in early January 2004, when Karnataka remained the last state holding out against the CBI probe. According to an article in the *Frontline* dated 2 January 2004, the Karnataka law and parliamentary affairs minister, D.B. Chandre Gowda, said that the state government was of the view that "there was no need for a CBI inquiry, since the specially constituted Stamp Investigation Team (STAMPIT) had almost completed its investigation and a special fast-track court had begun hearing the cases pertaining to the scam. If the Supreme Court or the Karnataka High Court were not satisfied with the investigation, they could direct that the case(s) be referred to the CBI." Echoing similar views, the chief minister of Karnataka, S.M. Krishna, said, "The Centre and certain political parties were calling for a CBI inquiry with the sole intention of politicising the issue, since 2004 was an election year."

Citing examples where the CBI had been unable to solve cases in Karnataka, Krishna said he had "no faith in the CBI". The Union government had also drawn flak from the Karnataka government for doing nothing to curb the spread of fake stamp paper, despite a letter written in June 2002 by the head of STAMPIT to the joint secretary, Ministry of Finance, warning of the dangers. The letter had stated, "It is essential to monitor the sales and dispatch of the various categories of security papers by the different security presses to various states. Any marked decline in the sale of a particular category of security paper should be an eye-opener to detect circulation of forged stamps immediately. It is urgently required to plug the loopholes in the system and take immediate remedial measures."

Notwithstanding their hard stand against the CBI, for Chief Minister Krishna and the Congress (I), the stamp paper scam was a hot potato as there were insinuations about the links of a few Congress politicians with A.K.L. Telgi. A regional newspaper was asking Krishna five questions every day on the alleged acts of omission and commission of the Karnataka Police investigating the stamp scam and the government's inaction. Surprisingly, the Opposition politicians (barring the BJP leader B.S. Yediyurappa and the floor leader of the All-India Progressive Janata Dal in the legislative assembly, B. Somashekar) had desisted from making any concerted noise pressuring the government for a CBI probe. Somashekar, who had been revenue minister in the Janata Dal government, claimed that the STAMPIT was a front to cover up the faults of the Congress government. Further, he alleged that Telgi had helped the All-India Congress Committee (AICC) session held in Bangalore in 2001 with money and had also picked up the tab of over sixty Congress legislators of Maharashtra (during the chief ministership of Vilasrao Deshmukh), who were lodged under cover at a resort in the outskirts of Bangalore. Telgi was given a stamp paper vendor licence when Deshmukh was the revenue minister of Maharashtra.

The Karnataka government made a quick volte-face and handed over the investigation to the CBI following the resignation of Roshan Baig from the state Cabinet on 4 January 2004. Baig's resignation and the Krishna government's surprise decision after months of resistance, gave the Opposition enough ammunition to attack the government. In both houses of the legislature, the Opposition demanded that the chief minister make a statement on Baig's role in the scam.

The Bharatiya Janata Party, which forced an adjournment of the assembly on 9 January 2004, insisted that the government had eventually let Roshan Baig resign as there was enough evidence linking the former minister to the scam. Jagadish Shettar, leader of the Opposition in the assembly, told *Frontline*, "Baig had gone abroad only to avoid being present during the legislative session."

Baig's position in the Cabinet had become tenuous after the surrender and arrest of his younger brother, Dr Rehan Baig, on 20 December 2003. Despite Rehan's assertions that his association with Telgi and Metro Corporation was limited to only palmolien and kerosene trade for a period of three months, and that he was unaware of Telgi's involvement in fake stamps until it became public in August 2000, the STAMPIT had uncovered a direct link between the Metro Corporation and the stamp paper racket. Rehan knew and worked with Telgi between 1995 and 2000, and hence became complicit. "The STAMPIT had even traced a mobile phone number that belonged to Rehan and which he allegedly used to transact in fake stamp papers" (*Frontline*, 30 January 2004).

State BJP leaders alleged that three persons had made big investments in various companies (such as Pearl Global Ltd, Delhi) on behalf of Telgi in Chennai and in New Delhi. One of them was a retired director general of police of Karnataka. The other two were J.L. Zutshi, a former chairman of the Indian Oil Corporation, and Suresh Mathur, the chairman and managing director of Petronet LNG. While Mathur didn't react, Zutshi and Deepak Seth, the chief managing director of Pearl Global, denied any involvement in the scam, as did Santhosh Gadia, a chartered accountant and a director of Pearl Global. He said he knew the former director general of police but did not have financial transactions with him.

Further, the Karnataka government invoked Section 268 of the Code of Criminal Procedure, 1973, to restrain Telgi's movement out of the state. It was feared that Telgi would spill the beans on his Karnataka contacts if allowed to do so. This, according to observers, was one of the main reasons why the Karnataka government was reluctant to hand over the case to the CBI. Unlike in Maharashtra, where the SIT had been working on the Bombay High Court's orders, the STAMPIT had been working directly under the Karnataka chief minister's office.

On the other hand, although the Centre had been making noises that Karnataka should hand over the fake stamp paper cases to the CBI (it even wrote a letter in June 2002 that the case should be handed over to the agency), it had not specifically asked the state to do so. In fact, Jaswant Singh, the Union finance minister, during a speech in Parliament, did not even refer to the allegations made by his own party members that the Congress (I) governments in Karnataka and Maharashtra were 'avoiding' a probe by the CBI. Jaswant Singh, however, said that the Union government had no problem whatsoever with 'who conducted the investigations', as long as the Centre was taken into confidence.

Kirit Somaiya, a member of Parliament of the Bharatiya Janata Party who represented Mumbai North-East at the time, raised the issue in Parliament (Lok Sabha debate papers) on 19 December 2003, stating that the country wanted the Maharashtra government to clearly scope the magnitude of the scam, whether it was Rs 300 crore or Rs 30,000 crore. He spoke about fake currency crossing borders (like terrorists) and unleashing economic terrorism in India, destabilising the economy, and wondered if the Telgi scam was in any way responsible. If that were so, the common man would lose faith in the 'Indian state' and would wonder whether the currency he was using was fake, or whether the stamp paper on which he recorded important transactions was illegal.

In November 2003, the finance minister assuaged fears in Indians worried about the validity of their transactions ranging from affidavits, bequests, marriage registration to sale and mortgage of property and financial assets. "Don't worry. Fake stamp papers already in use will not become invalid," Jaswant Singh said on the sidelines of the India Economic Summit, organised by the World Economic Forum and the Confederation of Indian Industries (CII). Top finance ministry officials later added the government would bring an ordinance to legalise transactions recorded on fake stamp papers between 1998 and 2002. Later, parliamentary approval would be sought to decree it into law. This comfort was important considering the panic that had spread across the country on account of markets being flooded with fake stamps. Singh said the government would move towards a non-stamp paper system. "Many nations now record legal transactions electronically, collecting a fee for storing such documents in a court depository. However, a shift to such a system will take time as courts throughout the country, down to the village level, will have to be computerised," Singh said (*The Telegraph*, 23 November 2003).

On 5 December 2003, Finance Minister Jaswant Singh dismissed allegations that his ministry had dragged its feet over the Rs 30,000-crore fake stamp paper scam for more than a year. He was reacting when asked about a newspaper report that S.M. Krishna had written to him as early as July the previous year about the possible involvement of security press officials in the Telgi scam. As part of his efforts to prevent such scams in the future, Singh said that "the government planned to introduce a paperless system by 6 to 8 weeks where stamp papers would be available in demat form, similar to the demat of shares in the capital market" (Rediff.com News, 5 December 2003). However, though security features were improved in physical stamp papers in mid-2005, the paperless avatar made its entry into the Indian financial system much later.

The Telgi scam rattled the Rajya Sabha, too. According to a *Times of India* report of 23 December 2003, the Upper House witnessed noisy scenes on 22 December 2003. Rajya Sabha members wanted Jaswant Singh to answer "where the stamp scam money was stowed away. Had it been used in the stock market or sent abroad, or was it used to fund terrorists?" Bal Apte (BJP) pointed fingers at the Karnataka government (Congress), accusing it of not allowing Telgi's interrogation and for resisting a CBI probe into the scam, despite its national character. He alleged that there was a reference to nineteen ministers in Telgi's taped conversations. Janardhana Poojary (Congress) counter-attacked the Centre, alleging that by insisting on a CBI inquiry (seen by many as acting as a stooge for those in power at the Centre), it was weakening the investigation.

Prithviraj Chauhan (Congress) joined the fray, alleging that there was no clear account of loss of revenue by the state machinery, but media reports suggested losses ranging from Rs 39,000 crore to Rs 60,000 crore. "The sale of the printing press in good condition as scrap, the smuggling of the designs, ink and paper all pointed towards complicity of the Nashik press workers, and I want accountability to be fixed," Chauhan said.

20

The CBI in Charge

The Special Investigation Team continued its investigation and periodically filed principal and supplementary charge sheets in the various cases in Maharashtra courts. Similarly, the Stamp Investigation Team was filing charge sheets for the Karnataka cases as were the other relevant authorities in other states, where the cancer of the stamp scam had spread. Yet, it was clear from the political posturing that the state of Maharashtra in late 2003 was finally keen to hand over investigation to the Central Bureau of Investigation. An announcement in the assembly was made to this effect by the Deputy Chief Minister and Home Minister Chhagan Bhujbal on 9 December 2003 (Rediff.com News, 9 December 2003).

Given the national character of the investigation and the various public and political pressures being mounted, forty-eight main cases (of the 200-odd ones involving A.K.L. Telgi) and allied investigations were transferred to the CBI vide a Supreme Court order dated 15 March 2004 in the Civil Writ Petition No.522 of 2003. These included twenty-three cases in Maharashtra alone with the Bund Garden case being the biggest both in terms of quantum of seizures and the fallout of allegations against those in public life. Also, several accused in this case (including Telgi and his associates) were charged in other cases as well. The Supreme Court further ruled that no high court in the country would entertain any prosecution petition related to the forty-eight cases transferred to the CBI and that a special court would handle all legal proceedings. The investigation bureau was also directed by the apex court to file periodic status reports with them and expedite investigations. The Supreme Court ruling of the transfer was followed up by a subsequent notification of the Government of India dated 23 March 2004. To maintain continuity in the proceedings, Raja Thakare, who was the special prosecutor of the SIT, filed his papers in the court on 21 April 2004 as prosecutor for the CBI.

Per the Supreme Court's directives, the SIT, the STAMPIT and other agencies handed their investigation, findings and evidence to the CBI by 13 April 2004. The CBI had moved an application before Special Judge S.M. Shembole (Special Court, Pune) seeking permission to interrogate all the sixty-five accused in Yerwada Prison, Pune, and received the green signal on 21 April 2004 (Rediff.com News, 22 April 2004). This included the prime accused A.K.L. Telgi who had been moved from the Bengaluru Central Prison to the Yerwada Prison in Pune, in 2004, as Telgi had expressed concerns about his safety. During the narco tests conducted on 22 December 2003, in addition to various other allegations and revelations, Telgi had mentioned that he knew some ministers, legislators and senior police officers in Karnataka. However, he said that he was afraid to reveal their names as "they had sent goons to his cell in the Bengaluru Central Jail, and he was worried about his own security" (Rediff.com news article on 10 February 2004).

The Telgi scam had captured the national imagination for its audacity, size and alleged complicity of the police, public sector officials as well as politicians. When the CBI filed its progress status report with the Supreme Court in August 2004, the latter gave it three months to complete the investigations. This was eventually competed on 5 December 2005.

However, the CBI had begun filing is charge sheets much earlier. The charge sheet against the prime accused A.K.L. Telgi was filed on 10 August 2004. Sixty-six other charge sheets were filed expeditiously and the CBI completed the onerous task on 26 July 2005, a little more than fifteen months after the cases had been assigned to them. Considering that the investigation/evidence had been handed over from the state agencies like the SIT, the STAMPIT and the others only in mid-April 2004, the pace of work was commendable.

In the Bund Garden case, of the sixty-eight accused, two expired during the pendency of the trial. Forty-three accused pleaded guilty to the charges framed against them. They were convicted. The main accused A.K.L. Telgi, too, pleaded guilty. Eighteen of the accused faced charges and applied for bail under various statutes.

Among the police officers named in the charge sheet by the CBI were former ex-Joint Commissioner of Police Shridhar Vagal, Deputy Commissioner of Police Pradeep Sawant, Assistant Commissioner of Police M. Mulani, Senior Inspector Gokul Patil, Inspector Prakash Deshmukh, Inspector Dattatraya Dal, Inspector Vashishtha Andale and Assistant Inspector Dilip Kamat. Samajwadi Janata Party MLA from Dhule, Anil Gote, Telgi's lawyer Rashid Kulkarni, and former Andhra Pradesh minister and Telugu Desam Party MLA Krishna Yadav were also implicated.

Mohammed Hafeez, one of Telgi's close associate, Telgi's wife Shahida and daughter Sana's names were included in the charge sheet following a letter written to the Maharashtra Deputy Chief Minister R.R. Patil in March 2004, alleging that Mushrif, the then additional commissioner, and Jaiswal, deputy inspector general and head of the SIT, had deliberately left these names out of the charge sheet. The charge sheet detailed the modus operandi of Telgi's deals in fake stamp papers and traced the rise of the scamster over a period, as well as the actual impact of the scam. The charge sheet confirmed that the analysis of various cell phones used by Telgi while in custody of the Crime Branch, Mumbai, from 28 October 2002 to 21 January 2003 had been conducted to link the members of his organised crime syndicate. Several witnesses had been examined to prove the use of the cell phones by Telgi's accomplices.

The charge sheet also investigated the role of former Union minister Ram Jethmalani. Jethmalani was interrogated in detail. The most challenging task encountered by the CBI was to file counter-replies to various applications for bail and discharges moved by those accused before the court of the special judge, and to contest various bail applications moved in the high courts and the Supreme Court.

Even with the above developments, the political rumblings refused to die down, perhaps because of the public perception that the 'big fish' had been incriminated, but not incarcerated. On 12 July 2004, Member of Parliament from Muzaffarpur (Janata Dal United) George Fernandes provided a personal explanation regarding certain remarks made against him by Sarvashri Raghunath Jha, Devendra Prasad and others in the Lok Sabha on 6 and 7 July 2004 (Lok Sabha Debate Papers). They had alleged that Fernandes had 'links' with the key accused in the stamp paper scam, Abdul Karim Telgi, and politician Anil Gote. A photograph taken at a public function in Dhule, Maharashtra, was exhibited to justify this allegation. Fernandes explained that in June 1999, he had received an invitation from Anil Gote to unveil a memorial statue for Param Vir Chakra Abdul Hamid, who had laid down his life in the war against Pakistan in 1965.

Fernandes claimed that he had travelled from New Delhi to Mumbai on 2 July 1999 and then with Narayan Rane (the then chief minister of Maharashtra), Gopinath Munde (the then deputy chief minister of Maharashtra) and Ram Jethmalani, noted lawyer and politician (the then Union minister of urban affairs and employment). He was present at the event held forenoon on 3 July 1999, and was on the podium with Rane, Munde and Jethmalani. They returned to Mumbai the same day, and Fernandes went back to New Delhi in the evening. Fernandes said, "I had no clue about the people who were on the dais at the function, except Mr and Mrs Gote. If a photograph shows Abdul Karim Telgi on the dais, a person whom I have never met in my life, to call this as 'links' is, to say the least, unjust." In the same debate, Fernandes also mentioned having travelled again on

26 October 2002 to Dhule for a similar function at the behest of Anil Ghote, along with Nitish Kumar (then Union minister for railways) and Ram Jethmalani.

While the matter died a natural death, the reason why such a high-level entourage travelled to Dhule at the invitation of Anil Gote not once, but multiple times, was never questioned.

In mid-2005, in a bid to counter the fake stamp menace after the scam, the finance ministry changed the design of stamp papers with intricate security features. The new design of the stamps of various denominations, from Re 1 to Rs 25,000, had been approved and production and supply had started in a phased manner. The Security Printing Press in Hyderabad was assigned the task of printing stamps up to a denomination of Rs 20, while the India Security Press of Nashik began printing denominations of Rs 50, Rs 100, Rs 500 and higher. Stamps worth Rs 10,000 to Rs 25,000 were reinforced with superior designs and security features.

The new stamp papers were printed on a special paper with security inks and special techniques. Besides, the new stamps were state-specific, with the names of the states printed indelibly on the stamps. They carried a serial number enabling them to be tracked. After efforts to improve the security of stamps were initiated in late 2003, the technical and revenue departments of the state and the Centre worked on this project for over a year. This, in addition to fortifying stamp papers with security protocols, included training the revenue officials to identify and segregate counterfeit stamps. (*Outlook*, 16 May 2005).

The trial of A.K.L. Telgi in the fake stamp paper case was held in-camera. It was decided to use the videoconferencing facility between Yerawada Jail, Pune, and the special court, Mumbai, for the entire trial hearing in view Telgi's poor health, security and other logistical reasons. The trial of the case was a milestone in the criminal justice system in using the technology of videoconferencing, with Telgi not being physically present in the court for any hearing but rather appearing in-camera from Yerawada Jail and later from Bengaluru Central Prison, where he was shifted in June 2008.

Shahida, Telgi's wife, surrendered to the special MCOCA court on 15 November 2005, "after having failed to appear before it on two occasions. A wailing Shahida, who was suffering from many diseases, besides being HIV positive, had to be lifted on to a wheelchair in which she was brought to the court. Shahida vomited twice in the court premises and looked very ill. The court directed that she be admitted to Sassoon Hospital for treatment. She was later released on bail." (Zee News, 15 November 2005)

On 17 January 2006, almost eleven years after the first case, CR 355/1995, against Telgi in the fake stamp scam was registered, the special CBI court judge, U.S. Salvi, pronounced Telgi guilty in this case on seven counts: criminal conspiracy, counterfeiting government stamps and cheating, among others. Telgi's associates Sanjay Gaikwad and Ram Ratan Soni were also convicted. Along with the imposition of fines, they were sentenced to ten years of rigorous imprisonment.

Telgi pleaded his case from Yerawada Jail via videoconferencing. "Clean-shaven but looking gaunt, he claimed that he was innocent of many of the charges. With folded hands, he pleaded for clemency because he was a diabetic, had been diagnosed HIV positive, and was dying. In fact, the defence asked the court to give Telgi minimum sentence because of his illness, but prosecutors argued that he was being given adequate medical attention" (*Frontline*, 10 February 2006).

Considering Telgi's rapidly deteriorating health, the prosecution impressed upon the court to expedite other cases against him. There was also pressure to force Telgi to reveal the extent of the scam and, more important, name those in high places involved in it. Special Public Prosecutor Raja Thakare told the media that Telgi was deliberately delaying the trial by promising to produce evidence that would implicate prominent people in the scam, but such documents were never produced, even when hearings were postponed.

This appears true given the startling developments in October 2004. On 30 October 2004, Telgi submitted a signed statement through his lawyer Harshad Nimbalkar to the special MCOCA court in Pune, stating that the kingpin in the case was not him, but a businessman from Kolkata named Mohammed Sayeed Mohammed Yasin, who was involved in the printing and sale of fake stamp papers. "He also claimed that he had received a threat to his life from one of the co-accused in the Yerawada Jail in Pune. Telgi had made his appearance in the court where he had pleaded for a fresh narco analysis test and brain mapping alleging that the earlier tests conducted in December 2003 were 'false and fabricated'. The plea was turned down." (Rediff.com News, 31 October 2004.)

Later in late February 2007, Telgi filed an application before the special MCOCA court seeking to turn approver, and be pardoned as an accomplice. This was in line with his stand from the beginning of the trial that he was neither the kingpin nor the main conspirator. (Rediff.com News dated 1 March 2007.)

Developments in other cases followed. On 24 March 2007, Telgi along with Bhadruddin, Irfan Ahmed, Wazir Ahmed Salik and Pradeep Kumar were sentenced to ten years of rigorous imprisonment and fined as well in a Karnataka case under the jurisdiction of the Peenya Industrial Area in Bengaluru.

21

Curtain Call

On 28 June 2007, Telgi was sentenced to rigorous imprisonment for thirteen years and fined an astounding sum of over Rs 250 crore on various counts in one of the main cases of the scandal, the Bund Garden case, hours after he had pleaded guilty. His guilty plea came as a surprise, for he had always said that he would 'take down many with him' if convicted. Perhaps, he had realized that it was the end of the road for him.

With evidence piling up thick and fast, not many of his powerful supporters coming to his rescue, and with his health rapidly failing, maybe he had accepted that the odds were irrevocably stacked against him. Perhaps he also realised that a guilty plea would help to reduce the punishment. A tearful Telgi stood with folded hands and appealed to the judge to be lenient as he was the only breadwinner in the family and was suffering from various ailments that had no cure. He also said that he was confessing at the behest of his wife.

This was the harshest punishment given to Telgi in any of the fake stamp paper cases that he had been convicted in Maharashtra and Karnataka, though Judge Chitra Bhedi of the special court opined that the ruling had been lenient given his confession and poor state of health. Had he opted for a protracted trial, punishment would have been far more severe, she said. Forty-three other accused in the case, who had pleaded guilty, too, were sentenced to rigorous imprisonment for up to six years, in addition to fines. CBI counsel Raja Thakare moved an application in the court seeking confiscation of Telgi's properties to recover the fine levied on him. There was a fair amount of confusion over the quantum of the fine. Various sources quoted amounts varying from Rs 50 crore to Rs 202 crore.

Finally, on 29 June 2007, "...the special MCOCA court issued the order of Telgi's sentence, ending the confusion over the actual fine slapped on him. Interestingly, Telgi had been fined Rs 252.28 crore, while the CBI's probe had maintained that the actual money involved in the scam was not more than Rs 172 crore. It had said that fake stamp papers worth Rs 3,000 crore that were recovered from Mumbai never made it to the market and, hence, couldn't be considered while deciding the magnitude of the case. Found guilty under five sections of MCOCA and seventeen sections of the Indian Penal Code, Telgi was sentenced to a maximum of thirteen years of rigorous imprisonment and fined a maximum of Rs 50 crore or an additional three years in jail in case of default, adding up to Rs 252.28 crore. The court order stated that while the actual sentences (under the various counts/sections) could run concurrently, the punishment awarded in case of default in payment of fine would have to be served separately. Therefore, if Telgi failed to pay up, his thirteen-year jail term could go up to thirty years, almost a life term." (*Hindustan Times* dated 30 June 2007.) Legal experts were of the view that the annals of Indian law had never seen such an astronomical figure being levied as a fine earlier. Also, many saw the judgment of Judge Chitra Bhedi not too lenient either. In light of the large fine and Telgi's possible inability to pay the same, Telgi's punishment would be a life sentence.

On 30 November 2007, Telgi and his four associates – Mohamad Ghas Shigvi, Sajid Khan, Maqdoom Tadkod and Kalim Bandaawaz – were sentenced to seven years' rigorous imprisonment by a special CBI court for their involvement in the death of his driver, Christopher

Bhatti, in 2001. On 25 March 2006, when Telgi and his associates had been charged with this crime, they had pleaded not guilty. Telgi, who was brought amid high security from Pune's Yerawada Jail, pleaded for leniency from Special Judge U.D. Salvi. "My life is like a bubble on water, it can burst any time," Telgi said, referring to his HIV positive status and diabetes. He said his wife was on her deathbed, and only his minor daughter was at home. "My mother and brother have passed away and I am the only one left to look after my family," Telgi said (*Indian Express*, 1 December 2007). Telgi, who was found guilty of a lesser charge of culpable homicide not amounting to murder, also pleaded that any sentence that he was handed out be ordered to run concurrently with the thirteen-year jail term he was already serving at Yerawada Jail in the Bund Garden case.

Judgment in a Chennai case followed on 30 January 2008 and special judge N. Velu sentenced Telgi to ten years' rigorous imprisonment (to run concurrently with the Pune court order) and penalties. Allowing the petitions filed by Telgi and four others pleading guilty, the judge convicted and sentenced Abdul Wahid, Balaji and Jacob Chacko to five years' rigorous imprisonment and another convict, Peter Kennedy, to three years, along with fines for all. The judge had earlier convicted and sentenced Sarfraz Nawaz, another accused who pleaded guilty, to five years' rigorous imprisonment in the case.

On 26 February 2008, a Delhi court framed charges against kingpin Abdul Karim Telgi and over twenty of his alleged associates for selling fake stamps in the national capital but absolved them of the stricter offence of printing the counterfeits. "The entire evidence shows how the accused had established offices in Delhi, recruited marketing executives and spread their business of selling counterfeit stamps. Mere possession and sale of such stamps cannot lead us to a conclusion that the accused were also guilty of printing them," CBI Special Judge Dinesh Dayal ruled.

The list also included Puran Singh, the sacked inspector. Five accused – Devender Mahajan, Amit Kumar, Ajay Grover, Jai Manchanda and Sanjay Raina – were discharged after the CBI failed to find any incriminating evidence against them. "It appears that these accused had joined M/s Capital Services (owned by Telgi) in order to make a livelihood without knowledge of its illegal activities," the judge said in his order (Rediff.com News dated 26 February 2008).

Similar judgments in other cases followed:

- 3 February 2009: Nine cases, eight involving fake stamps and one the possession of a fake passport. Six of these cases had been investigated by the police and three by the CBI. Telgi pleaded guilty in all the cases and was awarded five years' rigorous imprisonment for each case (to run concurrently).
- 13 November 2009: Seven years' rigorous imprisonment each in two separate cases by a local court in Churu, Rajasthan, along with fines. One case was related to a multi-crore stamp paper case in 1995, and another to the issuing of fake passports to labourers in 1994.
- 30 November 2009: Ten years' rigorous imprisonment (sentences to run concurrently), along with fines for Telgi and two of his accomplices, Shabbir Ahmed Sheikh and Sohail Khan, by the special Central Bureau of Investigation court in Bhopal. Jagjeevan Yadav, proprietor of Malwa Enterprises, Indore, and another accused, Abdul Gafur Mujahid, expired during the trial and investigation, respectively, and cases against them lapsed.
- 17 February 2010: Ten years' rigorous imprisonment along with fines for Telgi and twenty-one other associates in the 2003 Upparpet case, Bengaluru. Though the case had been initially filed against thirty-two accused, the judge acquitted eleven, including Rehan Baig.
- 14 June 2010: Ten years' rigorous imprisonment by a special court in Pune to be served by Telgi consecutively, after he had served the earlier sentences. An additional five years under MCOCA was served with both the sentences in this case to run concurrently. The case pertained to the arrest of two

persons, Rajgad Jaiswal and Avdesh Tiwari, from S.R. Travels in suburban Mulund, Mumbai, Maharashtra, who were allegedly selling fake stamps using the name of an authorised stamp vendor Kanchan Bhongale. Bhongale had reported to the General Stamps office and a case was registered at the Mulund Police Station in 2001. Fake stamps worth about Rs 25 lakh were seized from the duo. Ten persons were named as accused in the case, including Telgi. While Telgi pleaded guilty, four persons including a police officer pleaded 'not guilty' and faced trial. A police officer, Liladhar Nemade, died and the case against him lapsed.

- 29 February 2012: A special CBI court convicted Telgi and eleven others in one of the fake stamp paper scam-related cases but rejected an application by one of the accused, Ram Ratan Soni, to make former Maharashtra chief minister Vilasrao Deshmukh an accused. Soni alleged that it was during Deshmukh's tenure as state revenue minister that Telgi was granted the stamp vending licence, so he be impleaded in the case. The court, however, sentenced Telgi in cases registered at Colaba and the Cuffe Parade Police Stations in Mumbai, and at the Economic Offence Wing. The cases were later taken over by the CBI. Apart from Telgi, three police officials and a government officer were also convicted for assisting him. The allegations against Telgi and others were that they had sold fake stamp papers worth Rs 70 lakh to some major companies. Police officer Kulwant Parmar, who investigated the case registered at Colaba Police Station, A.B. Sonwalkar, who investigated the case registered at the Cuffe Parade Police Station, and Ganpat Jadhav, who was attached to EOW, were convicted for criminal misconduct. Parmar, Sonwalkar and Jadhav were sentenced to six, four and five years' imprisonment, respectively. Shrikant Rane, the officer from the stamp office, was also convicted. The other convicts were Shabir Shaikh, Mohmad Yasin, Ram Ratan Soni, Riyaz Mokashi, Mallesh Dhulannavar, Sanjay Gaikwad, Daniel

Kanikraj – all convicted for conspiracy and for assisting Telgi in the distribution and supply of counterfeit stamps.

Appearing on videoconference from a jail in Bangalore, Telgi said, "I have good faith in the judiciary. I am suffering from diabetes, heart disease, kidney problem and both my legs are paralysed. I need an urgent kidney operation. My health is deteriorating day-by-day. My wife is ill and on the deathbed (it was alleged that Telgi had passed on his AIDS infection to his wife). My only daughter is of marriageable age and there is no other male member in my family. I pray for minimum sentence. I am penniless and cannot pay the fine. I pray for leniency." (News 18, 29 February 2012).

- 10 October 2012: A Delhi court on Tuesday upheld Telgi's seven-year imprisonment along with fines in a New Delhi case, earlier awarded by a trial court. Telgi, along with other co-accused Abdul Gafur Mujahid, Anand G. Thorat, Sachin Munna and Ashfaq, had floated a company, M/S Prime Services, located at Nehru Place during 1997-98 for the unauthorised trading and selling of counterfeit stamps and non-judicial stamps in various parts of Delhi and adjoining areas. Telgi's plea to reduce the quantum of the sentence and fine was dismissed despite his submission that he was suffering from various health complications, including AIDS, and needed extra care and medication, and disparity in sentence would cause injustice to his family members.

A leading business daily, *Business Standard*, carried a report on 8 October 2004 that the Reserve Bank of India had penalised several public sector, private sector and foreign banks in the multi-crore fake stamp paper scam on account of poor adherence to 'Know Your Customer' norms, monitoring of depositors and nature of fund flows. Earlier in the same year, the RBI had sought details of over 160 accounts opened by Telgi and his associates in several banks. After a step-up in RBI inquiries and a formal order, the affected banks froze the related accounts. This was, however, three years after the arrest of Telgi, thereby perhaps enabling his associates to withdraw large sums from the many accounts. This was yet another example of not just poor measures of customer compliance rules and adherence by banks, but also delayed oversight and action by the regulator.

Telgi's health continued to deteriorate. When he was in Yerawada Prison, he had given an eight-page statement to his lawyer Milind Pawar, asking him to file an application under MCOCA that he was not being given proper treatment. "They are not bothered about me. From the way the Sasoon Hospital and others responsible are treating me, my impression is that some people want to see me dead soon," Telgi lamented. (Rediff.com News dated 7 September 2006.)

He was shifted to Parappana Agrahara Central Prison, Bengaluru, in June 2008, after he requested a transfer from Pune, citing the need for quick trials into all the cases pending against him in Karnataka as the reason. However, according to a news report (Rediff.com News dated 3 June 2008), Telgi preferred the cool climes of Bengaluru compared to the heat of Mumbai as he did the crispy masala dosas and the familial proximity. Of course, it could also be the VIP treatment that he was accorded here.

Though incarcerated, it was homecoming for him. "I feel safe here as the security is tight. I have been given a special cell and there is no problem. Coming back to this city was my biggest dream. It is like a second home to me, and I am very happy to be here. It is not because I am more comfortable in this jail, but the fact that my wife and daughter are closer to me makes me happier. I have been telling the investigating agencies that my wife is ailing, and I can meet her every day if I am lodged in Bengaluru. Moreover, my daughter wants to study further, and I need to be around, to advise her. I know that I don't have any freedom, but the weather and food in Bangalore suit me. There are over twelve cases pending against me in Karnataka, and I hope justice will be done soon. However, I won't say anything on the case as it is sub-judice. People say that I have been protecting several people in the case, and they keep expecting me to confess. Let me make this clear. I have nothing to confess." (Rediff.com News dated 3 June 2008.)

On 4 February 2011, Telgi filed a petition before the high court seeking to be excused from being taken to Pune, as per a production warrant issued on 18 January 2011, on account of his rapidly deteriorating health and the fear for his life in Maharashtra. "I have been suffering from neurological and other diseases. I have hypertension, diabetes, and HIV. My wife is also suffering from diabetes, hypertension and HIV and thyroid problems. My daughter also stays here. If I am taken away, I cannot communicate with them," Telgi said in his petition, which was eventually granted. Telgi appeared for all the subsequent hearings, regardless of the location of the case, from the precincts of Parappana Agrahara Central Prison, Bengaluru.

Despite medical care within the prison for diabetes and blood pressure, Telgi's health continued to worsen, and he was soon confined to a wheelchair. He was admitted with tuberculous meningitis to the Victoria Hospital in Bengaluru (a government hospital) on 16 October 2017. His daughter, Sana Talikoti, with her husband, Irfan Talikoti, a silk exporter with his office on Brigade Road, were at the hospital after Telgi was shifted from Parappana Agrahara prison to the government medical facility. Telgi was then moved to the intensive care unit on 19 October 2017 as his vitals failed.

Sana Talikoti told *Bangalore Mirror* (25 October 2017) that despite his condition, they were hopeful of a recovery as 'he is a fighter'. She also added that "prayers and sacrifices were being held for him at various places, from Rajasthan to his village in Belagavi". "He is also weak, and we are hoping that the prayers of his well-wishers will save him," Irfan Talikoti added.

Irfan and Sana also told *Bangalore Mirror* that though Telgi was under intensive care, he was aware of what was being told to him, which according to them was a positive sign that he might recover. "I was allowed inside, went up to him and gently shook his shoulders and told him that his grandson, Arman, was waiting for him to get well and meet him. We saw tears trickling down his right eye," Irfan said.

It was not just the family, but special prayers were held at various dargahs and places of worship from Ajmer to Khawja Bande Nawaz Dargah in Kalaburagi, Irfan said. He also added that goats were being sacrificed at various places, including at Telgi's village at Khanapur for his well-being. "His (Telgi's) biggest problem was that he could never say no to anyone. He has always helped people right from providing financial support, schooling children, digging borewells, constructing mosques and temples. More than anything else, he had full faith in the Indian legal system," Sana added. Irfan had also pointed out that it was unfair at this point to discuss his 'business' and 'scams'.

Irfan Talikoti, Telgi's son-in-law, who was the Youth Congress President, Khanapur Taluk, Belagavi, had created quite a stir when in December 2012 he was selected by former Karnataka chief minister B.S. Yediyurappa's newly launched political outfit, the Karnataka Janata Party (KJP). Although Irfan, then Sana's fiancé, was in no way connected to the multi-crore scam, people were surprised at his nomination to the party, especially since Yediyurappa was the one who had made the biggest noise about the multi-crore scam when he was the leader of the Opposition. Though KJP had been dismissive of Talikoti's involvement in the scam, political speculation was rife that it was a diabolical political move either to embarrass the BJP or perhaps use Talikoti's proximity to the Telgi family and knowledge about the scam against Yediyurappa's political opponents. Irfan had then hit out at his detractors saying that "he had an identity of his own and wanted to work for the development of his constituency" (Rediff.com News dated 27 December 2012).

However, Telgi suffered a cardiac arrest and couldn't be revived despite all resuscitative measures. He died at around 3:55 p.m. on 23 October 2017 at the age of fifty-six. He had been incarcerated for sixteen years. Even though Telgi died in the hospital, it was still considered as a custodial death since he was in judicial custody. In accordance with the prison manual, the post-mortem was conducted in the presence of a magistrate and the procedure was videographed. Telgi's wife Shahida, daughter Sana, and son-in-law Irfan were present at the Victoria Hospital during the post-mortem.

According to reports in *The Times of India* and *Deccan Chronicle* (29 October 2017), there was high drama at the funeral of A.K.L. Telgi (or Karim Lala as he was fondly called) on 28 October 2017 in Khanapur, "...when family members squabbled in full public view. When Telgi's body arrived, and Abdul Azim, his younger brother, went to take it out of the ambulance, a heated argument ensued. Irfan Talikoti, Telgi's son in-law, asked him, 'Why did you come to the funeral when you did not meet him earlier?' This enraged Azim's family, and they began quarrelling."

It appears that Abdul Azim fell out with A.K.L. Telgi and the latter's family when he failed to extend any support after the stamp paper scam kingpin's arrest. "Sana asked Abdul Azim and his sons to leave the house and told them not to attend the funeral. She said that her family would take care of the necessary rituals and that there was no need for any relatives to attend the funeral. Abdul Azim tried to convince Telgi's family that he was not allowed to meet Telgi when he was in the hospital in Bengaluru recently. Abdul Azim's two sons tried to attack Irfan Talikoti when the argument heated up, but the police intervened."

The situation was defused when Azim left the spot. Though Sana did not allow Azim's family to carry the casket to the burial ground, they were present at the burial site and the fracas escalated until the elders of the community intervened. The funeral prayers were conducted at Bahar Galli Mosque in the town, before the body was taken to the burial ground in the town's outskirts at 2 p.m., where Irfan performed the last rites. About 2,000 people had gathered at Lala's ancestral house as soon as his body was brought and some of his family friends from Telgi village, Bijapur district, were also present.

While his elder brother died a few years ago, Abdul Karim was the second sibling. The youngest brother Azim was the president of Khanapur town municipality. Azim was in jail for five years after the racket was busted. After being released from jail, he gradually built a career in politics. Shahida alleged that Azim's family had bought property thanks to her husband, but he deserted them when her husband needed help. The VIPs, political leaders and the big names who allegedly were recipients of Telgi's largesse were conspicuous by their absence.

Sources close to the family said that Telgi had spent large amounts of money on several social events, sports activities, weddings of the poor and in mosques for many years till he was jailed sixteen years ago. He had helped many unemployed youths from his town to get jobs, using his contacts. Many from Khanapur stayed with him whenever they went to Mumbai, in one of his many properties, which were all seized after his arrest.

On 31 December 2018, the Nashik sessions court in Maharashtra acquitted late Abdul Karim Telgi and seven others in a 2004 multi-crore fake stamp paper case in the absence of 'solid evidence' against them. This case involved RPF staff accused of purloining stamp papers belonging to the ISP, Nashik, from railway wagons.

Since Telgi, convicted in several cases in connection with the scam and sentenced to a long term of imprisonment, died while serving his jail term, charges against him were lapsed after his death. "Telgi's wife Shahida, a co-accused in many of the cases, his lawyer Rashid Kulkarni, his brother Abdul Azim, and his nephew Tabrez Telgi refused to please guilty." (*Pune Mirror*, 27 October 2017.)

According to an article dated 17 December 2017 in *DNA*, a leading English daily, Telgi's widow Shahida, while still an accused, applied in a MCOCA court (on 16 December 2017) requesting the investigating agencies to seize all properties of Telgi which had remained unencumbered. Seven of these properties were in Belgaum and two were in Bijapur, Karnataka. According to investigating agencies, Telgi used most of the money earned through the scam to purchase property, some of which were bought in Shahida's name and in the names of other relatives.

In her application, Shahida mentioned that it was Telgi's dying wish that the immovable assets he had acquired using money from the scam should be used 'for the benefit of the nation'. Shahida claimed in her application that "she was a God-fearing person and wished to come clean about the properties so that justice was served. She stated that she believed that every person had to repay his or her deeds and misdeeds on this earth itself, and she wanted to stay away from sin. Her faith in God and in the judicial system compelled her to inform the court about Telgi's unseized properties."

22

Famous Last Words...

Over two thousand people, a little over 10 per cent of Khanapur's population, attended the funeral of Telgi. A significant number, for none of them, other than the immediate family perhaps, were direct beneficiaries of his excesses. Yet, the modest fraction of his fortune which he had spent on social causes in Khanapur had perhaps earned him the dignity in death. And the shroud which covered him as he was interred in a nondescript burial ground in the town outskirts, covered more than his disease-ravaged remains. It hid the answers to the many unanswered questions that persist even after his death. Personal and professional truths, perhaps.

The Telgi scam is perceived by many to be more than just a financial fraud for loot and aggrandisement. If fake notes are seen as better funding vehicles for propelling terrorism than narcotics, the proceeds from fake stamps, too, could have been similarly misused, many argue. Fake notes make a mockery of national security and can sink a nation. Telgi's fake stamps, which had compromised the India Security Press, may have had the same potential and purpose.

How was it possible for a person of reasonable intelligence, yet one who had failed as a self-starter in his short stint in employment, to have such devious business acumen to reach dizzying heights of power and pelf? And then have the temerity to employ the loot to repeatedly mock, exploit and undermine the hallowed institutions of India? From police to politicians, from security printing presses to jails? Who were the real beneficiaries of his wealth? How was it possible for the scam figure to have dwindled to Rs 172 crores, less than 1 per cent of the lower range of earlier estimates? Was this a measure of the *profits made* or the *sales generated*? Was there political pressure at play? Was it possible that the Reserve Bank of India and the CBI moved too late to attach the numerous bank accounts and the wealth had flown by then? How do the unpaid income tax claims of Rs 190 crore and the fines levied by the court of over Rs 250 crore stack up, as do his vast number of properties, against the revised estimate, which is far lower than these figures? How was it possible for Telgi's wife, Shahida, to have offered nine unencumbered properties, valued at about Rs 100 crores, as late as December 2017, when Telgi's assets had ostensibly been seized to pay off the fine levied by the court and other claims from him? Is the excuse that these properties were in the names of Telgi's various family members acceptable when the CBI, income tax authorities, the Directorate of Revenue Intelligence, and the Reserve Bank of India were jointly investigating the value of the scam? And, if their collective might had missed these assets (and perhaps many more), how is their revised estimate of Rs 172 crore reliable and acceptable? How would the fate of investigations and the dispensation of justice have played out without Anna Hazare's PIL?

Perhaps, these are questions whose answers will never be found, despite the constant clamouring from many quarters to revisit the scam. There are too many big names involved. Names in politics, in the police, the prosecution and the judiciary. For, there are two facets aside from the perpetrator, which provide for the extent of corruption in any scam. Politics and the criminal justice system.

Let us address politics first. It's not the lack of legislation. Among the many, there is the Benami Transactions (Prohibition) Act 2016 (original act of 1988) which can be very effective in confiscating ill-gotten assets of politicians among others. According to media reports, till January 2019, the income tax department had confiscated assets worth Rs 6,900 crore under this Act (*The Mint*, 24 December 2020). Justic Jeevan Reddy, chairman, Law Commission, had drafted the Corrupt Public Servants (Forfeiture of Property) Act in 2003. The fate and use of this act is unclear. The Prevention of Corruption (Amendment) Bill, 2013, amended the Prevention of Corruption Act, 1988. The very fact that the first amendment to both this and the Benami Transactions Act came over twenty-five years later proves the low priority attached to the redressal of corruption. Certain amendments to the POCA bill were circulated by the government in 2015. A corrupt politician, whether in power or not, is as liable for criminal suit under the Prevention of Corruption Act as any other citizen. With the powers vested today with the Central Vigilance Commission, it should, therefore, be possible for the CBI to bring corrupt politicians to book. Yet, we know that reality is different.

Part of the problem is the credibility of the CBI with the states, especially those ruled by a different political party than that which calls the shots at the Centre. The CBI has often been referred to as 'the caged parrot' that sings the Centre's tune. There is fair evidence that when an investigation is not being monitored by the court, the agency, especially in its role as an anti-corruption watchdog, has seen enquiries, FIRs, cases and charge sheets filed or dropped or put on hold depending on who is in power in the Centre and what they dictate.

In October 2020, the Maharashtra government decided to withdraw the 'general consent' given to the CBI to investigate cases in the state. According to an *Indian Express* editorial on 24 October 2020, "Maharashtra is not the first state to flag this distrust of the federal agency: Andhra Pradesh, West Bengal and Chhattisgarh too have done the same in recent times. The current confrontation strengthens the perception that states in opposition see the Centre as weaponizing the agency to keep the heat on Opposition-led governments." The CBI, which is the only federal agency to probe corrupt officials attached to central departments like income tax, customs, GST and public sector undertakings, was recently forced to put on abeyance investigations into alleged fraud caused to public sector banks totalling over Rs 50,000 crore for want of general consent from states. (*The Economic Times*, 8 September 2021.) Considering this, the success or otherwise of the Telgi scam investigations and denouement if the cases had stayed with the state machinery such as the SIT or the STAMPIT is perhaps anybody's guess.

In addition to political confrontation which stymies investigations and the conviction process, the issue is also one of either political complicity or lack of political will or both, and there are supporting examples for each. The first example in point is the N.N. Vohra Committee report, shrouded in secrecy till this day, twenty-eight years later, notwithstanding the multiple changes in governments during this period.

A committee, headed by the then Union Secretary (Home) N.N. Vohra, was set up by the P.V. Narasimha Rao government in July 1993 to examine the link between crime syndicates, government functionaries and political personalities, following the shocking Mumbai blasts of March 1993. The committee that included members from the Research and Analysis Wing (RAW), the Intelligence Bureau as well as the CBI had unanimously said that during the 1993 bomb blasts, the criminal network in Mumbai was virtually running a parallel government. This was the first time that the seventy-year-old criminal justice system in India (essentially a penal system handed down as a legacy from the British) was under the scanner, barring the Code of Criminal Procedure which had been revamped in 1973.

The N.N. Vohra committee submitted its report expeditiously to the Ministry of Home Affairs on 5 October 1993, three months after it was established on 9 July 1993. In a startling disclosure, the report alleged that many Congress leaders, who were in influential positions in Maharashtra and Gujarat in the 1990s, had developed close ties with underworld don Dawood Ibrahim and his henchman Iqbal Mirchi. Partial contents of the report, limited only to eleven pages, were subsequently made public on 1 August 1995 in Parliament, whereas the full report ran close to a hundred pages. Despite a political controversy, Opposition clamouring and even the then Rajya Sabha member Dinesh Trivedi moving the Supreme Court, the complete document was never released. On 20 November 2020, advocate Ashwini Kumar Upadhyay filed a writ petition in the Supreme Court seeking concrete action on the Vohra Committee report. We await a development in the matter.

The police-politician nexus made it back to the headlines with the developments in March 2021, following the discovery of a bomb-laden SUV outside 'Atilia', the residence of industrialist Mukesh Ambani, with the arrest of police officer Sachin Waze by the National Investigation Agency, the transfer of Police Commissioner Param Bir Singh and Singh's letter making grave charges against the state home minister and the latter's rebuttal. Sounds familiar?

Another example is the India Against Corruption (IAC) movement and the fervour that it had generated in the anti-corruption protests in 2011 and 2012, which many will remember. India had hoped that the crusade by Anna Hazare and others with their Jan Lokpal Bill would expedite resolution of corruption cases. Yet, divisions amongst key members of the IAC's core committee eventually led to a split in the movement. Arvind Kejriwal left to form the Aam Aadmi Party, while Anna Hazare formed the Jantantra Morcha.

While laying the contextual framework of this book, we lamented the high rate of Members of Parliament who have criminal cases against them (a growth of 44 per cent in 2019 over 2009), despite the provisions of the Right to Information (RTI) Act, efforts of organisations such as the Association for Democratic Reforms and the number of Supreme Court judgments in this space. Yet, unless we have a qualification/entry criterion into politics, it will be impossible to cleanse the system, reduce culpability in politics and bolster political will. This must be the starting point if corruption in India is to abate.

Before we come to the second aspect, i.e., the criminal justice system, a submission on the legal framework must be made despite my limited knowledge of the law. I sincerely believe that it's time we change the legal framework for white-collar crimes. The collateral damage of these crimes should affect us as deeply as the sight of blood in a murder or the mutilation of humanity in a rape does. A crime of murder is one death. Why don't we see the thousands of hearths (and lives) snuffed out when Nirav Modi's factory workers or Kingfisher employees or independent stamp vendors lose their livelihoods? Shouldn't justice for both crimes be measured by the same yardstick? How can a bank which fails its due diligence process for customer acceptance and allows the financial system to be abused to perpetrate terror funding, get away with a monetary fine when the proceeds are employed to kill hundreds in a bomb blast? Shouldn't its licence to do business be suspended at least? Can we look at making certain white-collar crimes non-bailable offenses? We need to start thinking differently.

Today, when we see the judiciary step onto the turf of the executive often enough, the foot-dragging on the larger issue of corruption seems inexplicable. According to the National Crime Records Bureau (NCRB) statistics of 2019, the state of Maharashtra alone, which had topped the cases of corruption for the last four years, '... has had a conviction rate of less than 15 per cent' (*The Indian Express*, 3 October 2020). A state like Kerala has a conviction rate of over 60 per cent, while some states have had nil convictions. If conviction rates are the litmus test for success in justice, India's average of 16 per cent for corruption cases scores abysmally low. It must be noted, however, that low conviction is not always the result of the prosecuting agency's inability to provide evidence. Often, a sub-optimal outcome is the result of procedural red tape. For example, a government servant cannot be prosecuted without a sanction from the competent authority. For a constable, for example, the police commissioner must give sanction while in cases of senior officers it is the government. On most occasions the sanction, especially at the level of the government, is not forthcoming.

According to a RTI Foundation of India article of 19 December 2016, the National Crime Records Bureau throws up more interesting data. Between 2001 and 2015, a total of 54,139 cases were registered across the twenty-nine states and seven Union Territories (UTs) for corruption. During this period, people filed more than double that number (1,16,010) of reports about being required to pay bribes, on the popular website 'I Paid a Bribe'. In other words, the number of formal corruption cases registered are far less than actual events occurring. Shockingly, nil convictions were reported from states such as West Bengal (home to the famous Sharada scam), Goa, Mizoram, Arunachal Pradesh, Tripura and Meghalaya according to statistics published by the National Crime Records Bureau. In Manipur, only one case is said to have reached conviction.

In the same period, a little more than 5 lakh murder cases (5,01,852), 5.87 lakh cases (5,87,347) of kidnapping or abduction and 3.54 lakh robbery cases (3,54,453) across the country were reported. Corruption cases thus account for 10 per cent or a little more than other crimes reported and cases booked.

The compass of responsibility points therefore to us, too. Either Indians have become too benumbed or too inured to corruption to report it. It could also be that there is a severe lack of public confidence in the ability of anti-corruption agencies to investigate a complaint of corruption, collect evidence and put the case up for trial.

Clearly, a great degree of work remains in raising the levels of intolerance in the Indian consciousness against corruption and instilling in them a greater confidence that their efforts to highlight instances will be swiftly actioned. This is even more important where a citizen takes upon the onus of being the eyes and ears against corruption even though it may not personally impact him/her. We certainly need less examples of the helpless crusade of whistle blower Jayant M. Tinaikar, discussed in this book.

The criminal justice system in India has three important players, namely, the police, the prosecution and the judiciary. The police are usually the first to contact the victims, the witnesses and the accused, and hence play a key role through the course of investigation, particularly in the identification of and establishing the guilt of the accused during trial. Their moral conduct therefore has an immense bearing on the case. This book is replete with example of police complicity and hence underscores the need to strengthen this pillar of our criminal justice system.

In his very persuasive article on the importance of the police force in the improvement of the criminal justice system in India, R. Sri Kumar, who played a prominent role in the Telgi saga, highlights many areas for improvement. He observes that while police engagement should be more vigorous in cognizable criminal cases (such as murder, rape, dowry deaths, kidnapping, theft, criminal breach of trust, waging/abetting/attempting war against government of India, etc.), where a police officer can carry out investigations and make an arrest without a warrant, he regrettably gets more involved in non-cognizable cases (assault, cheating, causing simple hurt, forgery, etc.), which outnumber the former. Though, in the latter category, the police cannot begin any investigation without a court order (warrant).

People believe that the police should step in to resolve such non-cognizable cases and they take umbrage when directed to approach the court. In addition to the enormous time and resources spent on such matters which the police can ill afford, undue police interference can also give rise to malpractice and breed institutional corruption, such as minimising a cognizable crime and making it non-cognizable. It has been argued that the margin of difference between cognizable and non-cognizable offences should be done away with, and all registered cases should go directly to the jurisdictional magistrate, who can then decide what aspect of the crime needs to be investigated, and what needs to be further verified by the police, before a full-length investigation is launched.

The second problem according to Sri Kumar is that the investigating officer is ordinarily in charge of the investigation of a case until the final report is filed. Frequent transfers of officers in charge of the probes (mostly due to political reasons) affect investigation adversely. He also argues that though the Supreme Court has ruled repeatedly that in the field of crime investigation, the supremacy of the investigating police should be maintained, and the executive or the judiciary should desist in taking control of the investigation unless very strong grounds exist, investigating officers are changed frequently. Even when such a case has been transferred (as was the Telgi scam investigations transferred from the SITs and the STAMPIT to the CBI), the officer, who was originally in charge of the investigation, should be allowed to move court if he / she finds that the investigation is taking a wrong turn.

The third and a related issue highlighted by Sri Kumar is that during trial of cases, another investigating officer, called the holding IO, is responsible for placing the evidence before the court. The investigating officer who has filed the final report appears in the court several times as a witness and is often asked to help in the examination of key and crucial witnesses. During the trial and appeal stages, the officer's continued role and responsibility of keeping a close watch on the prosecutor's role is of paramount importance in not just seeing a responsible closure of the case, but in ensuring that documents, evidence and case properties are not compromised.

The fourth and perhaps the biggest issue is the lack of credibility of the police and investigation agencies. Sri Kumar laments the trust deficit which inhibits the police in performing their duties. Not only is the public scared to approach the police, but non-cooperation, witness hostility and general apathy result in the failure to secure a conviction. Sri Kumar feels that the judiciary can set an example in bridging this trust gap by allowing custodial interrogation as and when the police request it. One of the greatest challenges faced by the police is that police custody and interrogation is limited to only fourteen days, and they are unable to repeatedly interrogate an accused to verify the veracity of the statements made. Even when the accused is in judicial custody, repeated interrogation as and when fresh facts surface would greatly help in investigation.

Finally, Sri Kumar makes a strong case for an innovative, techno-legal solution to preserve evidence in a sound manner. A central repository for preservation of evidence should be set up in each district court with expeditious modernisation and digital transformation of the court *malkhana* or storehouse.

Perhaps, one of the most comprehensive efforts in improving

the criminal justice system (comprising police officers, judges, lawyers, prison officials, probation officers, etc.) was undertaken in 2000 when the Malimath Committee was constituted by the home ministry under the leadership of then deputy prime minister and home minister, L.K. Advani. The objective of the committee was to examine the fundamental principles of law and recommend ways to reform the criminal justice system to restore public confidence. It was headed by Justice V.S. Malimath, the former Chief Justice of Karnataka and Kerala. It submitted its report in 2003. The report has 158 recommendations, most of which were never applied. The reason ascribed often was that "the recommendations weighed in favour of the accused and did not adequately focus on justice to the victims of crime". One of the few accepted recommendations, allowing 'in-camera' court and trial sessions, permitted the Telgi cases to be completed using videoconferencing, as Telgi's poor health did not permit his physical appearance in court.

Since 2019, however, the Malimath Committee recommendations have again become the subject matter of discussion and one sincerely hopes that many of them will be implemented, with due concern and diligence on how the trajectory of crime and hence its redressal have changed since the recommendations were first mooted. The focus must be on the quality of justice rather than the number of judgments.

There are no easy solutions to the above in a democracy as large and complex as ours. Yet, they say, when you lose, do not lose the lesson. And every adverse event and every scam opens up opportunities to learn and redefine. That can only be the true measure of evolution, of progress.

If Telgi was questioned by the employees in large corporations/ smaller stamp vendors on how he was managing to offer large discounts compared to government norms or why the stamp vendor's licence wasn't in the name of the firm or proprietor, if he wasn't allowed the free run between 1995 to 2001, the stamp scam perhaps could never have assumed such colossal proportions. Greater awareness of and zero tolerance to corruption must be an imperative for each one of us, and we must make it our business. We cannot turn a blind eye only because we believe it doesn't impact us, or leave it for the official law keepers. Either we nip it in the bud when we encounter it in our vicinity or in our interactions or we report it as a responsible citizen.

If this is the only message that we take away, this book will have served its purpose.

APPENDIX

Stamping in India

In India, stamp duty is payable in respect of specified instruments in accordance with applicable Central or state stamp duty laws, on a fixed or ad valorem basis. The Indian Stamp Act, 1899, is the central legislation, while states have their own local stamp acts to deal with issues arising within that particular state. For example, The Bombay Stamp Act, 1958, now known as the Maharashtra Stamp Act (**MSA**), 1958, which came into force on 16 February 1959 is the law for stamp duty in the state of Maharashtra. The instruments and the applicability of the relevant law (Central/Union list below or state) are different and mutually exclusive.

To understand the legislative competence of the Centre and state to legislate on stamp duty, one must refer to the Seventh Schedule of the Constitution of India:

- Entry 91 of List I (Union List) of the Constitution of India mentions "Rate of stamp duty in respect of bills of exchange, cheques, promissory notes, bills of lading, letters of credit, policies of insurance, transfer of shares, debentures, proxies and receipts".
- Entry 63 of List II (State List) mentions "Rate of stamp duty in respect of documents other than these specified in the provisions of List I". Stamp duties may vary from state to state. Further, stamps printed and published in one state may not be valid in another state.
- Entry 44 of List III (Concurrent List) mentions "Stamp duties

> other than duties or fees collected by means of judicial stamps, but not including rates of stamp duty". This means that the power to levy non-judicial stamp duty is concurrent under Entry 44 of List III. However, the power to prescribe rates of non-judicial stamp duty is divided between the Union and the state by Entry 91 of List I and Entry 63 of List II, depending on the instrument type.

While some have been described below, the categories of stamps and stamp papers include non-judicial, judicial, court fee and copy papers, share transfers, insurance, special adhesive, foreign bills, hundis, revenue, notary, broker notes, etc.

Difference between document and instrument

Document is defined in the General Clauses Act, 1879. According to the definition, a document includes any matter written or described upon any substance by means of letters, figures, or marks or by more than one of those means, which is intended to be used for the purpose of recording the matter. The Indian Evidence Act, 1872, also defines document in a similar fashion. From the definitions, a document is a medium of recording a matter. It does *not* create, transfer, or assign any rights or liabilities.

Instrument is defined by the Indian Stamp Act, 1899. According to the act, an instrument includes every document by which any right or liability is or purports to be created, transferred, limited, extended, extinguished, or recorded. Thus, an instrument is a writing executed and delivered as the evidence of an act or agreement. Bill of exchanges, bonds, title deeds, leases, mortgages, promissory notes, etc., are treated as instruments. An instrument itself forms a legal act and such instruments should be stamped, unless specifically exempted. For any document to be admitted as evidence for any purpose, it shall be duly stamped.

All instruments are classified as documents, but all documents need not be instruments. However, it may be noted that many statutes use the terms 'document' and 'instrument' interchangeably.

What is meant by duly stamped?

The term duly stamped in relation to stamping of document/instrument means the duty chargeable and paid in accordance with the law in force at the time of execution of the instrument. If the instrument was duly stamped at the time of execution, any subsequent change in stamp law does not invalidate the document. A document on which stamp duty is duly paid is legally permissible and can be presented as evidence in the court of law.

What is stamp duty?

Stamp duty is an indirect tax and Central and state acts are revenue legislations especially enacted to raise revenue for the government. It is also important to note that under Article 268 of the Constitution, such stamp duties as are mentioned in the Union List will be levied by the Government of India but shall be collected in the case of Union Territories by the Government of India and in other cases, by the states within which such duties are leviable. Thus, the proceeds in any financial year from any such duty leviable within any state shall not form part of the Consolidated Fund of India but shall be assigned to that state. (*Note: The Indian Stamp Act, 1899, does not cover the state of Jammu and Kashmir.*)

Why is stamping of documents/instruments necessary

For a document to be valid or enforceable in a court of law, it must be properly stamped by paying sufficient stamp duty. In terms of the Stamp Act, and most state stamp duty laws, instruments which are chargeable with stamp duty are inadmissible as evidence in case appropriate stamp duty has not been paid. It is also essential that stamping on documents is done before or at the time of execution of the documents. However, under the Stamp Act and most state stamp duty laws, inappropriately stamped instruments may be admissible as evidence upon payment of applicable duty at a later stage, along with penalty of up to ten times the duty chargeable. Further, every person executing or signing otherwise than as a witness any such instruments chargeable with stamp duty, without the same being duly stamped, would be liable for monetary fines as well.

If a document is not duly stamped, the same cannot be rectified by mere annexing the stamp paper of the deficit value. In cases of document, which was not duly stamped by accident, it shall be produced before the Collector of Stamps. After proving that the omission was by mistake or accident, the position can be rectified by paying the deficit.

Documents not duly stamped must be presented to the Collector of Stamps within a period of one year from the date of execution. In case the period of one year has expired or the omission was not due to any accident or mistake, the rectification can be done only by paying the deficit duty, and penalty in court, when they are produced before the court in support of the claim. In certain states, the Stamp Act has provisions to inspect documents and impound insufficiently stamped documents during such inspection. In other states, insufficiently stamped documents can be impounded by the stamp authority upon production of such documents. For a document to be treated as properly stamped, the stamp of proper description and value should be used.

Vide the Indian Contract Act, 1872, an oral contract by which parties intend to be bound is valid and enforceable, but under certain circumstances contracts must be compulsorily written and registered.

Interstate documents

When a document is executed in two states, it should first be executed in one state on the stamp applicable to the said state of execution. The document should then be sent to the second state. If the rate of stamp duty is more in the second state, stamp for the deficit should be affixed before or at the time of execution. If the stamp duty in the first state is higher, the execution without affixing additional stamp would be valid.

Stamp papers

The stamp paper is a foolscap-size blank paper that is printed with a revenue stamp, like the one imprinted on currency notes or postal stamps.

It is issued by the government and usually carries a value of Rs10, Rs 20, Rs 50, Rs 100, Rs 500, Rs 1,000, Rs 5,000, Rs 10,000, Rs 15,000, Rs 20,000 and Rs 25,000.

Though every stamp paper carries a monetary value, it can neither be treated as a negotiable instrument nor exchanged like currency notes. The document is used for endorsing authenticity to official agreements. Documents with legal implications, such as lease agreements, buying and selling of property, business/contract agreements, loan agreements/financial deals, power of attorneys, affidavits, articles of association, memorandums of association, indemnity bonds, declarations, mortgages, and gift deeds among others are executed on stamp papers to make them legitimate and legally enforceable.

Types of Indian stamp papers

1. **Judicial:** Generally, judicial stamp papers are used for legal purposes. For instance, it can be used for proceeding with court cases or continuing legal procedures. These stamp papers are also known as court fee stamp papers as they are often used to avoid cash transactions with the court. A case may not be admitted by the court without the payment of court fees. This makes judicial stamp paper important.

2. **Non-judicial:** Non-judicial stamp papers are generally used for documents like power of attorney, sale deed, rent agreements, affidavit, transfer of immovable property like building or land, loan security, and mortgage or other important agreements.

   Under The Maharashtra Stamp Act, 1958, for example, sixty-two categories of documents are required to be legitimised by stamping them. Denominations available are Rs 10, Rs 25, Rs 50, Rs 100, Rs 500, Rs 1,000, Rs 5,000, Rs 10,000 Rs 15,000, Rs 20,000 and Rs 25,000.

Stamp papers are always bought from government-licensed stamp vendors, post offices, government treasury offices and courts. The concerned persons then write their mutual terms of the contract on the paper and lodge it with the court or concerned authority for legal validation.

This is an efficient and legal way of collecting taxes people owe to the government. It is also a passive way to get stamping documents legalised and authenticated without the obligation of submitting them to a responsible and authorised government authority.

The stamp papers must be purchased in the name of one of the parties involved in the contract/transaction.

Purchase of stamp papers

There are three different ways of paying stamp duty or fulfilling the formality of buying stamp papers for paying scheduled stamp revenue. These are:

1. Buying Stamp Papers
    a. Physical Stamp Papers
    b. E-Stamp Papers
2. Franking
3. Adhesive Stamps

E-stamp papers and physical stamp papers

Non-judicial stamp papers in India are available as e-stamp papers and traditional/physical stamp papers.

Details required while buying a physical non-judicial stamp paper: Names and addresses of the parties, document name and stamp paper value.

E-stamping (electronic stamping)

To contain counterfeiting, instances of human errors and to simplify the stamp paper process, the government introduced e-stamping in 2013. E-stamping is an electronic way of paying non-judicial stamp duty to the government.

E-stamping is currently available in nineteen states across India, with adoption by many other states underway. In fact, in a few states, for example, New Delhi, e-stamping is mandatory. For all e-stamps used in the country, the Central government has appointed the Stock Holding Corporation of India Limited (SHCIL) as the central record keeping agency (CRA). SHCIL is responsible for executing e-stamping, including user registration, e-stamping applications, and maintenance of records. It has designated authorised collection centres (ACCs), who are the agents between it and the stamp payer. In addition to the erstwhile stamp vendors, scheduled banks, company secretaries in practice and many other professionals, too, can be appointed as ACCs.

After ascertaining if the state government allows e-stamping, the applicant can download the e-stamping application form at the Stock Holding Corporation of India Limited website, and complete it with the following details: application date, whether the document is registrable or non-registrable, document description (what is the purpose of purchase of the e-stamp paper, whether sale of property, rent agreement, affidavit, etc.), property description, first party-seller/owner, etc., details (name, address, phone number, PAN and pincode), second party-buyer/tenant/transferee details (name, address, phone number, PAN and pincode), stamp duty payment details (purchased by whom, paid by whom, payment information – e-stamp paper can be purchased by either the first party or the second party).

The website offers information about which transactions require stamping. With the application form and requisite payment, the applicant needs to visit the closest ACC. The website has the addresses of the collection centres. Payment can be made by cash (for amounts below Rs 50,000) or by cheque or demand draft for higher amounts at the ACC. Online payment can be made on the Stock Holding Corporation of India Limited website, using debit cards, credit cards, pay orders, or other electronic means including real-time gross settlement (RTGS), national electronic fund transfer (NEFT) or through a direct account transfer. Upon submission of duly filled form and payment/payment proof (if payment has been made at Stock Holding Corporation of India Limited website), the e-stamping certificate is generated instantly, and handed over. In the system of e-SBTR (Electronic Secure Bank and Treasury Receipt), e-stamping facilities are provided at the authorised bank, thus reducing time and other administrative expenses.

E-stamp verification

Importantly, since the Stock Holding Corporation of India Limited website has all the data, e-stamps can be verified online by furnishing information such as name of the state, unique identification number (UIN), stamp duty type, and certificate issue date which expedites the verification process.

Benefits of e-stamping

- Convenience.
- Generation process is quick and easy.
- No problems of payment of additional charges as with paper-based stamp paper in case of fractional amounts/amounts different from correct denomination of stamp paper available.
- E-stamping is tamper-proof.
- All data is saved by the Stock Holding Corporation of India Limited.
- Authenticity can be verified on the website with the unique identification number.

Once e-stamping is stabilised, it will replace the system of physical stamp paper/franking. There are cons in the system of e-stamping as well. For example, if the e-stamp certificate is lost, a duplicate copy cannot be issued. Even though payment is made online, the actual stamp paper must be collected physically from the respective vendor. It is a challenge in the current-day situation (pandemic times of Covid) to collect the physical stamp paper.

The next problem faced in e-stamping is a late fee. If the payment is delayed, a late fee is levied. The collector has discretionary powers to accept delayed payments if an appropriate reason is given. The collector may not collect the late fee if the party approaches the collector on its own volition. Some state acts provide some flexibility to late payments. The Maharashtra Stamp Act, 1958, for example, allows payment of stamp duty the next day after the execution.

On 20 April 2020, the Ministry of Finance requested state governments to give proper instructions to the collector before collecting the late fee on loan agreements or any other instruments related to the loan. The communication has only requested the state governments and has not mentioned any directions concerning the penalty.

Franking

Franking is a technique of printing a mark on a document indicating that the stamp duty for the transaction has been paid. It is another method of stamping the documents. Special adhesive stamps franking licences are available. In this method, stamp along with value is imprinted on the document against payment of stamp duty. Unexecuted typed/printed document along with the requisite amount must be submitted to the *proper office*. The document is franked by an *authorised officer* with the stamp and is returned to the applicant. Franking machines are installed in many sub-registrar offices.

Adhesive stamps

Special adhesive stamps are used on prescribed documents. The stamps carry inscription such as insurance, notarial, share transfer, etc. Some state enactments stipulate that balance confirmation letters and acknowledgements of debt and security shall be stamped with special adhesive stamps. In such states, special adhesive stamps are being used instead of revenue stamps.

Cancellation of adhesive stamps

Adhesive stamps can be used in lieu of stamp papers, but the stamp must be cancelled by proper officers appointed under the stamp rules. In some states like Kerala, managers and agents of scheduled commercial banks are included within the meaning of 'proper officer'. In such states, use of adhesive stamps in lieu of non-judicial stamp papers is valid. As per Indian Stamp Act, every stamp on documents is required to be cancelled in such a way that it cannot be used again. Signing by the executant across the adhesive stamp is the easiest way of cancellation of adhesive stamps. If the stamp is not effectively/properly cancelled, it is treated as unstamped. If more than one stamp is used, all stamps should be cancelled. A non-judicial stamp paper can be cancelled by writing on the face of the stamp itself.

Revenue stamps

Revenue stamps are affixed on demand promissory notes, receipts, balance confirmation letters and acknowledgements of debt and security.

E-contracts

E-contracts are not paper-based. The main requirement of an e-contract is a digital signature. E-contracts are mainly used when the parties entering into an agreement are from different parts of the world.

Electronic signature is used for executing e-contracts. The e-signature comes into the picture through the Information Technology (Amendment) Act, 2008, and it is important to abide by the Indian Contract Act, 1872, while executing an e-contract.

Under Section 10A of the Information Technology Act, 2000, e-contracts have gained recognition to enforce any contract through electronic means. But under the First Schedule of the Information Technology Act, the sale of immovable property or any interest in a property is not included.

Stamping of e-contracts

There is no provision in the Indian Stamp Act, 1899, that specifically deals with electronic records and/or the stamp duty payable on execution thereof. Instruments are defined under the Indian Stamp Act as "includes every document by which any right or liability is, or purports to be, created, transferred, limited, extended, extinguished or record". While most of the state-specific stamp duty laws also do not specifically include electronic records within their ambit, some state stamp duty laws refer to electronic records. For instance, the Maharashtra Stamp Act, 1958, specifically refers to electronic records in the definition of the term 'instrument'.

Similarly, some other states like Delhi, Uttar Pradesh, Karnataka, Gujarat and Rajasthan also include electronic record within the definition of 'instrument', thereby imposing stamp duty on such electronic records.

Electronic contracts may be stamped either by taking the print of the document on stamp paper or by getting the printed document franked or, by procuring a stamp duty certificate by the process of e-stamping for the specific electronic contracts. However, stamping of electronic contracts, in such a conventional manner, like physical instruments, defeats the entire purpose of 'paperless' electronic contracts.

The stamp duty laws require suitable amendments to provide for an electronic stamping mechanism, thereby removing the requirement of physical/hard copies of the contracts. For instance, stamp duty on documents like memorandums/articles of association, can easily be paid electronically on the ministry of corporate affairs portal, irrespective of the different stamp duty payable under the state laws. A similar formulation providing for online payment of stamp duty and corresponding references of issuances of receipts/challans in relation thereto can also be introduced in the stamp duty laws. This formulation would, however, not work in respect of documents which require compulsory registration under the Indian Registration Act, 1908, such as sale deed, lease deed, instruments of gifts of immovable property, etc., wherein the registrar insists on physical copies of such documents with wet (physical) signature and adequate stamp duty.

It may also be worthwhile to consider exempting general agreements/documents (subject to nominal stamp duty rates) from payment of stamp duty, if they are executed electronically. Guidance can be taken from the stamp duty exemption available to (electronic) transfer of dematerialized shares, while stamp duty is otherwise applicable to transfer of physical shares.

Travails of the stamp vendor

With the advent of e-stamping, many erstwhile stamp vendors have struggled to conform to norms to obtain e-stamp vendors licences requiring common service centres (CSC) IDs, computer certificates, etc., even as various governments cap permissible sale volumes of physical stamps/stamp papers to promote e-stamping. There are, however, no limits to the volumes of e-stamps sold. Though the absolute earnings (averaging around 2.5 per cent on the value of physical judicial and non-judicial stamp papers sold) of the traditional physical stamp vendor has suffered because of the reduction in transactions in physical stamps, the incentive to become e-stamp vendors is minimal.

As the central record keeping agency, the Stock Holding Corporation of India Limited earns 0.65 per cent on the value of e-stamps sold and in turn pays a mere 0.15 per cent to the authorised collection centre. This is inadequate to cover the costs of most standalone stamp vendors operating as authorised collection centres, because they neither have the infrastructure, nor the resources of well-managed collection centres like banks and other professionals.

The e-stamping process works through a secure website in which the stamp vendor signs in with a login and password. After a data-entry process, where the names of the parties involved in the agreement, their PAN card details, and property description including financial transaction details are entered, the e-stamp is printed. Vendors deposit money with SHCIL against which they are allowed to print the stamps. When e-stamps are generated, the corresponding amount is deducted from the vendor's balance, and when it is exhausted, the vendor recharges the account online.

A vendor laments, "Each e-stamp takes five minutes for data-entry and printing. In an eight-hour workday, my staff effectively works for seven hours. I am only able to print a maximum of 130-150 e-stamps a day. To save on turnaround time, I have split the tasks. One person verifies the customer's details on paper, another then enters the data on a computer, the entries are then verified for spelling mistakes, and another person prints the e-stamp on another computer. Each man adds to the costs. Earlier, physical stamps were dispensed, noting just the bare details of the customer."

In addition to personnel costs, the costs of hardware or software malfunction repair are exorbitant too. A printer error, for example, results in damaged e-stamps, which cannot be reprinted. The e-stamping system doesn't allow reprint of copies of the e-stamp, to prevent misuse, but the amount stands deducted from the vendor's account. His customer, who perhaps has ordered a bulk number of e-stamps, doesn't reimburse the vendor. The vendors are demanding a refund policy for e-stamps rendered useless by hardware/software errors and spelling mistakes at 'data entry'. Monthly expenses to run a basic authorised collection centre are high. Salaries range between Rs 14,000-16,000 for a data-entry operator, a printer costs between Rs 4,000-6000, Internet connection another Rs 2,000 and monthly electricity costs above Rs 3,000.

The margin provided by the Stock Holding Corporation of India Limited is a pittance and clearly inadequate to cover these overheads, leave alone the costs of digital adoption. An advocate, who has also been a stamp vendor for the past fifteen years, and has had a loyal clientele comprising individuals, businessmen and companies in central Delhi, said, "If I were just an e-stamp vendor, my business would have been finished. Each stamp paper costs us Rs 7-8 in generating, but neither the government nor the Stock Holding Corporation of India Limited is reimbursing us this amount. We have no other option but to pass on this cost to the customer. Fortunately, I also provide a bouquet of other services including preparing agreements, affidavits and other registrable legal documents from which I earn profits."

(With inputs from articles in *The Hindu*, 22 June 2016, *The Pioneer*, 17 January 2014, *The Times of India*, 17 April 2015, *The Tribune*, 10 June 2015).

References

Cases, Application and Appeals, Writ Petition, Public Interest Litigation (PILs) by Judgment Dates

4 August 2003: Indian Law Report (ILR) Karnataka (KAR) 3702-3714. Stamp Investigating Team vs A.K.L. Telgi Cr P No. 1419 of 2003.

17 February 2004: Ranjitsing Brahmajeetsing Sharma and Others vs State of Maharashtra. Criminal Writ Petition. Nos. 3, 38 and 170 of 2004.

9 March 2004: Ranjitsing Brahmajeetsing Sharma vs Kisan Baburao Hazare alias Anna Hazare. Criminal Application No. 91 of 2004 in Criminal Writ Petition No. 865 of 2003.

16 July 2004: Ranjitsing Brahmajeetsing Sharma Retired (Commissioner of Police, Mumbai & Additional Director General of Police), vs State of Maharashtra and Others. Criminal Application No. 572 of 2004.

12 October 2004: The CBI vs Abdul Karim Ladsaab Telgi. Criminal Writ Petition No.157 of 2004.

23 March 2005: Syed Hammeduddin vs State of Andhra Pradesh (CBI). Criminal Petition No. 667 of 2005.

7 April 2005: Ranjitsing Brahmajeetsing Sharma vs State of Maharashtra and Others. Criminal Appeal No. 523 of 2005.

13 April 2005: Dattatraya Krishnaji Ghule vs State of Maharashtra and Others; Hitendra Manohar Vichare (2) vs State of Maharashtra and Others. Criminal Application No. 1202 of 2005; Criminal Application No. 1048 of 2005; Criminal Application No. 1666 of 2005.

14 October 2005: Dilip Pandurang Kamat, Abdul Rasheed Sikandarsab Kulkarni, Chenna Boyanna Krishna Yadav, Gokul Bhagaji Patil, Mohammad Chand Mulani vs State of Maharashtra and Others. Writ Petition No. 1483 of 2005.

19 October 2005: Ganga Prakash vs Union of India through, Finance Secretary, Department of Economic Affairs, Ministry of Finance, Ministry of Personnel, Public Grievances and Pension. Original Application (OA) No. 1130 of 2004.

25 January 2006: Anil M. Deshmukh vs State of Maharashtra (CBI). Case No. R.C-6/2004/E.O.U./VII, New Delhi (Crime No. 123 of 2000).

12 May 2006: Babanrao Tukaram Ranjane vs State of Maharashtra and Others. Criminal Appeal No. 640 of 2006.

5 September 2006: Ganga Prakash vs India Security Press, Security Printing and Minting Corporation of India Ltd. Decision No. 237/IC(A) 2006, F. No. CIC/MA/C/2006/0075.

18 September 2006: Mohd Chand Mulani vs Union of India and Others. Criminal Appeal No. 977 of 2006.

8 December 2006: Chenna Boyanna Krishna Yadav vs State of Maharashtra and Another. Criminal Appeal No. 1286 of 2006.

8 December 2006: Gokul Bhagaji Patil vs State of Maharashtra and Another. Criminal Appeal No. 1287 of 2006.

23 January 2007: Manoj Ramesh Mehta vs State of Maharashtra. Crime Report No.135 of 2002, MCOCA Special Case No. 2 of 2003).

9 February 2007: Dattatraya Krishnaji Ghule vs State of Maharashtra and Another; Hitendra Manohar Vichare vs State of Maharashtra and Another. Criminal Appeal Nos. 183 and 184 of 2007.

22 March 2007: Shridhar Sumant Vagal vs State of Maharashtra and Another. Criminal Appeal No. 411 of 2007.

17 April 2007: Nanjappa vs Union of India. Criminal Appeal No. 574 of 2007.

17 August 2007: State of Maharashtra and Others vs Vashishtha Rambhau Andhale. Criminal Appeal No. 1087 of 2007.

17 August 2007: CBI vs Pradeep Bhalchandra Sawant and Another. Criminal Appeal No. 1088 of 2007.

17-September-2007: Abdul Karim Telgi and Others vs State represented by Inspector of Police Central Bureau of Investigation EOU Chennai. Criminal Original Petition No. 25880 of 2007.

21 September 2007: Jayasimha vs State of Karnataka. Criminal Appeal No. 1275 of 2007.

17 January 2008: Puran Singh vs Union of India and Others. Writ Petition WP (Criminal) 2103 of 2005.

25 November 2008: Manoj Ramesh Mehta vs State of Maharashtra. Criminal Appeal No. 1868 of 2008.

17 April 2009: G.P.S. Rana vs Deputy Commissioner of Police (EOW). Appeal No. CIC/WB/A/2007/01652 dated 27 December 2007 under Right to Information Act 2005, Section 19.

27 October 2009: Abdul Karim Telgi Vs State of Karnataka. Criminal Revision Petition No. 974 of 2008.

14 December 2009: C. Madhu Mohan vs State of Andhra Pradesh. Petition under S. 482 CrPC for quashing proceedings in CC No. 2 of 2004, renumbered as CC No. 3 of 2007, relating to RC No. 4(E)/2004/CBI/EOW-I/EW1 of 2006.

8 April 2010: C.S. Balaji and Abdul Karim Telgi vs The State represented by the Inspector of Police, CBI, EOU VII. Criminal Appeal Nos. 436 and 766 of 2008.

15 June 2010: Jacob Chacko Theketala vs State of Tamil Nadu represented by the CBI, New Delhi, Camp at Chennai. Criminal Appeal No. 526 of 2009.

14 July 2010: Central Bureau of Investigation EOU-VIII vs Vashishtha Rambhau Andhale, State of Maharashtra. Criminal Appeal No. 763 of 2007

14 July 2010: Central Bureau of Investigation EOU-VIII vs Pradeep Balchandra Sawant, State of Maharashtra. Criminal Appeal No. 764 of 2007.

27 October 2010: Laxman Maruti Tirveer vs Central Bureau of Investigation. Criminal Appeal No. 45 of 2010, FIR 803/99.

27 October 2010: Vijay D. Patil vs Central Bureau of Investigation. Criminal Appeal No. 44 of 2010, FIR 803/99.

6 April 2011: K.A. Raghavendra Prasad vs State of Karnataka by SHO Bangalore City Market Police Station. Criminal Appeal No. 1385 of 2007 connected with Criminal Appeal Nos. 1462 and 1199 of 2007.

29 February 2012: Central Bureau of Investigation vs Puran Singh, Narender Singh, Om Prakash, Ratan Singh, Sanjay Bajad. CC No. 08/2011,FIR: 803/99 and FIR 878/00.

10 October 2012: Abdul Karim Ladsaab Telgi vs Central Bureau of Investigation (EOU-V) Criminal Appeal No. 21 of 2002.

4 January 2013: Sanjay Jaywant Gaikwad, Ram Ratan Shreenivas Soni, Abdul Karim Telgi vs State of Maharashtra and Union of India DCB, CID, CBI. Criminal Appeal Nos. 410, 486 and 710 of 2006.

3 April 2014: Abdul Karim Telgi, Sohail Khan, Shabbir Ahmed Sheikh vs Union of India Through Central Bureau of Investigation, A.C.B. Criminal Appeal No. 58 of 2010 (Arising Out of S.T. No. 109/2005), Criminal Appeal No. 150 of 2010 (Arising Out of S.T. No. 109/2005); Criminal Appeal No. 148 of 2010 (Arising Out of S.T. No. 108/2005); and Criminal Appeal No. 57 of 2010 (Arising Out of S.T. No. 108/2005).

11 May 2015: Shri Ganga Prakash vs Union of India through its Secretary, Department of Economic Affairs, Ministry of Finance, North Block, New Delhi, and Ministry of Personnel, Public Grievances and Pension through its Secretary, Department of Personnel and Training, North Block, New Delhi. OA No. 162 of 2014.

17 December 2015: Deepak Anand vs Union of India and Others. Writ Petition (C) No. 3903 of 2011.

18 July 2016: Central Bureau of Investigation vs Puran Singh, Gaurav Aggarwal, Abdul Karim Telgi, Om Prakash, Ratan Singh, Sanjay Bajad. New Case No. CBI/49/2016, FIR 878/2000.

11 January 2017: Ganga Prakash vs Union of India and Another. Writ Petition (C) 8696 of 2015.

11 July 2017: Abdul Karim Telgi, Dr K.H. Jnanendrappa, Dr K.M. Channakeshava vs State of Karnataka by Madiwala PS and the CBI. Criminal Appeal Nos. 1187, 1123, 1241 of 2007

12 July 2017: Abdul Karim Telgi vs State of Karnataka, Upparpet Police Station through the CBI. Criminal Appeal No. 360 of 2010

14 July 2017: Vittal Maruthi Sungar and Others vs State of Karnataka (Upparpet PS) CA Nos. 387, 321, 296 of 2010 and No. 130 of 2011.

31 July 2017:. Mr A. Nizamuddin vs State of Karnataka by Madiwala Police investigated by the CBI. Criminal Appeal No. 1190 of 2010.

3 August 2017: State of Karnataka (Madiwala Police Station Bengaluru through the CBI) vs Abdul Karim Telgi and Others. Criminal Appeal No. 87 of 2011 (Crime No. 545 of 2000).

8 August 2017: Shamshad Ahmad vs State of Karnataka, Upparpet Police Station. Criminal Appeal No. 708 of 2010.

4 September 2017: Anand Thorat and Others vs the CBI. Criminal Appeal Nos. 660, 360, 457, 414 of 2009 and Nos. 510, 338 of 2011.

8 April 2021: All U.P. Stamp Vendors Association Vs Union of India and Others. Writ C No. 11738 of 2020.

Income Tax Cases by judgment dates

22 December 2010: Abdul Karim Ladsaab Telgi vs Assistant Commissioner of Income-tax, Central Circle 1(1), Bangalore. I.T.A. Nos. 1062 to 1067/ Bang/2009 (Asst. Years 1996-97 to 2001-02).

23 December 2010: Abdul Karim Ladsaab Telgi vs Assistant Commissioner of Income-tax, Central Circle 1(1), Bangalore. I.T.A. Nos. 1048 to 1054/ Bang/2009 (Asst. Years 1996-97 to 2002-03).

23 December 2010: Abdul Karim Ladsaab Telgi vs Assistant Commissioner of Income-tax, Central Circle 1(1), Bangalore. I.T.A. Nos. 1055 to 1061/ Bang/2009 (Asst. Years 1996-97 to 2002-03).

4 September 2013: The Commissioner of Income Tax Central Circle, Assistant Commissioner of Income Tax Central Circle 1(1) vs Abdul Karim Ladsaab Telgi. I.T.A. No. 811/2008 and I.T.A. No. 812/2008.

Papers, Articles and Blogs

'Use of Modern Scientific Tests in Investigation and Evidence: Mere Desperation or Justifiable in Public Interest?', Abhyudaya Agarwal and Prithwijit Gangopadhyay, West Bengal National University of Juridical Sciences (2009), 2, NUJS L Rev 31.

'The Truth Behind Truth Machines: A Psycho Legal Enigma', Dr G.K. Goswami and Siddhartha Goswami, DCS (Forensic Sciences and Law), Honorary Professor National Law University, Delhi, and National Forensic Science University, Gandhinagar.

'Fair Trial vis-à-vis Criminal Justice Administration: A Critical Study of Indian Criminal Justice System', Neeraj Tiwari, Indian Law Institute, New Delhi.

'Narco Analysis and its Evidentiary Value in India', Barcelona Panda, National Law University, Raipur (2011) PL July S-36.

'Trusting the Police: Challenges of Criminal Investigation and Trials in India', R. Sri Kumar, Approaches to Justice in India (2017).

'The Flaw in the Law', Karan Kapoor, 22 October 2019, Malimath Committee Recommendations.

Articles, RTI Foundation of India.

Lok Sabha Debate Papers.

Blog: Vohra Committee Report 1993, Sanjeev Sabhlok, 26 December 2010.

Blog: Telgi Stamp Paper Scam must be exhumed, Capt. Ajit Vadakayil, 6 December 2014.

Blog: Stamp Duty and its Relevance, Agama Law Associates, Commercial Law Blog 14. January 2016.

Blog: E-contracts in India and its Relevance, Agama Law Associates, Commercial Law Blog, 3 June 2015.

Blog: Stamp Duty and Stamping of Documents, CelebrateBanking.com, 3 January 2017.

Resources: National Digital Library of India, India, *Kanoon*, Judgments High and Supreme Courts, Newspaper articles, references and archives.

Magazines: *India Today, Outlook*.

Books

Reporter Ki Diary (Diary of a Reporter): Sanjay Singh. Published 2004.

Dangerous Minds: S. Hussain Zaidi and Brijesh Singh. Published 2017. Chapter 5.